# Guns, Violence, and Identity among African American and Latino Youth

*A book in the series:*

# Criminal Justice Recent Scholarship
Edited by Marilyn McShane and Frank P. Williams III

# Guns, Violence, and Identity among African American and Latino Youth

Deanna L. Wilkinson

LFB Scholarly Publishing LLC
New York

First published 2003 by LFB Scholarly Publishing LLC.
First printing in paperback, 2004.

Library of Congress Cataloging-in-Publication Data

Wilkinson, Deanna Lyn, 1968-
  Guns, violence, and identity among African American and Latino
youth
/ Deanna L. Wilkinson.
      p. cm. -- (Criminal justice : recent scholarship)
Includes bibliographical references and index.
  ISBN 1-59332-009-4 (alk. paper)
  1. Youth and violence--New York--New York. 2. Youth with social
disabilities--New York--New York--Psychology. 3. African American
young men--New York--New York--Social conditions. 4. Hispanic
American young men--New York--New York--Social conditions. 5.
Violence in adolescence. 6. Neighborhood--Social aspects. 7. Identity
(Psychology) in youth. 8. Firearms--Social aspects. I. Title. II.
Criminal justice (LFB Scholarly Publishing LLC)
  HQ799.2.V56W55 2003
  303.6'0835'097471--dc21
                                        2003007666


ISBN 1-59332-009-4 (casebound)
ISBN 1-59332-089-2 (paperback)


Printed on acid-free 250-year-life paper.
Manufactured in the United States of America.

This book is dedicated to the loving memory of my father, Daniel J. Wilkinson, Sr.—August 6, 1943-June 14, 2002.

# TABLE OF CONTENTS

Page

# LIST OF TABLES

## ACKNOWLEDGEMENTS

My list of debts from this project is long. Financial support for this work was provided by grants from the Harry Frank Guggenheim, Centers for Disease Control and Prevention, National Insitute of Justice, and the National Science Foundation. Lois Mock, Jim Mercy, and Mary Alice Yates provided meaningful feedback on the development of the study. In addition, the manuscript could not have been completed without considerable support from the William Penn Foundation and Jean Hunt in particular. The opinions are solely those of the author. Special thanks to Jeffrey Fagan, principal investigator, for his support, suggestions and commmets.

Most importantly, I am deeply indebted to the young men who were willing to share their life histories with the interview team. I hope that my interpretations and presentation of their stories provide insights that help shape policy and practice.

I would like to acknowledge the many contributions of my field research staff. This project would not have been possible without them. Rich McClain, Whetsel Wade, Davon Battee, David Tufino, and Jason Mercado inspired me with their resilience and personal growth during the project. I am grateful for the opportunity to get to know and care about five extraordinary individuals. Each member brought something special and unique to this study. They showed considerable courage to do something visible and different from what most individuals their age were doing in these neighborhoods. They lived many of the experiences described in this book and continue to struggle for survival in these dangerous neighborhoods, they call home. I think my understanding of the social worlds of inner-city adolescent males was enriched most through my conversations and debates with the interviewers. Week after week the stories poured in about what my field interviewers observed, experienced, heard about, feared, and/or grieved. The frequency of violent events in their neighborhoods shocked and outraged me.

I gratefully acknowledge the research assistance of Marlene Pantin, Ed Wilkinson, Lori Davie, Alex Figueroa, Valli Rajah, Adam Trister, Jorge Nunez, Wilson Cruz, Michael Perez, Richard Vargas, and Javier Tufino. In addition, I am grateful to Christopher Tennant and Keith Gooch for not being afraid to criticize my work and helping me to improve my writing. The staff at Friends of Island Academy deserves special appreciation for generously providing me access to their clients and programs. Specifically, I thank Clinton Lacey, Lonnie Shockley, Neftalti Humenez, Christine Pahigan, Beth Nunez, and B. Davis.

I have been fortunate to have many excellent teachers and mentors over the years. I would like to acknowledge Richard Peterson, Chris Carlson, Holly Hollibaugh, and Charlotte Vaughan at Cornell College; Dennis Rosenbaum, Michael Maltz, Mindie Lazarus-Black, and Joseph Peterson at the University of Illinois at Chicago; Jeffrey Fagan, Elin Waring, Mercer Sullivan, Don Gottfredson, Todd Clear, Ron Clarke, Drew Humphries, Gerhardt Mueller, and Ko-lin Chin at Rutgers University. My colleagues at Temple University have also provided support for my work. Specifically, I would like to thank Ralph Taylor, Alex Piquero, Edem Avakeme, James Fyfe, Phil Harris, Joan McCord, Ellen Kurtz, and Susan Hamerschlag.

Finally, I need to thank my brother Ed Wilkinson for putting up with me during the difficult years of data collection and analysis. Thanks go to my husband Keith Gooch for encouraging me to finish this project and to my son William for bringing so much joy into my life.

## INTRODUCTION

In 1994, I was beginning my dissertation work in criminology and was also volunteering with ex-offenders in New York City. The academic literature I read at the time made it clear that adolescent violence (especially gun violence) among inner city youth had reached unprecedented numbers, but did little to describe the nature, processes, or contexts of youth violence. In contrast, the lay media provided a powerful and shocking explanation of this new wave of gun violence - a generation of super-predators, a concept that I saw no support for from either the criminological literature or my personal experience interacting with inner city adolescent and young adult males. The study described in the pages that follow was undertaken to gain a better understanding of the social worlds of violent adolescent males in two New York City neighborhoods and the violent events that they experienced. It consisted of life history interviews with 125 violent offenders to get detailed descriptions of 306 violent or near violent events situated in the contexts of the young men's social worlds. The study attempted to understand youth gun violence by examining the dynamic contextualism[1] of urban neighborhoods, the influence of these social processes on socialization, social control, and behavior, and the role of guns in shaping norms and behaviors. The interviews were analyzed using the latest techniques in qualitative methods to organize the data into recurrent themes and patterns. What emerged was a heterogeneous picture of violent events shaped by ecological processes that had consequences for the social identities of urban adolescent males. The most powerful part of this book is the window that it provides into the social worlds of violent adolescents by documenting how the most recent youth violence epidemic led to adaptations in the everyday lives of inner city adolescents.

### The Epidemic of Adolescent Gun Violence

Although violence has been a recurrent theme for decades in urban delinquency, youth gun violence has become more prevalent and more concentrated spatially and socially in the past two decades. Starting in 1985, gun violence among teenagers rose sharply in prevalence, it

---

[1] Robert Sampson argued that criminology would benefit from shifting focus from one monolithic explanation of crime to multi-level perspectives (1993). Dynamic contextualism "recognizes and attempts to join developmental and historical insights, event structures and community context, qualitative narratives and causal explanation and time and place." (Sampson, 1993: 426)

*1*

diffused quickly through a generation of teenagers, it sustained a high prevalence and incidence for over five years, and it has declined steadily for nearly a decade since. The most recent peak was far higher than the previous peak, but its decline through 1994 was also more pronounced than either of the two earlier epidemics. Cook and Laub (1998) show that nearly all the volatility in adolescent homicide rates for the past 30 years is the result of rising and falling gun homicide rates. Despite these steep declines in gun homicides nationally, there were twice as many victims of gun homicides in 1997 compared to 1984 (Fingerhut and Christoffel, 2002). While gun homicides among adolescents increased rapidly following the onset of the crack crisis in the mid-1980s, it is unclear whether these homicides can be traced to business violence in the drug trade, or to other situational and ecological forces during that time.

The widening gap between gun and non-gun homicides was more pronounced for older adolescents. The growth rates for gun homicides by adolescents of all age categories were similar, but rose more sharply for older adolescents ages 18 to 24, compared with younger teens ages 13 to 17. Throughout this time, non-gun homicides remained nearly constant for both age groups. Moreover, the rise in the percentage of adolescent homicides by guns was pronounced for most types of non-family victim-offender relationships: gang-related homicides, robberies and other felonies, brawls and disputes, and other known and unknown circumstances (Cook & Laub, 1998, Table 6: p. 56).

By the early 1990's, the relative risks for gun homicide victimization of adolescents had reached epidemic proportions. During the early 1990s youth violence was more lethal, guns were getting into the hands of young people more than ever before, and fear levels were increasing among youth. Since 1984, gun homicides among adolescents ages 12 to 17 nearly tripled, from fewer than 600 victims in 1984 to a peak of more than 1,700 in 1993 (Snyder & Sickmund, 1999). Deaths of adolescents due to firearm injuries are disproportionately concentrated among nonwhites, and especially among African American teenagers and young adults. During the early 1990s young African American men were dying and getting injured at staggering rates at the hands of other African American youth armed with firearms in our inner cities. Deaths of adolescents due to firearm injuries are disproportionately concentrated among nonwhites, and especially among African American teenagers and young adults. Since

1988, the firearm death rate among African American male teenagers 15-19 years exceeded the death rate due to natural causes or any other cause. Young African American males were 4.7 times more likely to die from firearm injuries than from natural causes (Fingerhut, 1993). Similar increases were reported for other age-sex-race groups—highest among African American males.

Okay, so the youth violence epidemic was predominantly the result of the increased use of guns. What do we know about the patterns of gun carrying among youth? The literature on guns and adolescents is characterized by broad surveys that gauge how often students bring weapons to school, and how their outlooks have been affected by the presence of firearms (Harris, 1993; Sheley, Wright, & Smith, 1993). Studies of nationally representative samples of adolescents in schools, selected (often urban) samples of adolescents in schools, and target samples of criminal justice or criminally involved offenders show that guns have become a central feature of the context of adolescent life (Wilkinson and Fagan, 2001). Estimates of gun carrying in school during this time ranges from 0.1 percent (NCVS-SS, 1995) to 15 percent (Harris, 1993). These rates of gun carrying are much higher among inner city and criminal justice involved youth (Decker & Pennell, 1995; Huff, 1998). Specifically, among criminal justice involved youth the range carrying (anywhere) was 22 percent (Decker, Pennell, & Caldwell, 1997) to 50% (Sheley & Wright, 1995). Gun carrying and use is higher among youth involved in drug selling and gang activity (Decker et al., 1997; Huff, 1998; Inciardi, Horowitz, & Pottieger, 1993; Sheley & Wright, 1995). Across a wide range of sampling and measurement conditions, adolescents consistently report that guns are easily obtained, frequently carried, readily used, deemed necessary for self-defense and survival, and influence teenagers' views of routine social interactions (Wilkinson & Fagan, 2001). These trends persist even after a nearly decade-long decline in youth gun violence.

Why do certain youth carry and use guns? Recent survey research shows that offenders and high school students alike report "self-defense" as the most important reason for carrying firearms (Harris, 1993; Kennedy, 1993; Sheley & Wright, 1995). Fear is a recurring theme in juvenile gun acquisition, and the escalating adolescent "weapons race" can be traced in the literature to the 1970s.

The survey-based studies provide a starting point for understanding adolescent attitudes and patterns of behavior related to guns and violence; however an in-depth examination of the social world of violent adolescent males has been lacking until now. Although the scope of the youth violence problem was becoming very clear by 1994, our ability to make sense of the challenges facing adolescents growing up in violent environments was generally lacking. From existing studies, it is unclear whether firearm use by adolescents is part of a generalized pattern of adolescent violence or a maladaptive developmental outcome. That is, research on adolescent firearm use has not yet analyzed the interactions of the characteristics of the individuals involved, the interpersonal transactions and interactions between the parties, or how the presence of guns affects the outcomes of these interactions.

The literature on adolescent gun violence raises more questions than it answers. For example, what factors bear on the decisions of young males to carry weapons, to place themselves in circumstances where weapons are likely to be used, and to use violence, including gun violence? What roles do family background, neighborhood environment, peer associations, school experiences, and employment have on involvement with violence and guns? What role do guns play in the decision-making processes of adolescent males? What are the motivations and provocations for gun carrying and use among a sample of violent youth? What does the heterogeneity look like? Why use violence in some situations and not others? How do violent youth perceive risks, threats, and opportunities? What role does violence play in shaping adolescent social identity? How do youth make sense of violent experiences—both when they are perpetrators and when they are victims? How does the community, either through parents, neighbors, school officials or criminal justice agents, assist youth in making sense of their violent experiences? How might the rich data on the youths' social worlds be used to develop effective prevention/intervention strategies? This study provides answers to some of these questions.

Despite our limited knowledge of the nature and circumstances of gun violence among youth, the media and some academics, rushed to conclusions. Alarmist statements and destructive labels were instrumental in vilifying young urban males. For example, in 1995 Dr. John Dilulio, then Professor of Political Science at Princeton University, wrote about the violence problem in America. He projected the coming of new class of young violent offenders that he called "super-predators." According Dr. Dilulio "ever-growing numbers of hardened, remorseless juvenile criminals are creating a group of 'super-predators' that has not yet begun to crest. Americans are sitting atop a demographic time bomb of youth offenders who maim or kill on impulse, without any intelligible motive for rehabilitation" (Dilulio, 1995; 1996; Fox, 1995; 1996). His warnings did not just speak about adolescents but also suggested that children were already lost as well. For example, Dilulio (1995) wrote: "We're talking about boys whose voices have yet to change. We're talking about elementary school youngsters who pack guns instead of lunches. We're talking about kids who have absolutely no respect for human life and no sense of the future." The prevailing argument in the popular press during the early-to-mid 1990s was that children, especially minority boys, of that day were drastically more evil than earlier generations. Franklin Zimring and others have effectively disabled Dilulio's characterizations of this new generation of young violent offenders by showing that the claims were not grounded in solid research evidence. The sound bites and images of African-American youth killing other African-American youth undoubtedly fed public fear and "get tough" policies. More recently Dilulio has backed away from these statements and admitted that he had made a mistake. Despite his change in position the term super-predator continues to capture headlines and sell books (Elikann, 1999). The main irony of this now unproven theory of doom is that very little of the discussion that followed had much to with protecting those individuals who would likely become prey in the predatory environments characteristic of gun and drug infested neighborhoods. It was easier for the public to get behind strategies to remove youth from the community through 'get tough' policies that would hold youth responsible for their actions without regard for the deeper issues underlying the crisis. By getting inside the heads of violent youth we gain insights into multifaceted world that provides almost no support for the existence of so-called super-predators.

This book documents the many ways in which adolescent males cope and adapt to their dangerous and often unpredictable environments. The neighborhoods in this study were significantly more violent compared to New York City as a whole. The interviews retrospectively document the experiences of young violent offenders with violence for the two-year period before the interview, thus their accounts provide a perspective of what was happening in 1993-1996.

The book explores on the social worlds of young males who are among a segment of the American population that is at the highest risk of violent death. This study sheds new light on the ecological processes that shape behavioral expectancies and social identities of urban adolescent males. By interviewing youth who are at the extreme end of the spectrum of violent behaviors we get a fuller understanding of the complex social processes that create and sustain environments in which violence is deemed necessary.

Violent events are examined in detail in order to understand the complex social processes that affected adolescent decision-making and dispute resolution in a context of danger. The book documents how the availability and frequent use of guns, coupled with the perception of fear and hostile intent has altered dispute-handling processes. The research also demonstrates how adolescents use violence to achieve social status or identities in economic contexts with attenuated pathways to adult roles. The analysis is focused on understanding decision-making during violent events by examining the convergence of context, arousal, information processing, normative processes, and situational factors from a developmental perspective.

**About the Presentation of the Interview Data**
The interview excerpts include rough and offensive language. In order to draw the youth out ex-offenders from the Neighborhoods conducted the interviews. The language included is simply how youth talk. My goal was to make them feel comfortable, to talk freely, and therefore, I hired people who could talk to them as equals in the language they spoke. The best interviews of 125 included herein resemble listening in on private conservations between friends. This quality strengthens the study. I purposely decided not to substantially edit or clean up the interview excerpts because there is more to learn from hearing the voices of youth in their own words. In addition, censoring their words would have distorted the intended meanings of the discourse. Respondents used the word "nigga" frequently to refer to other people in their lives (both friend and enemy). Like it or not, this term is a prominent feature of inner city youth culture. In some cases words placed in parentheses have been added to clarify the meaning of a statement. Readers will probably need to flip to the back of the book to the glossary of slang terms in Appendix B.

# CHAPTER 1
# Setting the Empirical Context

Youth violence must be understood within the context of human development and life course pathways. Adolescence is a time of stressful development, manifested by changes in physical appearance, social status, and cognitive abilities. It is a developmental period characterized by physical stress, underdeveloped coping skills, and high vulnerability (Van Gundy, 2002; Hamburg, 1974). It is a prolonged period, beginning with hormonal changes and ending with the transition to adult social roles, typically employment. In modern American society, this period extends well into the early twenties reflecting shifts in family, economic, and educational aspirations (Furstenberg, 2000). Cognitive ability shifts during adolescence from concrete to abstract thinking. Growth in cognitive functioning occurs gradually as youth gain experience with diverse, often contradictory sets of issues. The pace of development varies widely among individuals.

Adolescence is marked by a series of social transitions, including entry into junior high school and differentiated school tasks, increasing use of the peer group as a critical reference group for exploration of social roles, exploration of opposite-sex relationships, and changing relations with parents and other adults. Youth begin spending considerably less time with parents and other adults and considerably more time with peers. Adult expectations of teenagers are changing at the same time that adolescents' perceptions of self also are undergoing basic changes. It also is a time of pursuit of some universal goals of adolescence: social affiliation, task mastery, social identity, and autonomy (Van Gundy, 2002). Furstenberg (2000) argues:

> "this phase of the life course establishes a youth-based social world that is age segregated, partially buffered from adult control, and relatively turned in on itself. This transformation encourages the development of a youth culture that is impelled to distinguish itself from adulthood and can establish its own system of rewards. To a great degree, the problematic features of adolescence and the transition to adulthood are structurally created and maintained by social institutions that isolate youth from adults; ironically, this is done to prepare them for future roles (Furstenberg, 2000: 897).

The developmental processes of adolescents vary by race, social class, gender, community context, and family background. Racial and economic inequalities shape the experiences of minority youth in ways that are not clearly understood. African American scholars argue that African American youth have to confront issues related to developing their ethnic identity by reconciling their identity in relation to the majority position through assimilation, alienation, withdrawal, and integration (Corbin & Pruitt, 1999). The experiences of youth occur across multiple contexts including neighborhoods, family, school, employment, and peer groups. Apart from family, social interactions occur among groups of similarly situated youth within schools or neighborhood peer groups. Although most scholars agree that each context is important rarely are young people's experiences examined across each context in one study (Furstenberg, 2000). These contexts circumscribe social networks, and daily interactions within these networks give rise to potential disputes and violence in three ways.

First, there are recurring interactions among individual youths. Adolescents see each other daily in school, on the journey to and from school, in their neighborhoods, and in a range of social activities including parties and athletic events. Individuals rank each other in these contexts through a variety of social comparisons. These processes naturally give rise to competition and disputes.

Second, bystanders are present in contexts of adolescents' lives.—they witness and participate in disputes. They confirm and withhold social status. The presence and behavior of bystanders can critically affect the escalation of disputes into violence (Decker, 1995; Felson & Steadman, 1983; Tedeschi & Felson, 1994). Witnesses to disputes are arbiters of their outcomes and often the main arbiters of status. Accordingly, they play a crucial role in the initiation and settlement of disputes, at times encouraging violence for their own vicarious pleasure or raising the stakes of a conflict so high that violence becomes a necessity to the participants in the dispute. From children on playgrounds to adolescents in street-corner groups, witnesses are a part of the landscape of social interactions and influence decisions on how to conduct social relations or settle disputes.

Third, the social position of the inner-city affords limited avenues for children and adolescents to obtain the social status and roles available to children in other ecological contexts. Inner-city residents tend to withdraw from organized communal life (Anderson, 1990).

.......ᴜ peer groups dominate social roles, and the opportunity for broader participation in community life (after-school groups, volunteer organizations, or supervised athletics) often is limited by a lack of adequate local resources (Short, 1996). Accordingly, adolescents often are unable to demonstrate the types of refined skills that bring status in later years. Alternatives to conventional status attainment, then, may be limited in the inner city to manifestations of physical power or domination, athletic performance, verbal agility, or displays of material wealth. Social status inordinately depends on one's position within social hierarchies, and for males those hierarchies often are established through manifestations of physical power or fighting (Guerra, Nucci, & Huesmann, 1994; Guerra & Slaby, 1990). The continual demand for personal "respect," coupled with limited avenues by which to attain it, sets up conflicts that often are resolved through fighting, an available pathway to high status. The social exchanges within the socially isolated youth networks provide specific motivations and social values that may limit the range of behavioral choices once conflicts arise.

Prior research has shown that violence serves specific social and/or psychological functions. Researchers have articulated three main goals of aggressive actions: to compel and deter others, to achieve a favorable social identity, and to obtain justice (Felson, 1993; Katz, 1988). These functions, which provide the motivational component for violence, can be understood in the context of adolescent development. Previous studies identify the possible functions served by adolescent violence—including social control (Black, 1983), identity and reputation (Anderson, 1999; Goffman, 1983), material acquisition (Katz, 1988), domination and conquest (Felson, 1993; Katz, 1988; Oliver, 1994; Polk, 1994).

Contingent decision-making by adolescents is not *ad hoc* for each event, but reflects cumulative knowledge gained through both participation in and observation of violent interactions. This involves socialization processes that begin prior to adolescence and are refined along the way through interaction and practice. Adolescents are likely to look to the streets for lessons on the rules of gun fighting, learn from experience in conflict situations, and practice moves they have observed others performing in handling disputes on the street (Anderson, 1990; Anderson, 1999; Canada, 1995; Oliver, 1994; Sullivan, 1998). We are beginning to understand the processes of learning and diffusion of this sort of gun "knowledge" in specific urban research locations.   There may be a number of social interactional, developmental, contextual, cultural, and socio-economic factors that impinge on the decision-making processes of young males in violent conflicts.

The development of scripts, the processes of decision-making, the social definitions of conflict and other functions served by violence form in specific social contexts.   These contexts shape normative definitions, imperatives or expected behaviors, costs and rewards of violence.   Firearm violence represents an extreme of a continuum of violence in the dynamics of inner city youths.   Yet only a few studies have examined the current social worlds of young inner city males in depth (Anderson, 1990; Anderson, 1999; Canada, 1995; Sullivan, 1998; Sullivan, 1989; Sullivan, 1997) and even fewer studies have examined violent events among adolescent males.

The analysis of violence in an event framework explicitly recognizes the dynamic interactions of individuals with one another, with other persons in their social networks or situational contexts, and with neighborhood contexts that bear on the course of violent events. Prominent researchers have called for innovative studies that employ research methods that simultaneously examine the dynamic contextualism of violence (the person in context influences on violence) (Sampson, 1993; Short 1998).   In addition to the study of communities and groups, this approach also requires an analysis of events themselves.    Discerning the functions of violence requires an analysis of violent events, but events are the products of ongoing dynamics within communities: the influence of contexts combines with individual characteristics to shape events that accumulate toward developmental outcomes.  These dynamics, in turn, are situated in a set of normative influences — codes, for example — that reflect the sum of these interactions.

Gun violence involves a series of decisions, and an explanatory framework must include a decision-making framework.  Decisions to carry guns, to bring oneself to a setting where guns are likely to be present, to show a gun or make a threat with it, to pursue a dispute that may turn deadly, and ultimately to use the gun, are decisions that reflect the convergence of arousal, anger, opportunity, and context. Consistent with the rational choice perspective, the actor makes a choice to engage in violent behavior because it seems to be the best alternative available in the situation. We know that adolescents are poor decision makers, with limited capacity to weigh consequences (Steinberg & Caufmann, 1996). They also may lack the cognitive capital to understand the range of potential consequences, or to fashion strategies that may exempt them from gun violence.

In sum, event-based studies are needed to analyze interactions that involve young males and firearms. This approach does not deny the importance of the individual attributes that bring people to situations, such as "disputatiousness" (Luckenbill & Doyle, 1989), but recognizes that these situations involve other processes that shape the outcomes. Events are analyzed as "situated transactions," including rules that develop within specific socio-cultural contexts, the situations and contexts where weapons are used, the motivations for carrying and using weapons, and the personality "sets" of groups where weapons are used. There are "rules" that govern how disputes are settled, when and where firearms are used or avoided, and the broader significance of firearms in adolescent culture. These processes must be understood in order to have any success in intervening in future potentially explosive situations. Thus, research must examine both the symbolic and the instrumental meanings of firearms in the lives of young males.

## EVENT PERSPECTIVES
Criminological theories tend to focus on identifying the differences between those who engage in violent activity from those who do not. A myriad of variables are repeatedly modeled to account for these differences, including proscribed structural opportunities, socialization, personality traits, learned normative patterns, biological factors, and the lack of social controls. While many of these factors are captured in the current study, the central research questions explored in this book are the conditions and interactional processes under which actors choose to use violence at some times and not others. More precisely, given a sample of violent offenders, the goal is to identify the motivational and situational factors that produce violent encounters. Most studies rely upon official statistics or survey-based data with bias samples to test existing theories. A multi-level explanation of violent behavior among adolescents is lacking; current criminological theories generally fail to specify the interactions and overlap of social context, violent situations, and individual factors. To address this deficiency, I examined the utility of existing theories that include individual and event level

processes, namely symbolic interactionism and the social interactionist perspective.

## Symbolic Interactionism and Adolescent Violence

Symbolic interactionism provides a framework for understanding events in context and the social identities that emerge from human interaction.  Symbolic interactionism offers a useful perspective for examining of transactional aspects of violent behavior among two or more individuals especially because it is a theory of contextualized action. According to Blumer (1969), "human interaction is mediated by the use of symbols, by interpretation, or by ascertaining the meaning of one another's actions." (Blumer, 1969:70).  For Blumer, human action is processual  (or process-based) and begins with observation/sensation resulting in an "indication to the self" which is noted and interpreted in order to construct a proper response.  It is through this process of self-indication that an individual digests information and begins to formulate a decision for future action.

Blumer argues "social action is lodged in acting individuals who fit their respective lines of action to one another through a process of interpretation." (Blumer, 1969: 84). There is a social learning process that occurs where individuals develop an understanding of how to act in certain social situations based on previous experience and repetitive behavior over time.  Blumer claims that individuals are constantly interpreting the actions of others in structured social situations and often individuals confront conflicting definitions or interpretations of the situation. The conflicting definition forces the adaptation of new actions for a particular set of circumstances.  One of the central ideas of symbolic interactionism is the "taking each other into account." Blumer states:

> Taking another person into account means being aware of him, identifying him in some way, making some judgment or appraisal of him, identifying the meaning of his action, trying to find out what he has on his mind or trying to figure out what he intends to do. Such awareness ...becomes the occasion for orienting oneself and for the direction of one's own conduct. One takes the other person and his action into account ...throughout the period of interaction.  One has to keep abreast of the action of the other, noting what he says at this point and that point or interpreting his movements as they

appear, one after another. Perceiving, defining and judging the other person and his action and organizing oneself in terms of such definitions and judgments constitute a continuing or running process. (Blumer, 1969: 108-109)

Blumer also notes that an individual also takes his or her own actions into account and makes interpretations to him or herself. For Blumer, interactions take on "careers" of their own through repeated interpretation, decision, action, reinterpretation, decision, and counteraction by the parties involved. He claims that the interpretation is made based on the actor's "purpose, aims, or directions." These interpretations can also be based on prior experience in similar situations or misread definitions of a situation (scripts). Blumer notes that social interaction is mostly stable and predictable, but variations of action are to be expected. Blumer also suggests an explanation for defused interactions or the de-escalation of events that might otherwise have resulted in some (probably negative) action. He explained that certain social cues in the situation may inhibit behavior and cause an individual to hold back his expression of "inclinations, impulses, wishes, and feelings" until more "profitable" situation arises. According to Blumer, third parties and other onlookers are likely to alter the interpretations of the situation and the subsequent plan of action (Blumer, 1969: 111).

Goffman offers many insights into the dynamic social processes of human interaction. His concepts such as the "character contest" and "impression management" have been used widely in criminological research, including studies of both homicide events and gang violence. Goffman examined the ways in which a person presents an image of himself to others and develops a view of others as social actors. In addition, he analyzed the ritualistic aspects of social interaction in a variety of social contexts. Goffman defines interaction as "...the reciprocal influence of individuals upon one another's actions when in one another's immediate physical presence." He claims that self-identity is essentially social, that is, dependent on the responses of others for construction and retention. One of the many concepts he introduced was dramaturgical analysis of social interaction (or performance). He describes two kinds of communication in which individuals participate: "expressions *given*" and "expressions *given off*." According to Goffman, impressions *given off* are most important in conveying meaning about the actor within a social situation.

Thus, an actor can manipulate the impression received by projecting a certain definition of the situation he enters. Goffman explains that "first impressions" are crucial in determining the next stage in most interactions. Other participants in the situations will most often confirm the original definition of the situation consistent with how others around them react or register the event. Goffman claims that open conflict over a definition of a situation would be a rare occurrence (Goffman, 1959: 10). Goffman explains:

> In noting the tendency for a participant to accept the definitional claims made by the others present, we can appreciate the crucial importance of the information that the individual initially possesses or acquires concerning his fellow participants, for it is on the basis of this initial information that the individual starts to define the situation and starts to build up lines of responsive action. ...As the interaction among the participants progresses, additions and modifications in this initial informational state will of course occur, but it is essential that these later developments be related without contradiction to, and even built up from, the initial positions taken by the several participants. It would seem that an individual can more easily make a choice as to what line of treatment to demand from and extend to the others present at the beginning of an encounter than he can alter the line of treatment that is being pursued once the interaction is underway. (Goffman, 1959: 10-11)

According to Goffman (1959), people are to some extent involved in giving staged performances to different social audiences. Individual behavior is "scripted" to the extent that scripts are used to convey the kind of impression (or situational identity) an actor wants others to perceive. He argues that different audiences may have different preconceptions of the actor and the actor may have varying degrees of experience projecting alternate impressions in new situations. The importance of status and reputation (impression *given off*) in this social context influences the scripts an individual may choose when confronted with a public dispute. One could argue that based on the knowledge available at the start of the event, an individual will choose a script that casts him or her in the best light.

Symbolic interactionism is generally criticized for overlooking the macro-level forces that shape micro-level processes. Later in his career, Goffman began to focus on linking the micro-dynamics of social interaction with the macro-level forces working to structure such interactions. Goffman (1983) argues that there is an "interaction order" (a set of ground rules and moral obligations) that imposes constraints on interaction. Goffman suggests that actors use language and shared cultural knowledge ("general resources") to make decisions during social interactions. People create meaning in face-to-face interactions by drawing on local agreements, definitions and understandings that are upheld during an event. The lesson of an event may continue into the future as the parties have future contact. Goffman uses the term "baggage" to describe the cumulative memory (history or biography) of handling previous encounters. He suggests that the "baggage" automatically affects how those currently engaged in a social situation will relate to each other. In Goffman's opinion, "social structures don't 'determine' culturally standard displays, merely help select from an available repertoire of them" (Goffman, 1983: 11). The current study uses rich life history narratives to explore the existence and effects of "cumulative baggage" on adolescent violence.

## Social Interactionist Perspective on Violence

Both structural and situational context is important in understanding violent behavior. Actors are situated in a variety of organizational and role positions, such as school, family, work, neighborhood, and peer group settings. The human interactions in these settings shape beliefs, attitudes, and behavior. These social contexts need to be understood as dynamic and having multiple influences on individuals and groups. The situational or event-based perspective on victimization encourages researchers and practitioners to think about the co-production of a violence experience. Many kinds of victimizations are not one-sided events. The outcomes reflect a dynamic interplay involving the victim, offender(s) and others who may be present in a specific context. The situational or event perspective emphasizes the precursors of the event, including the locational and situational factors that bring people together in time and space; transactions that indicate how the interactions among participants define the outcomes of their actions; and the aftermath of the event, including the reporting to the police, the harm done, and the redress required. This perspective has been especially helpful in thinking about the causes and correlates of violence among inner-city youth.

Interest in understanding the transactional dynamics between offenders and victims really began with Marvin Wolfgang's seminal study in which he found that 26% of homicides could be described as victim precipitated, that is, the victim played a role (either active or passive) in initiating the violent event. Alcohol use was also a common theme in those homicide situations. He also noted that 50% of homicides involved multiple offenders (Wolfgang, 1958). Wolfgang interpreted this finding as partial evidence for a subculture of violence hypothesis. He argued that there is a segment of society that generally holds attitudes and values that are supportive of violence as an accepted means of social interaction.

Studies of violent events as situated transactions examine the intersection of individual personality and situational factors in which violent outcomes result, what Toch has called "contingent consistency" (Toch, 1986: 28). The social interactionist perspective emphasizes the role of social interaction over other "personality" explanations in aggressive behavior (Campbell, 1984; Campbell & Gibbs, 1986; Canada, 1995; Luckenbill, 1977; Moore, 1978).

This perspective integrates concepts from symbolic interactionism and rational choice perspectives to examine violent interactions. Luckenbill (1977) argued that the likelihood of violence reflects the progression of decisions across these stages. There are contingencies within each stage, and the contingencies are shaped both by external influences (contexts such as bystanders), and social interactions of the individuals in deciding to escalate or defuse the event. Felson describes the dynamics of violent incidents similarly to Luckenbill and Doyle, calling the sequence of events a social control process. Violence is a function of events that occur during the incident and therefore is not predetermined by the initial goals of the actors (Felson & Steadman, 1983).

Tedeschi and Felson (1994) argue that if investigators carefully examine the sequence of activities in events that have been previously classified as "irrational," "impulsive," or non-goal directed from the actor's point of view, they will usually find that the behavior is instrumental. This type of imperfect decision-making that appears irrational is simply what Clarke and Cornish (1985) refer to as "bounded rationality" (Clarke & Cornish, 1985). Katz (1988) suggests that even the most seemingly irrational violent acts have a logic and predictable sequence (Katz, 1988). Tedeschi and Felson's (1994) articulation of the social interactionist perspective departs greatly from previous work in the area of violence research, primarily because of their claim that all violent behaviors (coercive actions) are instrumental, or goal-oriented behavior. Tedeschi and Felson (1994) suggest that several factors affect the decision-making process, including cognitive processes (scripted behavior), emotion, alcohol/drug consumption, and impulsivity (Tedeschi and Felson, 1994).

Both Katz (1988) and Felson (1993) identified three main goals of aggressive actions: to compel and deter others, to achieve a favorable social identity, and to obtain justice. An interactionist perspective, concerned with the actor's point of view, focuses on describing the factors that produce conflict and those that inhibit it. This approach emphasizes on three central issues for understanding violence: the escalation of disputes, the role of social identities, and the role of third parties. Instrumental behavior is considered learned behavior because individuals learn about expectations, incentives, and inhibitions. The actor has expectations about what actions should follow his use of threats and/or punishment, as well as the probable costs of that action. These expectations, based on whatever information is processed at the time of the event, may be incomplete or distorted.

The role of bystanders and third parties in the evolution of interpersonal disputes contributes significantly to their outcomes (Black, 1993; Decker, 1995; Felson, 1982; Felson, 1984; Oliver, 1994). In their comprehensive review, Tedeschi and Felson (1994) describe a variety of roles that third parties play, including instigator, peacekeeper, cheerleader, and bouncer. In a public dispute, third parties constitute the audience, and their reaction has a strong effect on youthful actors. In dispute situations, the identities and associations of observers of potential conflict can deeply influence the thoughts, feelings, and behavior of the actors. For example, Felson (1982) found that when a dispute occurred between parties of the same sex, the presence of third parties increased the likelihood that a verbal disagreement would turn into a physical fight. Given the nature of peer relations during adolescence and their social activity patterns (frequent interaction with peers), third parties or bystanders may play an even greater role in "co-producing" violent events. These issues are examined later in the book.

## Violence as Self-Help

When normative law is weak, the uses of violence suggest a self-help dimension that illustrates Black's (1983) "self-help" or "crime as social control" dynamic. Law is a physical and social externality with weak legitimacy for inner city adolescents.2 In areas where legal controls are weak, the externality of law moot legal norms, and self-help becomes a codified and normative basis for action. Street codes that are actively reinforced exert a strong normative influence on how social interactions are interpreted, how disputes are resolved, and how limited social standing is allocated. Combined with the social and cultural isolation of inner city life, legal proscriptions of violence are functionally weak compared to a "code" that values violence and continually defines its strategic value.

The ritualization of violence as social control is a sign of the replacement or supplement of formal law and social rules with street codes and values (Anderson, 1999; Black, 1993). Street codes emphasize toughness and quick, violent retribution for transgressions against one's sense of self or insults to one's reputation. Such transgressions become grievances, and a response is mandatory (Anderson, 1999; Wilkinson, 2001). A failure to respond is a sign of weakness, and the ensuing loss of status is unacceptable. In contexts where formal social control is seen either as oppressive (serving an external dominant class) or illegitimate, street codes become normative and adopt the moral dimension formerly reserved for the law or other social institutions.

As a response to the conduct of someone else, violence can be a form of self-help. For example, in the context of perceived wrongs or grievances, violence may be seen as a moral behavior in pursuit of a form of justice. Some violence is an effort to achieve retribution, restitution, or compensation for perceived wrongs (Black, 1983; Luckenbill, 1977; Tedeschi & Felson, 1994). Whether the violence is done with cool precision or in an impulsive outburst, the arousal of

---

[2] The limited material returns from compliance with legal norms undermine the legitimacy of sanctions. See, for example, Meares (1998), Fagan and Freeman (1999), and Sullivan (1989).

anger can be initiated by the desire to respond to a perceived assault against one's person or reputation. Much gang violence takes on this retributive form, when one gang commits an assault against the person or honor of a member of another gang. In this case, *collective liability* is assigned to all gang members for the actions of one. Gang codes call for a swift response, and the retribution often takes the form of an 'eye for an eye.' Similar acts of retribution occur when perceived slights are directed at family members or boyfriends/girlfriends. In the course of a dispute, maintaining dominant status or face requires a response to an assault against one's honor or status (Felson & Steadman, 1983). Certain homicides have long been regarded as a form of self-help. From Wolfgang's victim-initiated homicides to battered women's self-defensive homicide, self-help has motivated the use of lethal violence against the actions of another. Collective liability and self-help may be important concepts in understanding street violence among youth.

## GUNS IN CONTEXT

Several specific lines of research on the contexts of violence (e.g. gangs, drug markets, robberies) provide insights into gun use. These literatures suggest that gun use is infrequent and contingent, part of a context of *situated transactions* noted by Luckenbill (1977) and Felson (1993). In fact, many of these studies are somewhat casual in reporting the presence of guns, noting that they are common features of these scenes. One consequence is that gun events have not been carefully analyzed.

For example, gangs have always been social units in which weapons were prevalent, but the presence and types of weapons have changed the stakes and calculus of gang violence. Huff (1998) reports that 75% of gang members compared to only 25-50% of non-gang youth owned a gun. Sanders reported that 38% of incidents of gang violence in San Diego in 1988 were drive-by shootings, up from 16% in 1981 (Sanders, 1994). Although gangs favored drive-bys more than 20 years ago (Miller, 1975), the increase in the use of manufactured (compared to homemade) guns has de-emphasized the importance of fighting in resolving gang conflicts. If gangs are an important context of gun use, the growing number of gangs and gang-affiliated youths may have increased market demand for guns. As gangs emerge in new cities and new gangs form, and more adolescents consequently join gangs, the simple probability of a conflict between gangs and gang members grows (Fagan, 1992). During periods of instability, both within and across gangs, the likelihood of disputes is especially high (Spergel, 1989). If guns prescribe the rules and nature of settling gang conflicts, the likelihood of disputes settled by guns increases together with the frequency of conflict.

Although drug markets are another context in which gun possession is common, the precise relationship between drugs and guns is uncertain. In previous qualitative studies, guns have been characterized as necessary tools of the drug trade to protect money, protect dealers from assaults and robberies, to settle disputes over money or drugs, to secure territory, and to preempt incursions (Fagan & Chin, 1990; Goldstein, Brownstein, Ryan, & Belluci, 1989; Sommers & Baskin, 1993). Young males may be more vulnerable to gun use and victimization in drug markets than their older counterparts. They may lack experience or other affective skills to show the toughness necessary to survive.

As open air drug markets shrank homicides by and of young males continue to rise or remain stable until the mid 1990s (Reiss & Roth, 1993). Many homicides seem to be unrelated or tangential to drugs, involving material goods or personal slights. The increase in homicides may at one time have reflected the expanding drug market. Homicides in the mid 1990s, more than a decade after the emergence of crack markets, may reflect the residual effects of those markets. That is, guns that entered street networks during the expansion of drug markets remained part of the street ecology even as the drug economy subsided (Blumstein & Rosenfeld, 1998: Blumstein, 2002).

Firearm use in robbery is one of the most feared crimes in America because of its unpredictability and threat of serious harm. Especially among adolescents, robberies often are unplanned or hastily planned events, the result of the instantaneous confluence of motivation and opportunity (Zimring & Zuehl, 1986). Guns provide a tactical advantage in robberies, even beyond the advantage first created by the selection of time and circumstances that undermine the victim's expectations of safety. In an examination of patterns of force in robbery, Luckenbill (1980) found that choice of "coercive lethal resources" (i.e., weapon or no weapon) determined the offender's opening move and the subsequent patterns of behavior in the robbery event. Luckenbill concluded:

...based on the observations of the interviewed offenders, that offenders with lethal resources open the transformation process with a threat of force, whereas offenders with nonlethal resources open with incapacitating force. (Luckenbill, 1980: 367)

Similarly, Skogan (1978) suggested that lethal weapons impact on the type, timing, and sequence of events that characterize robbery. In Skogan's analysis of the hypothetical "life without lethal weapons," he suggests that offenders would face more resistance from victims (including fighting back or running away), would use an increased amount of physical force to gain compliance, and would select more vulnerable targets in robberies. In reality, we have experienced an increase in the availability and lethality of firearms. Under these conditions offenders tend to take on more "risky or harder" targets, anticipate little or no resistance when faced with a lethal weapon, and rely upon threat of force (which may or may not be followed by the use of force). As Skogan (1978) notes, offenders can achieve more with lethal weapons, and less effort is required (Skogan, 1978: 68). Cook (1980) found that robbery victims were more likely to be injured by unarmed offenders than by offenders carrying a firearm. He concluded that victims were sufficiently intimidated by the weapon to more readily comply with the offender's demands (Cook, 1980). However, Cook notes that the presence of a firearm opens the way for a robbery to become a homicide (Cook, 1983).

While firearms may often be present during robberies, their use in the course of a robbery may reflect other contingencies (Zimring & Zuehl, 1986). There are predictable stages for the robbery event, and when responses fail to meet the robber's expectations, threatened violence may turn to actual violence in order to gain compliance or to return the event to its planned course (Feeney, 1986; Skogan, 1978). Force, including the firing of guns, often is not gratuitous in robberies, unless a robbery becomes a stage for acting out toughness or meanness. Difficulties are introduced in robbery situations when victims (or, for that matter, third parties) do not adhere to the robbery "script." At that point, the offender is faced with the decision to back up his lethal threats with action. This stage in the event may be complicated by a young offender's limited reasoning ability. Adolescence is a developmental stage during which abstract reasoning about the consequences of using guns and the cognitive capacity to read social cues are incomplete (Kagan, 1989). The adolescent robber may see choices in these situations as "black and white" or "all or nothing." During the course of a robbery, the (presumably inexperienced) teenager armed with a gun becomes an unstable actor in a scenario the outcomes of which are dependent on a predictable set of interactions between the robber and his victim. It is when the initial definition of the situation strays from robbery to a threat, personal slight, or conflict (in the wake of resistance) that seemingly irrational violence occurs.

## THE VIOLENT SOCIAL WORLDS OF YOUNG MEN IN THE INNER CITY

Research on interpersonal violence has emphasized the characteristics of individuals or communities, while generally neglecting the contexts in which violent events unfold. Despite the well-documented contextual nature of violence, few studies have thoroughly examined both the social worlds of young inner-city males and the violent encounters they face. Inner-city neighborhoods characterized by extensive "resource deprivation" (Land, McCall, & Cohen, 1990) or "cumulative disadvantage" (Sampson, 1997) purportedly skew conflict resolution toward lethal or potentially lethal violence involving firearms.

The symbolic and instrumental meanings of violent behavior develop in a specific socio-cultural context, and we expect that they will reflect the physical and social isolation that young people experience in inner cities. This context may shape how young males develop a range of behavioral styles and evaluate the contingencies of behavioral choices. Advanced segregation (Massey & Denton, 1993) and social isolation (Sampson & Wilson, 1995) in inner-city communities create social boundaries that effectively seal off adolescent networks from the potentially moderating influences of other social contexts. In these circumstances, cultural diffusion transmits such views and behavioral norms quite efficiently (Tienda, 1991).

High levels of exposure to violence, including witnessing or participating in the death of peers, friends, family members, or neighbors, have become a way of life for many inner-city adolescents. Inner-city adolescents are exposed to a limited set of problem-solving techniques, and when conflict or threatening situations occur violence often is seen as one of the few options available. Adolescents simply do what they know in these situations. The handling of one situation by violent means affects an individual's approach to the next situation and so on. The costs of violence, including death by gunfire, are rated very low in this context (Anderson, 1999; Kotlowitz, 1991). The irony of this position reflects the internalization of a cynical view toward a living a long life among young inner city males. Futures, especially for males, are seen as tenuous both in terms of survival into adulthood and any hope of achieving mainstream measures of success in life. As Sheley and Wright (1995): argue:

Lacking an attainable future, or at least the belief in one, and absent models of deferred gratification and conventional success, it is all too easy to see how life can quickly become a quest for the immediate gratification of present impulses, a moment-to-moment existence where weighing the consequences of today's behavior against their future implications is largely pointless (Sheley & Wright, 1995: 160). Thus, what may appear as a problem of impulsive violence may in fact reflect a calculation of the benefits of restraint compared to the short-term payoffs from high-risk acts of violence.

In the study neighborhoods, behavior is driven by fear, young people believe that life is dangerous, that anything (fatal): can happen at any time, and that having a gun is a necessary, if not attractive, option. The more guns are present within adolescent social networks, the more they seem normative and the more inured kids become to the realities of guns. In an environment in which many individuals see themselves as having no power or control over the dangers and fears they face, guns provide a means to reduce fear and regain some defense against ever-present threats and enemies. Some young males may decide that the option of defense through gun use is too attractive to pass up, especially when weighed against the social and mortality costs of not having a firearm accessible. Decisions about gun use are often related to building tough identities and achieving social status in the neighborhood and among peers.

The complexities of developing positive social and personal identities among inner-city minority males are both structurally and situationally determined. Anderson (1994): states:

The inclination to violence springs from the circumstances of life among the ghetto poor --the lack of jobs that pay a living wage, the stigma of race, the fallout from rampant drug use and drug trafficking, and the resulting alienation and lack of hope for the future (Anderson, 1994: 81).

Thus one could argue that an inner-city context as described in detail by Anderson (1994): limits the scope of the repertoire available for the actor. The code of the streets operates both at the micro- and macro-levels through social interaction, cumulative definitions of conflict situations, and replicated support for the code. Actors are situated in a variety of organizational and role positions, such as school, family, work, neighborhood, and peer group settings. The human interactions in these settings shape beliefs, attitudes, and behavior. These dynamic social contexts need to be understood as dynamic and having multiple influences on individuals and groups. The data presented in this book illustrates that prestige is granted to those inner-city males who are tough, who have gained respect by proving their toughness, and who behave as such in public. These findings are consistent with several other studies. Majors and Billson (1992): explain the structural difficulties young African American males encounter in identity development:

Masculine attainment refers to the persistent quest for gender identity among all American males. Our society defines manhood through measures of responsibility and the ability to be a good provider for self and family. For black males, this is not a straightforward achievement. Outlets for achieving masculine pride and identity, especially in political, economic, and educational systems, are more fully available to white males than to black males. ...The black male's path toward manhood is lined with pitfalls of racism and discrimination, negative self-image, guilt, shame, and fear (Majors & Billson, 1992: 31).

Messerschmidt (1993): offers a theory of *crime as structured action* which suggests that crime is a resource for 'doing gender' that is carried out differentially by race, age, gender, and class position in society. Messerschmidt (1993): uses published data from three studies (Chambliss, 1977; Schwendinger & Schwendinger, 1985; Sullivan, 1989) to illustrate the race-, gender-, social class-relationship between different types of crime and male identity formation or what he called 'doing gender.' According to Messerschmidt (1993), the internalization of hegemonic masculinity ideals of dominance, control, independence, daring, and power lead to different forms of masculinity.

After careful consideration of the literature, he found that racial-minority males, like lower-working class whites, were most likely to embrace crime as a method of achieving these ideals. He states, "Participation in street violence, a more frequent practice when other hegemonic masculine ideals are unavailable (e.g. a job in the paid labor market), demonstrates to closest friends that one is 'a man'" (Messerschmidt, 1993: 110). According to his theory, using violence to *do gender* involves making strong distinctions between the masculine ideal and feminine traits. Performing well in violent situations brings manly status, while poor performance is typically classified with feminine descriptors.

In the chapters that follow I describe the respondents' social worlds in their own words. While the primary focus of this book is on violent events and event-level analysis, narratives describing the personal life histories of these violent actors allowed me to link social context to identity development and provide vivid examples of personal development in an ecology of danger in which the use of violence is both normative and resourceful. To gain insight into the contexts in which violent events occurred, important aspects of life experience (neighborhood life, exposure to violence, social control, family, peer groups, school, and employment): were examined.

CHAPTER 2
# The Research Process

The author, in collaboration by Dr. Jeffrey Fagan, conducted the original study at Columbia University from 1995 to 1998. Interviews were conducted with a targeted sample of 125 active violent offenders from two New York City neighborhoods. The primary field methods were in-depth interviews and biographical methods focusing on the social and symbolic construction of violent events (Cornish, 1993; Cornish, 1994). The interviews were quite detailed, and in addition to the violent events of primary interest, cover a wide range of topics including neighborhood violence, family experiences, school, employment, friends, guns, drug use, and future goals. Finally, respondents were asked to reconstruct three violent events: one where guns were present and were used, one where guns were present and were not used, and one where guns were not present. Data were collected on at least one violent event per person, with an average of 2.44 events per individual. Events included both "completed" and non-completed violent situations; the latter group included events where violence was avoided in a variety of situational and social contexts. "Peer" interviewers were used to increase interviewer-respondent rapport and enhance data collection efforts. Proximate age, race/ethnicity, and gender matches between the interviewer and interviewee were deemed necessary for success of the study.

The study design included sampling from two primary targeted pools: a recently released sample of young violent offenders and a matched sample drawn from the study neighborhoods. Eligible respondents were males, from 16-24 years of age, who either were convicted of illegal possession of handguns or other violent offenses (criminal justice sample), or who, upon screening, were identified as actively involved in these behaviors in the past six months (neighborhood sample). The recently released sample consists of young men who were released from Rikers Island Academy between April, 1995 and December, 1996[3] and who, upon release, entered a membership program called *Friends of Island Academy,* Guys Insight on Imprisonment for Teenagers (G.I.I.F.T.).[4] The neighborhood

---

[3] The interviews were conducted from June, 1995 and March, 1997.

[4] *Friends of Island Academy* (Friends) is a non-profit organization founded in

samples were generated using *chain referral* or *snowball sampling* techniques (Biernacki & Waldorf, 1981; Sommers & Baskin, 1993; Watters & Bieracki, 1989; Wright & Decker, 1997).

The study sample included an array of respondents that, in qualitative terms, reflect what are thought to be the characteristics of both violent offenders and violent events. The sample consists of individuals who have completed a period of criminal incarceration for a violence-related offense and those recruited from the study neighborhoods. The sample for this analysis is exclusively male and minority: 44.8% African American, 41.6% Puerto Rican American, and 13.6% Caribbean or mixed ethnicity. The majority of respondents (58.4%) resided in East New York and 41.6% resided in the South Bronx. Nearly half (45%) had been recently released from Rikers Island or another correctional institution, while the rest were recruited from the study neighborhoods. The average age was 19.3 years old with 24.8% of respondents at the modal age of 18 years old. Respondents provided detailed descriptions of a total of 306 violent events that occurred in the two-year period prior to the interview, an average of 2.44 events per interview, with a range of one event [16%] to 10 events [0.8%]. Additional characteristics of the sample are presented in TABLE 2-1.

The primary justification for including only active violent offenders in our sample was that we were interested in the social processes of violent events among individuals who had multiple events to report (to overcome the base rate problem). While the results will not be generalizable to the larger adolescent male population or even the neighborhoods, we learn about the cognitive landscapes of active violent offenders. We selected two neighborhoods for this study primarily to control for the effects neighborhood differences may have on violent behavior.

---

1992. Friends provides educational, vocational, and mentoring services to young men and women who have left the educational Academy (alternative high school) at Rikers Island. Guys Insight on Imprisonment for Teenagers (G.I.I.F.T.) Pack is a program for youth run by the youth membership of Friends. The main approach is peer counseling and outreach where ex-offenders assist soon-to-be released offenders to make positive changes by learning from their mistakes. G.I.I.F.T. Pack members regularly engage in public speaking at Rikers Island Academy, New York City schools, community based organizations, and in local media outlets.

**TABLE 2-1: Sample Characteristics (N=125)**

| Variable | % | N |
|---|---|---|
| Neighborhood | | |
| East New York | 58.4 | 125 |
| South Bronx | 41.6 | 125 |
| Sample Source | | |
| Recently Released (Jail) | 45.0 | 125 |
| Neighborhood Chain Referral | 55.0 | 125 |
| Age | | |
| Mean | 19.3 | 125 |
| Median | 19 | 125 |
| Modal | 18 | 125 |
| Race/Ethnicity | | |
| African American | 44.8 | 125 |
| Puerto Rican American | 41.6 | 125 |
| Other Islands or Mixed | 13.6 | 125 |
| Structural Position | | |
| Completed High School or GED | 19.4 | 120 |
| Enrolled in School | 26.4 | 120 |
| Currently Employed (legal) | 11.4 | 114 |
| Raised in 2 Parent Family | 16.8 | 119 |
| Mean Family Size | 5.4 members | 104 |
| Respondent is a Father | 46.9 | 104 |
| Risk Factors/Violent Behaviors | | |
| Ever Owned a Gun | 96.8 | 125 |
| Median Age of First Gun | 14.0 years old | 73 |
| Involved in Violence | 99.0 | 125 |
| Involved in Drug Economy | 84.3 | 121 |
| Ever been Incarcerated | 89.7 | 117 |
| Ever Witnessed a Serious Violent Incident | 91.4 | 125 |
| Reported a Gun Event | 79.2 | 125 |
| Experienced feeling like a Punk/Herb | 72.9 | 96 |

The two neighborhoods are among the worst off in terms of poverty and violent crime in the City of New York. The socio-demographic and violent crime profiles (1990) of the two neighborhoods selected for this study are summarized in TABLE 2-2. Compared to New York City as a whole, East New York and the South Bronx have significantly higher rates of unemployment, fewer high school graduates, higher percentages of families below poverty, a higher proportion of the population below 25 years old, and higher minority populations. The homicide rate was 2.24 times greater in East New York and 3.41 times greater for the South Bronx than the overall rate for New York City. As shown in TABLE 2-2, both East New York and the South Bronx also had significantly higher rates of robbery and assault.

This study employed a number of exploratory methods and nonstandard features that allowed us to collect data that are unique and rich. The original idea for this study emerged from discussions in Dr. Jeffrey Fagan's graduate seminar on violence at Rutgers University in 1994. Jeff and I worked closely together to develop the research design and secure funding for the study. A team research approach that included local experts was considered the best way to get close to the phenomenon of interest for this study. Differences in age, gender, street knowledge and language, identity, and race prevented me from gaining direct entry into the social worlds of young violent inner city males. However, *Friends of Island Academy* (hereafter *Friends*) provided an ideal setting for developing a fruitful research partnership. Prior to initiation of the actual study, I devoted one evening per week to developing a trusting relationship with our "lay experts" over a one-year period. I was introduced to the men's group as a graduate student who wanted to mentor, tutor, listen, and generally support the young men in their efforts to successfully reintegrate into the community. In the beginning I was skeptical of my ability to gain access and felt pretty uncomfortable because I felt like an outsider. I was convinced that my race, gender, educational achievement, and physical appearance would prevent me from getting in. The first several meetings were awkward but eventually I participated actively in the discussion, gained the trust of key youth in the organization, and gained open access to talk with the young men.

**TABLE 2-2.** Neighborhood Socio-Demographic and Crime Profiles, 1990

|                                  | East New York | South Bronx | New York City |
|----------------------------------|--------------:|------------:|--------------:|
| **Total Population**             | 161,359       | 77,234      | 7,322,564     |
| % Males under 9                  | 20.32         | 22.56       | 14.34         |
| % Males 10 to 14                 | 9.93          | 10.34       | 6.62          |
| % Males 15 to 19                 | 9.85          | 10.17       | 6.89          |
| % Males 20 to 24                 | 9.01          | 9.97        | 8.15          |
| % Males 25 to 59                 | 42.15         | 38.41       | 49.43         |
| % Males over 60                  | 8.71          | 8.51        | 14.54         |
| **Ethnicity**                    |               |             |               |
| % Non-Hispanic White             | 9.45          | 1.70        | 43.19         |
| % Non-Hispanic Black             | 47.94         | 30.51       | 25.22         |
| % Hispanic                       | 38.38         | 66.88       | 24.35         |
| % Non-Hispanic Other             | 4.16          | 1.26        | 6.68          |
| **Employment**                   |               |             |               |
| Unemployment Rate -Males         | 15.00         | 19.90       | 9.30          |
| Unemployment Rate -Females       | 13.40         | 18.40       | 8.70          |
| **Education**                    |               |             |               |
| % Persons 25+ with < HS Educ.    | 46.70         | 62.60       | 31.70         |
| % Dropouts Aged 16-19            | 16.50         | 22.90       | 13.50         |
| **Poverty**                      |               |             |               |
| % Families Below Poverty         | 29.00         | 49.40       | 16.30         |
| % Female Head Families B. Pov.   | 45.60         | 63.70       | 35.30         |
| % Female Head w/ kids B. Pov.    | 54.50         | 71.60       | 48.10         |
| **Violent Crime**                |               |             |               |
| Murder Rate Per 100,000*         | 64.25         | 97.97       | 28.70         |
| Robbery Rate Per 100,000*        | 2142.63       | 2676.28     | 1329.99       |
| Assault Rate Per 100,000*        | 1749.10       | 2112.20     | 940.80        |

*A three-year average of 1989, 1990, and 1991 FBI Uniform Crime Report statistics was used to compute these rates.

Sources: New York City Department of Planning, 1993. *Socioeconomic Profiles 1970-90.* New York: Dept. of City Planning. New York City FBI Index Crime Reports (Uniform Crime Report).

reciprocal relationship with two-way
.... and respect between professional researchers and "lay
experts" was essential for the study to succeed. I alternately served as
advisor, teacher, student, employer, friend, coach, and mentor to twenty
potential peer interviewers, all of who would have met the criteria to
participate in the study. Lay members of the research team had
personal experience with violent activities, including firearms offenses.
Most of these young men had gained powerful reputations on the
streets (for past violent behavior and/or current anti-violence outreach
work) and were granted respect and trust in their neighborhoods. Six of
the young men were residents of the study neighborhoods. Their
contributions to the study aided recruitment, protocol development,
data collection and interpretation.

The primary goal of this research was to capture thick descriptions
of events including firearms use to generate hypotheses and elaborate a
theoretical framework for understanding violent events among
adolescents. In-depth interviewing is the most appropriate method to
record information about specific events and to allow respondents to
reflect on those events.[5] The unit of analysis for the study included
both individuals and events. For interviews in which respondents
described more than one event, each individual served as his own
control, avoiding person-event confounding. Narrative interviews took
one to two hours to complete. The interviews were tape-recorded and
fully transcribed. The audio taped interviews were transcribed into
case-specific files that, upon cleaning, were integrated into a highly
complex relational database using QSR-NUD*IST 4.0.

The interviews consisted of conversations about events and their
contexts, based on semi-structured but open-ended and highly flexible
interview protocol. The benefit of this approach is that it allows
respondents to introduce new topics or issues not previously considered
by the researcher in the initial design phase. The use of prompts or
probes was highly dependent upon the level of specificity with which
the respondent described the situated transaction. The interviewers
prompted respondents to clarify points and elaborate on initial

---

[5] There are generally three sources of data for event level research: (1) official
case reports from police investigations and court proceedings, (2) survey-based
measures of event activity, and (3) ethnographic or qualitative interviews.
Interviews provide the richest data.

descriptions of their actions and perceptions. The interviewers were trained throughout the data collection period in techniques to elicit detailed information on respondents' life histories and violent events. Study procedures and techniques improved over time; therefore, many of the early problems n were overcome during the data collection period.[6]

## USING PEER INTERVIEWERS

Ex-offenders were involved in a variety of different roles on the research project, including advising, facilitating, locating and interviewing respondents. Bringing ex-offenders into the process as contributing members of the research team greatly enhanced the quality of data collected. This "lay expert" turned researcher approach has been used most successfully in field studies of drug addicts (Dunlap et al., 1990; Walker & Lidz, 1977; Williams & Kornblum, 1994), and gang members (Hagedorn, 1988), and in education research (McLaughlin, Irby, & Langman, 1994). The approach is considered appropriate for a study of gun users because it enhances researchers' ability to access a typically hidden population, to gain understanding into what happens in violent situations, and to overcome the methodological limitations inherent in survey-based methods.

Peer field researchers served as advisors on this project during the early stages of protocol development and in the chain referral sampling strategy. They also advised the researchers about apparent holes in the data regarding the types of violent events that occur in their neighborhoods, thus directing future sampling decisions. As noted above, the young men also served as facilitators and locators of potential subjects and social settings for the study.

The use of peer interviews attempted to bridge developmental, generational, and cultural gaps by having a supportive peer with whom life experiences could be discussed. Effectively communicating with young men who are at a very difficult transitional stage of human

---

[6.]The unevenness of data content and quality presented only minor problems for the study. For example, many of the early interviews did not include certain questions that we realized were relevant only after numerous interviews had been conducted. Those topics are simply missing for respondents interviewed using the earlier version of the protocol. While missing data are always problematic, it is less troublesome in qualitative studies such as this.

development and who typically converse using a slang version of the English language would be difficult even for the most streetwise researcher. But the young men serving as peer interviewers for this study were experienced with violence or had recently gone through the same difficult issues while making the transition from adolescence to adulthood. The familiarity peer interviewers had with those issues improved the validity of the data collected. They could easily establish a rapport with subjects, understand the issues that were discussed, and could clearly communicate with the respondents. In addition, our ex-offender interviewers had experienced the difficulties of making the transition from crime to legitimate employment, school, or volunteerism. This status differentiates them from the subjects, but the interviewers were trained to not show any value judgments or react impressionably to respondents' stories. In most studies, where "indigenous observers" were used, the individuals employed as researchers already had been established in "paraprofessional" or "grown-up" lifestyles and career patterns (See Dunlap, et.al. 1990; Walker and Lidz, 1977), but that was not the case in this study.

**Training Peer Interviewers**

In this research project, the interviewers had an important influence on the quality and richness of the data. Interviewer training was an ongoing and elaborate process that focused on teaching peer interviewers about the purposes and sponsorship of the research, the procedures for protecting respondents' confidentiality, ways of being sensitive to respondents, interviewing techniques, the importance of developing a rapport, and communicating effectively with potential respondents. Training also included role playing; mock interviewing; peer and researcher critiques of each interviewer's style; explanations of how to use probes, reference points, sequencing, memory aids, and cross checks to assist in the recall of information; identifying and screening potential subjects; a full review of the informed consent procedures; and transcription of taped interviews.

First, I interviewed each peer interviewer and became familiar with his personal story and general philosophy about the causes of violence. In turn, I shared my own personal story and motivation for conducting violence research. This open personal dialogue helped to bridge the social distance between the researcher and the peer interviewers. The youth were surprised to learn that I had grown up in a welfare-dependent household, experienced a great deal of violence in my childhood, and had struggled to overcome class-based prejudices. We bonded over reminiscing about our common experiences of eating processed cheese and waiting in long lines for vaccinations and booster shots at public welfare health clinics. Next, the interview crew began interviewing each other and other young men who were members of G.I.I.F.T. Pack as part of the training process. I debriefed the interviewers after each interview for the first four months of data collection, and weekly thereafter. Individual coaching seemed to be the most effective tool in teaching the peer interviewers to collect useful and detailed information.

During the data collection process, weekly debriefing meetings provided additional training support and feedback to the research staff. The field crew members recorded their personal reflections on the interviewing process in a weekly audio journal. I listened to the tapes and/or read transcripts and then reviewed them with the interviewers to identify specific recommendations to improve the interviewers' data collection skills. Group feedback also was important for repeatedly reminding everyone of the study goals and sample selection requirements. After some obvious misunderstandings, the training approach was redirected toward explaining methodological issues around sample selection, bias, and research design. One common mistake interviewers made early on in the study was to interview any candidate who was available regardless of whether or not he met the study criteria or to settle for shallow answers that did not provide enough information to make inferences. A series of readings, handouts, and formal exercises were developed as training tools using examples from the recorded interviews. A significant amount of time also was spent training on the screening and sampling procedures. This individualized learning process was ongoing throughout the study.

The research team experimented with a variety of different styles regarding language, wording, and level of formality of the interview guide. At first, we used a list of general interview content domains to guide the interviews. This approach did not produce consistent data. We determined that a more detailed but highly flexible guide yielded more systematic data collection. Throughout the process, the interview guides were modified to enhance the quality of data we were collecting and to explore topics and ideas that emerged during the data collection process. The final interview protocol is including in Appendix A.

The peer interviewers were allowed to develop their own style and modify the interview guide as needed into a more "street smart" language. It was up to the researchers to coach the young men to elicit the necessary detail and to monitor the overall quality of the interviews. They were taught to allow the research subjects to introduce topics or issues that the researchers had not considered beforehand. As recommended by Cornish (1993:28), sections of the interviews on focusing the procedural developments of violent events used a "free elicitation" approach with active prompts in an effort to record the offender's own script, and to optimize individual variation. Many of the interviews were extremely conversational in tone; some of the best interviews resembled conversations between two old friends or classmates. The use of prompts or probes was dependent upon the level of specificity with which a respondent described a given transaction. The interviewers prompted respondents to clarify points and further elaborate their actions and perception. The interviewers employed techniques such as probes, reference points, sequencing, memory aids, and cross checks to assist in the recall of information. Use of these research tools varied over time as the peer interviewers learned various strategies and received feedback from me. Throughout the interviews, the lay researchers followed up on topics that had been raised by asking specific questions, encouraging respondents to describe experiences in detail, and constantly pressing for clarification of the respondents' words. The respondents were aware that their conversations were being recorded but understood that their responses would be kept in strict confidence.

## THE DATA COLLECTION PROCESS
The data collection process for the study proceeded at a relatively slow and steady pace over a period of 20 months. To avoid problems with lengthy delays between completion of interviews and transcription of the audiotapes, semi-formal debriefings were conducted with the staff after each completed interview. The debriefing process also served to monitor the quality of data collection and to allow interviewers to share feelings and discuss any problems that may have surfaced. For example, in one particular situation an interviewer was confronted with a safety issue during an interview. A respondent became angry during the father question sequence and he happened to be armed with a gun at the time of the interview. The interviewer, Jason, was able to calm the

respondent and end the interview peacefully but he was clearly affected and more concerned about his personal safety during the interviewing process from that moment forward. This situation lead to a policy on screening for gun carrying during the interview appointment and gun removal prior to the start of an interview.

Each interview was audio taped to relieve the interviewers of the burden of taking notes and to eliminate the artificiality imposed by that process. Recording the interviews enabled the interviewer to create a more conversational interview environment, devote complete attention to the respondent, and concentrate on the discussion. The tape recording also gave the researcher a genuine accounting of what transpired during an interview. The open-ended interviewing technique (non-structured answer format) also created a context in which informants could speak candidly and in their own words. Interviewing locations were carefully chosen to ensure privacy of conversations. Most interviews were conducted in an isolated private room to avoid any interruptions or possible eavesdropping by others. Respondents were paid $25 for their interview and were given subway tokens for travel to and from the interview site. Payment was made at the end of the interview although it was not contingent upon the completion of the interview. For safety reasons, interviewers never carried more than $50, or two stipends, at any time.

Each of the focal respondents was informed in detail about the nature of the study, its sponsors, sources of funding, objectives and goals, probable duration, and the likely extent of his time and participation. Before beginning the interview, a respondent was to have definitively affirmed that he was giving his informed and voluntary consent to act as a respondent in this study. Following the completion of an interview, respondents were asked about their comfort with the conversation and were offered the opportunity to speak with a counselor to address any anxiety or emotional distress from recounting unpleasant experiences.

## Recruiting Respondents

A detailed screening protocol was used to ensure that respondents met the eligibility requirements of the study. All locators and field researchers were trained explicitly on the screening procedures to ensure that only individuals who met the criteria were included in the study. The staff did not interview a potential respondent until a full screening interview had been completed and eligibility was established.

The peer interviewers recruited respondents and completed a formal screening process for interviews. Approximately 1 to 4 weeks before their release, potential participants were introduced to the study during weekly peer counseling sessions held by a youth counselor from *Friends*. The peer counselor described the basic goals of the study and encouraged young men from the two study neighborhoods to participate. It should be noted that the main purpose of the "prep class" was to talk to the young men about making changes in their lives upon being released from jail. Mention of the study inside the jail and the peer counselor's involvement in the study were considered important steps in beginning to establish rapport with potential subjects. However, to comply with requirements mandated by the institutional review board, no formalized recruitment or screening was conducted inside the jail. Upon release from Rikers Island, potential subjects sought assistance from *Friends* and were fully screened for eligibility by the same youth leader they met while on Rikers Island.

Criminal justice samples provided only one population of violent offenders. After recruiting and interviewing the majority of the criminal justice subjects, the research team began to identify and recruit individuals who had not been convicted for violent offenses, but who were active in the same behaviors and lived in the same neighborhoods as the participants in the criminal justice sample. Like many who commit illicit behaviors, non-convicted violent actors make up a low-visibility population. Identifying a pool of presumed offenders requires sampling of natural interactional units using chain referral or "snowball" sampling techniques (see Fagan, 1989; 1994; Sommers and Baskin, 1993; Biernacki and Waldorf, 1981). To achieve comparability in both neighborhood and demographic characteristics, respondents in the criminal justice samples were asked to nominate potential respondents to populate a non-convicted neighborhood sample (N=74). Respondents were asked to nominate or refer "someone like you, from your neighborhood, who frequently resolves his personal conflicts with violent actions, has a big reputation on the street for violent behavior, or has been involved in a serious violent confrontation in the past six months." Individual cases from the neighborhood pool of respondents were matched to the characteristics of individual respondents from the criminal justice sample based on the dependent variable (violent experiences) and on certain predictor variables (e.g., exposure, demographics, etc.).

The peer interviewers also used their personal neighborhood contacts and interviewed members of their old social networks and other youth members of *Friends* assisted in reaching out to potential respondents and recruiting them for interviews. As described above, *Friends* staff members were trained as both locators and interviewers. Because of their past situations, they were considered to have unique knowledge about and access to violent offenders, which aided in the selection, recruitment, and interviewing of eligible respondents. These "lay researchers" also were able to more easily develop referral chains because they may already have been familiar with potential respondents or may have been more likely to have others reveal their potential to them. Locators, who also were associates of the potential respondents, relied upon existing personal ties to facilitate interviews. During the recruitment of the neighborhood samples, referral chains were monitored as they developed for each of the five peer interviewers. Interviews were analyzed with an eye toward directing and guiding existing and future referral chains. As the data were gathered and analyzed, emerging patterns and subgroups were incorporated into future sampling. The chain referrals, agency referrals, and "cold" contacts were mapped for each interviewer. The chain referral samples were limited to five linked individuals to avoid clustering effects in the data.

The initial sample consists of 51 young men who were released from Rikers Island Academy and who upon release sought the assistance of Friends. The neighborhood sample (N=74) was identified and interviewed using chain referral sampling techniques after the majority of the criminal justice sample was collected. Involvement in gun use activities was a main consideration for inclusive in the study. The match between the criminal justice sample and the neighborhood sample is complicated by the fact that the criminal justice participants are "help-seekers" while most neighborhood respondents are not. In the analysis, I examine the similarities and differences in attitudes and behavior between the two subgroups and report these findings accordingly.

### Reflections on the Team

Ten youth leaders were employed as interviewers and locators during the course of this study. Five individuals conducted the interviews over a twenty-month period. Approximately 12 additional young men were involved in advising and recruiting roles on the project.

Each of the field crew members had a unique experience with learning the "ropes" of interviewing. Some were very skilled and seemed to be naturally talented at interviewing, while others were uncomfortable and unsure of themselves as interviewers. A common problem for the interviewers was their inability to listen effectively without jumping into (and sometimes dominating) the conversation by adding stories of their own past criminal behavior. All of the interviewers had to learn how to be patient, wait for the subject to finish speaking before asking the next question, and to be cautious about revealing too much personal information. In the early practice interviews, subjects were frequently cut-off in the middle of their stories that resulted in a loss of data. Fortunately, we were able to allow the interviewers to learn from their mistakes by carefully scrutinizing every interview and providing detailed feedback.

Several members of the interview crew welcomed this feedback and worked hard to develop and improve their interviewing skills. In the group meetings, everyone on the team contributed by tutoring each other on interviewing techniques and techniques to handle difficult situations. Reflections on the data collection process for one interviewer are provided below.

Rich M. was a 23-year old ex-offender (in 1995) who conducted over 20 interviews for this study. He was a strong leader, had great communication skills, and was very motivated to make change. His knowledge and personal history of life in East New York, Brooklyn allowed us to get a window on the social world of violent offenders that is often difficult to capture. He described himself as someone who has truly "been there" and seen it all. I was struck by his street savvy, leadership ability, and knew instantly that he could make a great member of the research team. In 1995, he was the president of the G.I.I.F.T. Pack and a young man who could command a certain level of respect from other young men who come to *Friends* for assistance. He had been employed part-time by *Friends* for less than one year, and in that capacity, he regularly spoke to incarcerated young men about changing their lives.

The skills that made Rich M. well suited to be a peer interviewer also created unexpected obstacles for the research. Fortunately, we noticed several problems with his interviews during the early stages and worked to correct them. He had a tendency to conduct G.I.I.F.T. Pack related outreach during the interviews. In addition, he had strong convictions about "how stupid" the killings on the street were and sometimes spoke about it during the interview. I found that it was difficult for him to make the transition from the role of youth counselor to interviewer. The portions of the interview in which he asked the questions and allowed the subject to answer were excellent. It was obvious that Rich was able to gain the trust of the subjects and develop a great rapport. He was able to get subjects to talk openly about a wide range of criminal behaviors and other negative outcomes. His style of interviewing was very relaxed and conversational which seemed to enhance his data collection efforts.

Although I offered almost constant feedback after each interview, it took additional effort to get him to understand the implications of his approach for the research process. I found that replaying portions of the interviews in which he stepped outside the interview guide was helpful in redirecting his focus for future interviews. I continued to monitor the quality of his interviews very closely and offered suggestions throughout the process. The interviews changed dramatically over time. They became more standardized, free flowing, focused, and detailed. Occasionally, he reverted to giving speeches and doing outreach during the interviews but overall this problem dissipated. In addition, he was permitted to make any kinds of "preachy" or judgmental statements after the interview was finished. These strategies helped tremendously and his interviewing skills gradually improved throughout the study.

Using peer interviewers was undoubtedly the biggest challenge for the study. The strategy always seemed like a trade-off, I traded control for depth and rapport. Working closely with the interview crew required incredible energy, devotion, and patience. Trust came slowly for the young men on my team although belief in the "good of the project" came rather quickly. What I was asking from my interview crew was very difficult especially when most had never worked in a "real" work environment prior to their employment as interviewers. As a researcher, I had certain aims I needed to accomplish in this project and most of those were dependent on my ability to work closely with

the devel[...] [...]se I was not conducting the
interviev [...] nterviewer was extremely
importan [...] ter the fact and we did not
design the study to include more than one opportunity for gathering
data with the same subject. The interview protocol was one vehicle
with which I attempted to build a solid relationship by working out
problems with wording and content relying heavily on the crew
members' ideas and suggestions.

## DATA ANALYSIS

The method of analysis in this study incorporated both induction and
deduction. Data analysis for this study comprised a number of stages,
including open coding (Strauss, 1987), sifting and sorting (Wolcott,
1994), categorizing, coding in teams and checking for consistency, and
examining interactions between and across categories and cases. The
typescript files were created, printed, and coded in an interactive
process. While reading the interview content, a topic name (code) was
inserted beside each excerpt categorizing the theme(s) of what was
being discussed.[7]

The interview content was deconstructed into themes and emergent
patterns. The coding process evolved throughout the data collection
process. Each code was explicitly defined; where necessary, multiple
codes were used. These codes then were assigned addresses in the
database system. Additional notes and memos were written at the case,
node (category), and intersecting location. Both individual- and event-
level variables were sorted according to categories that were identified
through careful reading and analysis of the data. The details of the
specific data domains are presented in subsequent chapters. The event
coding schemata for the event analysis is presented in Appendix C.

Using QSR NUD*IST, a commercially available relational
database, each text string or series of text strings was given an address
code for easy retrieval and analysis. These analyses were intended to
describe and interpret the social world of young inner-city violent
offenders and the structural and processual components of violent

---

[7] The lay expert researchers worked closely with the researcher by helping to
identify patterns, suggesting interpretations, and validating the investigator's
interpretations. These efforts facilitated the coding and analysis of the data and
permitted checks for consistency in classification among members of the
research team.

events. Several matrices were developed as a heuristic device for making assessments of the reported components of violent events. The detailed narratives were used to reveal the many contingencies and factors within and across events. Finally, the clustering or intersections of these dimensions of violent events were examined to identify consistent and recurring patterns of interaction and context that describe the contingencies that launched them. Patterns of motivation, decisions, third-party involvement, action, tactics (including weapons), and contexts or settings were analyzed within violent transactions. Different explanations for the same incident were compared, negative cases were examined, and multiple interpretations were developed where appropriate (Becker, 1998; Kvale, 1996; Miles & Huberman, 1994).

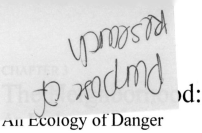

# The Neighborhood:
## An Ecology of Danger

This chapter is the first of four interrelated chapters that attempt to layout the contextual ecology in which the young males in this study are situated. I start with neighborhood context because so much of the violent behavior that is described in subsequent chapters needs to be understood in the contexts available to these young people. None of the 125 young men who were interviewed for this study felt that their neighborhoods were safe places to grow up. In the pages that follow I present quotes that illustrate some of the dominant themes that characterized how these young men perceive their neighborhood environments. Embedded in many of the descriptions is a sense of pessimism that conditions will not change although many youth acknowledge that there are people in the neighborhood trying to make a difference. The common set of complaints about the neighborhood included drugs (use, addiction, market competition, and legal consequences), violence, guns, tension or hypersensitivity between residents, a general lack of unity, a lack of viable employment opportunities, a lack of social and recreational alternatives for young people, an abundance of negative role models, and the absence of effective social control agents.

This chapter demonstrates that the level of danger for young males in these neighborhoods is extremely high; the individuals interviewed are exposed to violence daily. Neighborhood youth are armed with handguns, guns dominate conflict interactions, and guns are necessary for protection especially for those involved in illegal activity. Much of the violence is motivated in part by justice seeking behaviors in the absence of effective social control agents. Adult-youth relationships are precarious at best; outlooks for the future are quite negative for these young men.

We purposely selected East New York and Mott Haven for this study because of the rates of violence and correlates of violence including concentrated poverty, high unemployment, and low educational attainment. The picture that emerges from the statistical data provides little information about how residents of those neighborhoods negotiate safety; perceive social threat, or protect themselves from harm. The young men we interviewed had many opinions about their neighborhoods and described the ways in which violence permeates their experiences. They were asked to discuss the day-to-day activity in the neighborhood, the level and frequency of violence, the level of illegal activity on the street, their perceptions of safety, their assessment of the economic and political resources, their assessment of collective efficacy, and their assessment of agents of formal social control.

Respondents often characterized their neighborhood as a "war zone," a dangerous and unpredictable place where violence was expected and could erupt out of a variety of situations. Violence plays a major role in defining the quality of life in the neighborhoods. Public behavior on the streets is regulated by a general knowledge that life could be taken away at any moment (by guns, primarily). Three excerpts are presented to describe the neighborhoods:

INTERVIEWER:[8]  Ah, tell me about your neighborhood?
ROBERT: It's mad, drug addicts out there, niggas selling drugs all the time, shooting niggas for no reason, for stupid shit. Like niggas looking at other niggas' girls, they fighting. Niggas beaten up in, on this girl, you want to go get a gun.

VICTOR:  What has it been like?  It's been rough, shitty. Everybody, a lot of people getting killed.
INT: What do you think is the biggest problem in your neighborhood?
VICTOR: Shootings, drug selling. Robberies, murders all that.
INT:  Is there a lot of violence?
VICTOR:  Daily.

MALIK: You had to fight for yours.  You had to earn your own respect, and you don't even have to be causin' trouble, you gets picked on or something, or it could be jealousy, animosity, people jealous of you, your wealth, you get a new pair of sneakers. It could be anything. That's why it's stupid. [I'm} really tryin' to get up outta there though.
INT: How would you describe your neighborhood in terms of safety? Is it safe compared to other New York areas?
MALIK: It depends.  Safe how?  Your mother try to make it safe for you or does the community?

---

[8] To save space INT is used to identify the interviewer as the speaker. Pseudonyms were assigned to respondents to protect personal identities.

MALIK: ...pen. That's what -- that's
t... ke, you come outside, you
don't know if you comin back in. That could be your last day
walkin' or somethin,' so I really can't say it's too safe, you
know. It depends you -- if you goin' to school, you in school,
that when they try keep you safe there. But,once you outside...

INT: Why do you think that your neighborhood is so violent?
FERNANDO: Violent because of ignorance and I guess as
young they were only taught to fight for their shit, while the
two kids were there fighting. The parents are like, they didn't
say, they didn't teach them, yo, don't play with your hands.
That's not respectful. They would be like, oh, look, laughing.
Laughing. Let them go on, I am saying. Now for the safety,
we still got programs and a lot of them being cut, but we could
adapt and build stuff. And cutting these programs, I guess, the
family has to, the family structure comes together, because
they you just find yourselves to be bored.

Concerns about personal safety and self-protection are paramount
for young urban males in East New York and Mott Haven because the
environment is perceived as dangerous and the threat of predatory
crime is ever present.

Continuous exposure to injurious or lethal violence has had lasting
effects on the young men in these areas. The threat of violence in the
neighborhood shapes attitudes, perceptions, behavior, and social
identity as the next two examples demonstrate. Derek explained:

DEREK: Please, safe, if it was safe, when I come out of my
crib, I wouldn't have to carry a burner. If it was safe, when I
come out of my crib, I got to watch my back from all angles.
If it were safe, I wouldn't have to do that, I would be able to
come out, go where I want to go, move how I want to move
and don't worry about who watching me, who trying to get
me, so it ain't safe.

GABINO: Safe. If you ain't in your house, you ain't safe.
And even when you in your house, you know, something
could happen.
INT: Like what?

GABINO: Like you be, you could be in the living room watching TV and next thing you know, "bow bow," gunshots through the windows. They might not be for you, but, you know. Bullets, bullets have no, you know, no names.

Two strategies are described as essential for safety in the neighborhood: banding together with others and getting a gun for protection. The evidence suggests that young men combine these strategies. One young man explained that young men cannot rely on the police for protection but rather they find safety in numbers:

INT: So how would you describe your neighborhood in terms of safety?
STACEY: Ain't no... It's only safety in the family, that's it right there. The little crew that you clique with.
INT: Yeah.
STACEY: That's the only safety. You can't...you can't depend on police, cause they scared half the time. They don't want to come up in there. They don't wanna...they trying to go home to their family. If you...if you don't got no unity in your own clique, your own family then that's the only safety you got. Safety in numbers right there.

INT: How would you describe you Neighborhood in terms of safety?
CARLOS: Psst, the only safety we got is each other man. The guys that hang around the block that's the only safety we got. We look out for other kids on the block and that's about it. That's the only safety we got.

INT: Is it safe to compare it to other areas in New York City?
WILSON: No. Not at all. The area is not safe at all because of the violence. To me, in my own opinion, cops is scared. The cops can't even maintain it to a certain level that they would like it to be. They could do it in other neighborhoods, cause that's the amount of violence in the streets also.

Themes of "insider" versus "outsider" status, which have been documented consistently in studies of violence, clearly play a role in neighborhood safety (Anderson, 1999; Strodtbeck & Short, 1968; Sullivan, 1989; Whyte, 1943; Wolfgang & Ferracuti, 1967). The next several examples demonstrate how many young people experience their neighborhoods:

> INT: Alright how would you describe the East in terms of safety?
>
> RODNEY: In terms of safety?
>
> INT: Is it safe?
>
> RODNEY: It's alright you know what I mean it's not safe and it's not a hazard, it depends on how the person carry themselves, if you look for trouble most of the time you find it you know what I mean a lot brothers like to beef, but if you out there and you're really not looking for trouble 9 out of 10 times you'll be safe.

> INT: How would you describe your neighborhood in terms of safety?
>
> DAMONE: It is not safe at all. Anywhere you walk down the street you could get mugged or something or robbed.
>
> INT: If I was to walk to down the block would they start trouble with me?
>
> DAMONE: Yeah. You probably look like a herb to them, there is a lot of black people over there. A lot of black over there. That's their turf.
>
> INT: What is mostly out there like blacks, just blacks or?
>
> DAMONE: A lot of blacks, a few Hispanics but mostly blacks. That's the projects, there is a lot of blacks. You got to know people out there to really hang out there. Like me. I know a lot of people out there so I could hang. If you ain't from around there you will probably get into a little trouble something like that. Niggas probably try to rob you or play you or something like that.

The next example presents a variation on this theme. Here Austin described the heightened sensitivity to personal slights, insults, looks, and identity challenges in his neighborhood as a source of danger. He compared his perceptions of how people behave in his neighborhood to how he thinks people behave in white neighborhoods. Austin explained:

> INT: So how about, in terms of safety, how would you rate where you are from?

AUSTIN: Where I live? This ain't really no place to live. You can't be safe out here, when you out here, you can't be safe. Ain't got no safety in the world to be out here. Now if you go to a white neighborhood, you'll be safe, cause they ain't doing nothing. What they doing? They minding their business just chillin', that's all they doing. Don't get me wrong it's bad [in] every neighborhood, but this neighborhood right here, it's off the hook, it's off the hook. They dying back and forth, for bullshit, look at a nigga the wrong way now a days, get shot in your head for no reason. They just clap [shoot] you up. Niggas will be like, what the fuck you looking at, all that other shit. That's why I stay away from niggas man, [not] trying to get into trouble like that.

Similarly Samuel describes the dangers that male outsiders would face in the neighborhood. He concludes that the way that physical appearance and nonverbal communication are critical in terms of whether or not a male will have trouble traveling through the neighborhood. Females, according to Samuel, will not face the same dangers. When asked how he would describe his area in terms of safety he reports:

SAMUEL: It ain't safe really to walk over there. Like it depends on your appearance too. A girl could walk through there with no problem but a guy walking through there is gonna get a lot of eye contact. Some people keep walking, some people ask for it.

Repeatedly respondents report that the neighborhood is safe to "insiders" and those individuals who carry themselves correctly. Safety depends on self presentation—avoiding being seen as an outsider.

A few respondents felt that the neighborhoods were safe even for strangers as long as individuals who entered the neighborhood did not start trouble or try to control others. He explained:

INT: How would you describe you neighborhood on the terms of safety?
OMAR: It's alright, it's alright, you could walk over there and ain't nobody gonna mess with you. {by you, he meant the

interviewer, a tough looking young male of Hispanic origin},
Just don't act up and try to rule shit, rule the street.
INT: So is there a lot of violence?
OMAR: If you look for it you gonna find it.

The illegal drug business is the most frequently cited source of danger in the neighborhood. Respondents are well aware of how dangerous street life can be especially for people engaged in activity related to selling or using drugs.

INT: How would you describe your neighborhood in safety compared to other areas?
RANDY: Not so safe because of the drugs in the Projects involved. There are killing and fighting. Stuff like that.

INT: Why you think your neighborhood is so violent?
RIC: My neighb... 'Cause it's overcrowded drug areas, it's it so overcrowded that either for the new peoples to come they got to fight for theirs, or there's no room for no new people. Every year there's somebody coming out of jail claiming their property. Different faces every year.

Respondents acknowledge that drug dealers are responsible for neighborhood violence. Interestingly, youth feel that the neighborhood is safe for people who stay inside their homes and people who avoid the drug spots. Three examples are presented:

INT: How about it terms of safety, how safe is it?
TONY: It's not really safe.
INT: Who is it safe for, is it safe for you?
TONY: Some people.
INT: some people like who?
TONY: Like the people that don't be messing with the drugs and don't be working with getting drugs or none of that.

JAMAL: Safety? Don't come outside if you want safety. Stay in the household with your loved ones. Don't come out here, and don't come and stand on my corner.

BRANDON: Man, the safe part about it, man. The safe part about it is being in the crib (house) and staying away from the projects man. That's the safe part about it.

The next example shows that young men are aware of the reputation that a neighborhood may have but the reputation does not necessarily represent the experiences of all youth. His story suggests that at one time he had been deeply involved with violent activity on the street but was currently striving to avoid street violence by staying indoors. He explained:

> INT: How would you describe your Neighborhood in terms of violence?
> HAKEEM: They say this is the most violentest 'hood there is. But I don't see it.
> INT: What about safety?
> HAKEEM: It seems safe to me, now. I tell you it seems safe to me. I think I'm about that age where I don't hang out like that wild anymore, chilling.

In addition to safety issues related to criminal activity, perceptions of safety are shaped by unfortunate accidents involving firearms. Bryce was particularly troubled by this situation because the young deceased girl was an innocent victim and her death was pointless in his mind:

> INT: So um in the last two years what you think violence has gotten worse or better, has it increased or decreased?
> BRYCE: Worse.
> INT: It got worse? You don't think it got better? Why you say it got worse?
> BRYCE: People getting killed, recently. pssst.
> INT: You know somebody that recently got killed?
> BRYCE: Yeah my friend name Yasmine.
> INT: Word?
> BRYCE: From the other side of the projects.
> INT: Word. What happen?
> BRYCE: Kid playing with a gun shot her in her chest.
> INT: Word!
> BRYCE: In.. In this girl house and they dragged her in the hallway and she just died.
> INT: Word! Damn that's fucked up. So what happen to the kid?
> BRYCE: He locked up.

## GUNS AND THE ECOLOGY OF DANGER

Within this context, guns play a big part in conveying a sense of personal safety. Perceptions of neighborhood safety as described in this chapter reflect a variety of concerns including: individual status as an insider versus an outsider; competition over turf, girls, and drug business; violent reputations; belonging to a clique or group; active involvement in drug selling; hanging out in or near drug markets; carrying guns; and lack of adequate social control. The interview data demonstrated that guns were pervasive and had been part of the street scene for over a decade. According to many respondents guns were getting into the hands of youth at much younger ages than just five-to-ten years earlier when the respondents were growing up. Respondents felt that young males were arming themselves primarily for protection especially if they were involved in drug selling. Cal explained why he believed that many young males in his neighborhood were carrying guns:

> INT: So who's carrying the guns out there? Like what age?
> CAL: You got, you got everybody carrying guns. You got the girls carrying guns, you got the shorties.
> INT: You don't know what reason they carrying guns? CAL: They just want to be down with everybody else, you know. And the one thing is, another thing is, a lot of people dropping in the 'hood. People dropping, so everybody walking around, they ain't safe, they don't trust nobody, that's why they got another reason for a lot of homicides. The reason is trust—don't nobody trust nobody. Everybody growing up, trying to get that money, everybody try to knock each [other] off. So everybody say just 'ah fuck it' ...everybody just grab the ghat, just be walking around. So it just be a jungle out there.

Respondents described an abundance of guns in their neighborhoods ranging from small handguns to the latest military-style automatic weapons. Consistent with other research (Sheley and Wright, 1995), the nine-millimeter is the most popular caliber handgun although .22s, .25s, .38s, and .45s also were commonly used. The sale and distribution of firearms generally occurs surreptitiously through social networks. Respondents reported that most young males (i.e., 14 to 30 years old) could and did have guns in their neighborhoods. Guns were available on the street to nearly everybody who has the means to purchase, share, borrow, or steal them. Even people with less powerful identities can get access to firearms through associates, family members, or local drug dealers. One respondent explained the dangers he and his friends faced when "borrowing" guns from his father's stock pile:

> JEROME: The first time, ...was when I was in Catholic school, as a matter of fact. My father used to have guns in the house.
>
> INT: Oh?
>
> JEROME: My father had guns in the house and he had a two-five, a thirty-eight and a two-two. ...We used to fuck around with his guns a lot and we took all... his guns and left him with a shotgun 'cause he had a shotgun too. Left him with a shotgun, 'cause we had gave the two-five to my friend. ...My other friend we let him hold, um, the thirty-eight and ...matter of fact, we lent all of them out. Everybody claimed they lost it, everybody ended up dying.
>
> INT: How?
>
> JEROME: Everybody got shot. My man J. ...he died, I don't know what happen, I just know he got shot twice in the head. My man D., got shot, like, a whole bunch of times in his chest. And, um, my man L., he got shot in his head too.
>
> INT: They all got killed?
>
> JEROME: They all got killed.
>
> INT: And what was the reason they was borrowing these guns, they had beef?
>
> JEROME: No. They just wanted to hold them.
>
> INT: What happen? ...they went out there doing stupid shit and they got caught in the mix?
>
> JEROME: Yup. And these is the people that we grew up with and stuff, the only friends we had, the only friends we knew.
>
> INT: And they all got killed. How did that make you feel?
>
> JEROME: It had me fucked up 'cause even before we lent them the gun, it was cool. And, um, it's like when, after we let them, when we let them hold it, it seemed like... They changed into they world. I was what, I was in the, um, we was in the seventh grade. We used to mess with the eighth and ninth graders. It was like everybody was scared of us 'cause everybody knew we had guns.

As shown in Table 2.1, 91.8% of the sample reported that they had possessed a gun at some time in the past (ever had a gun). The mean age of gun acquisition was 14.4. An even higher percentage reported that they had ever fired a gun (93.8%). The mean age for firing a gun the first time was slightly younger at 14.2 years old. Respondents owned an average of 3.8 guns. 29% carried on a daily basis; another 52% carried on an occasional basis. Seventy-three percent of respondents reported easy access to guns in their neighborhood. Seventy-four percent had used a gun in a crime and 41.8% reported that they had been arrested for a gun or gun-related offense. According to 50.4% of respondents, guns were acquired primarily for protection.

Respondents reported that their own experiences with guns, which began as early as eight and as late as sixteen, were central to their socialization. Having a powerful gun was valued both for intrinsic and extrinsic reasons. Guns may have fulfilled a variety of personal needs for adolescents, including power, status, protection, recreation and a sense of belonging. These processes began at a young age, often before adolescence, as boys are being socialized into gun use on the street (also, see Sullivan, 1989; Anderson, 1994; 1999).

Many respondents fondly recalled their first firing experiences. These stories reflected a curiosity about guns and a fascination with the feelings of danger and power that guns represent. Most initial gun firing situations were non-violent in nature. Many young men, for example, shot a gun for the first time either off the roof, out the window, in the stairway, in the park, in the schoolyard, at the range, etc. These firing situations were often characterized as "testing the gun," a "rite of passage" into manhood, and an activity to do in conjunction with other kids. Holidays such as New Year's, Halloween, and the Fourth of July are often "accepted" days to fire guns in celebration or as an expression of freedom.

The frequency of gun carrying varied from daily to only in times of ongoing conflict with others. Gun carrying was most frequent at night, when young males were going to a party, wearing gold or other valuable possessions, selling drugs or hustling, and when with peers. We observed that respondents' carrying habits reflect the newness of the gun (they carry a new gun more frequently at first), the novelty of having a gun, routine activities, involvement in an ongoing conflict or "beef," and the level of police presence in the neighborhood. In the case of ongoing disputes, respondents attempted to be prepared for the moment when the dispute would escalate into gun violence. It is understood that using a gun to harm an opponent is the most effective way to handle the situation, both in terms of what is expected on the street and what an individual has to do to maintain a respected identity. Most often, respondents reported having a gun close by in case it was needed during a spontaneous conflict or retaliatory situation. They described many instances in which they had time to prepare for a potential attack by going inside their building to retrieve their guns or sending others to get them. Individuals actively involved in drug selling, for example, usually either carried a firearm or stashed it in the drug spot in case of possible robbery or territorial attack. The carrying and anticipated use of guns by respondents' peers also influenced their decisions to carry and use guns. Several members of a group may carry in anticipation of conflict, running into an old rival who is "sleeping" (off-guard, unarmed and alone), or just in case an opportunity arises to commit an easy robbery.

The majority of respondents found it easy or very easy to obtain a gun. Guns flow through connections or networks of friends or family associates. Most respondents had experience obtaining guns, many described buying guns out of state, and many others were given guns by older brothers, cousins, or drug dealers. According to some respondents gun prices were lower and there were fewer restrictions outside of New York. Respondents mentioned Pennsylvania, Virginia, North Carolina, South Carolina, Georgia, and Florida as points of purchase. Respondents provided limited detail on the exact methods of acquiring guns. The interviewers failed to effectively probe the topic to get beyond vague generalities about the process. One young man described his experiences in the Southern United States:

> MATT: Experience of buying it? It was to the point, to purchase a gun, you ain't have to have no I.D.
> INT: Was it easy?
> MATT: Yeah, it was a lot easier. You had ain't have to go through all the paperwork and wait a couple of days, you order it, just get it right there and then. You got the money, boom boom. Down south, not here.
> INT: What's the going price for, what would you say for a 9 MM?
> MATT: A good price? A buck fifty. ($150)
> INT: A buck fifty, where's that coming from, downtown?

MATT:  No, down South.
INT:  Down South, oh true that.  What about up here?
MATT:  Up here, around like three hundred, probably some shit like that.

## ALCOHOL & DRUGS IN NEIGHBORHOOD LIFE

Clearly, drugs are a background factor of gun violence in the South Bronx and East New York, in that they are part of the cultural landscape that influences perceptions and behaviors of residents of those neighborhoods.  But drugs also are in the foreground of gun violence in those neighborhoods, in that they have an immediate, apparent influence on the processes and outcomes of violent events. Drug use, drug selling, and drinking are some of the most commonly identified activities that facilitate violence.   Together, drugs and alcohol are a pervasive influence on the daily lives of young people, impacting behavior in several ways.   Rampant drug use and drug selling supersede other activities as social contexts for interactions, conflicts, and public stages for status attainment in these neighborhoods. These events, in turn, contribute to and form the codes and expectancies that regulate street behavior and foster the "ecology of danger."

Drug and alcohol use was cited as the most common type of social/recreational activity for young males.  Over one-half of respondents reported being high or drunk on a frequent—often daily—basis.  Drug addiction is also widespread among respondents' family members, friends, and neighborhood associates.   One respondent described his world in terms of selling and using drugs:

> ARLO: All my fucking people I know in my building, my fucking neighborhood, they have [sold drugs] in their life or they are still doing it right now.
> INT: How long have they been doing that for?
> ARLO: In my neighborhood, mostly, you know, [the] last six months.  Then a new nigga comes in and he wants to take over your fucking spot.
> INT: Is guns a part of that scene in your neighborhood?
> ARLO: Yes, it's part.  When niggas try to front on you with the loot, and when niggas want to take over your fucking spot, or your property, they are going to pull out, so you got to be ready too.

INT: Do your friends drink or use drugs in your neighborhood?

ARLO: That's the only thing to do. I think it's part of depression. Niggas don't know what the fuck to do with their lives, so yeah, that's what we mostly do. We fucking drink and smoke.

INT: How often?

ARLO: I would say, fuckin,' it's like breakfast, lunch, and dinner. Three course meal! [laughs].

The drug economy was described as the primary means of financial support for most of our respondents. For many, they are the second or third generation of drug dealers in their neighborhoods and have been socialized into the drug trade by older family members. Most respondents described being drawn into drug selling by the lure of "easy money" and having the means to acquire the clothes, jewelry, sneakers, guns, and other accessories needed for social acceptance and popularity on the street. They described growing up seeing older guys profiting from the drug trade in terms of money, material possessions, and interpersonal rewards (respect).

Gun carrying and use are central features of the drug business. Access to guns is widespread, and not limited to those involved in the drug trade. Our data suggest that the reasons for gun use by drug dealers are essentially unchanged over the past decade (Goldstein 1985, 1989). Recognition of the etiological relevance of drug trafficking to violence has resulted in a more careful formulation of theories regarding the relationship between the drugs and violence. There are several influences on violence that occur in the context of street-level drug distribution. Violence may be used to enforce organizational discipline or resolve business disputes. Disputes over drugs and drug paraphernalia are common among users and sellers, and territorial disputes are common among drug sellers. Street-level sellers may skim profits from mid-level suppliers or crew bosses; in the absence of legal recourse for illegal activities, such disputes are likely to be settled either by economic reprisal or by violence. When causal factors are examined, violence in drug dealing can be viewed as an extension of behaviors that are associated with efficiency and success in legitimate businesses (Black, 1983; Hadegorn, 1997).

The social milieu of drug selling/buying areas and the presence of money and drugs is conducive to both robbery of sellers and users for either cash or drugs. One respondent described the risks involved in maintaining a drug spot and how a gun is a necessary tool of the trade:

INT: Why did you have the gun on you that day when you was with your father?

PATRICK: 'Cause... we was hustling, yo. When you out there in the street, ...the stick-up man could come. And I'm not going to let nobody stick-up me and my pops. 'cause if a stick-up man come and you got over $5000 worth of drugs on you, you got money, he going to kill you, , so I just had to protect me and my family, yo.

Another respondent described his attempt to enforce street justice by shooting a drug addict who robbed his friend's drug spot:

INT: Alright, what happened? Describe, you know, it.

ARMANDO: I go–I was turning in my block and shit and I see this nigga and shit. So, boom, I was pitching --pitching, doing my thing. This kid came on and shit, my man, shit, he came out, and I like 'yeah, do this real quick, cop this bundle for me real quick.' So this dude was holding it down while I was gonna be back, 'cause I gotta go to the store. So I, like, I'm goin' to the store and shit, this other nigga from the other spot went to my spot and took the shit. So my man came back, he was [an] addict, they robbed me--they robbed me, motherfucking nigga from the other spot. I went over there nicely and said 'that was my shit, where my shit at?' It was like, 'I don't know.' The guy went upstairs, [I] got five of my niggas ...we was ready to set it. First nigga, the nigga that got robbed, my--my man that got robbed, he had a--a nine, he just blast that nigga right in the face. And from there it was just on. It was shooting. Caught a nigga in the leg--I caught a nigga in the leg and in the chest and in the stomach --caught a nigga in the stomach.

INT: What kind of gun you have?

ARMANDO: I had a nine, too.

INT: What started it? They--he --

ARMANDO: They robbed my man.

The relationship between drug use and violence may be spurious. The reciprocal nature of the drug business and violence may influence the decision to participate in drug selling, i.e., individuals averse to violence may avoid street-level drug transactions, leaving only those willing to engage in violent behaviors as participants. Self-selection of violent individuals for participation in the drug business also may increase the likelihood of violence during drug transactions. For example, Fagan (1989) found that the link between drug selling and violence among youth gangs was strongest for those gangs most frequently involved in violence generally.

## NEIGHBORHOOD RESOURCES AND SOCIAL COHESION

Respondents generally described their neighborhoods as lacking in resources and community cohesion. Respondents were asked about whether they knew of community leaders, professional people, and religious leaders in their community. The majority did not know of any individuals who would fits into the first two categories and most reported that they knew religious people but not the leadership.

Many respondents felt that community centers were important for preventing violence in their neighborhood. Frequently in neighborhoods without community centers youth would lament about how the centers could help make the neighborhood a better place for children. In some cases community centers, playgrounds, and youth programs did exist in the past but were not longer in operation.

> INT: What about, how about the community, the community is together like?
> TYRONE: Not really man, nobody know nothing when stuff happen.
> INT: Yeah.
> TYRONE: So, they, they ain't together.
> INT: What about people, people of the church and stuff?
> TYRONE: Yeah....the church across the street from my building. That half of my project go to.
> INT: How about social and recreational activities for kids, like things to do, places to play at, monkey bars, swings, stuff like that?
> TYRONE: They messed that up when they changed the projects around man, when they rebuild the front, the front of my projects, ain't none of that no more.
> INT: They took all that out?
> TYRONE: Took all that out.

These violent offenders may have a skewed view of their environments or, perhaps, they describe the reality of these distressed communities.  An example of this perception can be seen in many fashions but particularly with perceptions of legitimate community authority.  These negative perceptions are easily recognized in the sentiment expressed by one respondent:

> INT: Do you feel the community leaders in your neighborhood are doing their part to reduce violence?
> EDDY:  Ain't no fucking community leaders no more.  Who the fuck got a leader? Spanish people ain't got a leader.  Black mother fuckers ain't got not leaders, they ain't got shit.

## Perceptions of How Adults View Adolescent Males

Ninety-four respondents described their perceptions of relations between adults and young people in the neighborhood.  This question was especially interesting to me because one of the topics that came up frequently in the young men's support group that I had initially participated in was a strong resentment of the judgments that adults made of young African American and Latino men.  One entire weekly session focused on this issue.  Several young men described examples of how they felt all of society viewed them as predators, how people on the street would clutch onto their bags as they approached (as if he was planning to attack that person), and that most people expected the worst from them. One articulate young man reflected on how once he started to physically mature through puberty people started treating him differently.  I did not write down his exact words but I distinctly remember the tears in his eyes and the crackle in his voice as he described how painful it was for him to see fear and distrust in the eyes of strangers and neighbors alike.  He longed for the days before he matured into an adolescent because from his perspective "society stopped caring, stopped hoping, and stopped seeing him as a human being."  This particular young man did not enjoy evoking fear.  This interaction left a lasting impression on me although I have no way of knowing how common these feelings are among young minority men. These themes were evident in Anderson's ethnographic study of social interaction in Philadelphia neighborhoods (Anderson, 1990).

Researchers rarely ask young people to describe their relationships with adult figures in their communities.  Little is none about what factors shape an adolescent's perception of adult –youth relations.  I posed the question in a generic way with the hope of getting a sense of the degree of involve adults have with youth on the street.  In many of the responses the respondents offered more than one answer and often described situation-dependent opinions. The selected quotes provide more detail of how the respondents talked about the relations between youth and adults in their neighborhoods.

ART: I feel they give them respect cause they scared of them. cause of a lot of the brothers in my 'hood, around my age and them older and a little younger they don't really, they like careless and shit they don't really think about shit. So that's why they got the adults over there scared to death and shit.

INT: What type of relationship do you think most adults have with teenagers and young men in your neighborhood?
RUSTY: I don't think they have no kind of relationship with them.
INT: Explain yourself?
RUSTY: Because there is a lot of adults will see things going on with kids and they are the one that's suppose to set the example for us being kids, and a lot of them don't set the example, the example that they set is drugs and alcohol.

QUINCEY: Nah it ain't like it used to be back in the old days, it's like they ain't got no respect for them, I mean. They young one's ain't got no respect, for the old one's. And the old was is scared to death of the young, 'cause everybody packing ghats and shit.

HAKEEM: I think they intimidated by teenagers.
INT: Explain?
HAKEEM: Cause the little teenagers they wild. They wild so you know adults, maybe not the young adults but the older adults are defiantly intimidated by them. They may not, cause around here they might put a cap in that ass.
INT: Do they respect them?
HAKEEM: Nah they ain't got no respect.

TERRILL: [In] my neighborhood most of them are scared of them.
INT: Explain.
TERRILL: Because the young kids today walk around with this sag and busting new styles. You know they didn't grow up like we grow up. So they petrified of us cause they think

wrong. Well they have a good
relationship, the older guys don't try to school the little guys,
tell them to stay out of trouble. Even though the older guys
still be in trouble.

Today's urban youth must confront challenges to their personal
safety as they negotiate their neighborhoods and struggle for survival in
the context of poverty and extreme violence. Norms supportive of
violence to resolve conflicts, achieve status, and establish manhood are
ever present and passed down from the previous generation (see
Anderson, 1990; Fagan and Wilkinson, 1998; Wolfgang and Ferracuti,
1967). These adults, who represent the "old head" class, often fail to
positively influence today's at risk generation. In turn, these youth
frequently fail to recognize or respect the legitimate adult authority
within their communities. Interestingly enough, young people appear
to adapt to this role reversal by turning their illegitimate pursuits into
"accepted" or at least tolerated activities that ensure "survival."

Anderson (1999) describes the withdrawal of adults from public
spaces in inner city neighborhoods. He also describes the
consequences of that abandonment. The so-called adults in these
neighborhoods have allowed the power of establishing and maintain
social order to in favor of youth who are perceived as ruthless and
dangerous. The power and control over public spaces transferred to
youth as adults prematurely withdraw from their legitimate roles of
exerting informal social control over youth. Our analysis suggests that
adolescents perceive this abandonment as further evidence of the lack
of adult legitimacy. Neighborhood adults assume the role of mentor for
many youths whether they realize it or not. An adult that supports
illegal activity can influence a young person to lead a life of crime. An
adult that supports schooling and education can serve as a positive role
model. Our respondents describe a general lack of positive role models
in their lives. Many respondents felt that male role models in the
neighborhood could either influence children to be future hustlers or
scholars. According to respondents, many older citizens were not even
aware of the influence they have on the younger generations.

The decline of neighborhoods, increasing crime rates, rising
unemployment and poverty, and general failure of institutions to cope
with increasing service demands with decreasing resources has reached
almost crisis proportion in the inner city. Sampson and colleagues
recent test of social disorganization theory showed that "collective

efficacy" –the notion that neighbors will intervene in several problematic situations– reduces the risk of violence at the neighborhood level (Sampson et al. 1998). In neighborhoods where residents have little interpersonal contact with their neighbors, distrust each other, go their own way, fail to intervene with children, and withdraw from any type of organized community life an accumulation of negative outcomes can be found. Inner city neighborhoods have historically been described as generally lacking the necessary ingredients to maintain social order and control over youth and adult criminality. Participation is generally the lowest in neighborhoods that need crime/drug prevention the most. Residents of low-income, high crime, heterogeneous communities are the least likely to become involved.

The worlds of adolescents, especially violent adolescent males (who are viewed by many as ruthless predators) are rarely examined or understood. This section described how those so-called street-oriented youth view their neighborhoods in terms of social control. In our interviews we gathered relevant information regarding the social control processes operating at the neighborhood or often block level. These young men comment on the roles that they see "adults" play in intervening behaviors, informal social control, and social relations with youth. Here respondents describe how adults would respond to a variety of scenarios of crime and disorder (See Taylor, 2002; Gibson, Zhao, Lovrich, and Gaffney, 2002; Sampson, Earls, and Raudenbush, 1998). Recall that the processes of social control within the context of respondents' family situation were described in an earlier chapter.

It will become clear in the pages that follow that these young men failed on multiple fronts and were caught up not only in a lifestyle where violence was likely, but have been cognitively shaped by that violence. The reader should be mindful that this sample is not representative of all young men in these neighborhoods, but rather is a selected sample of active violent youths.

# CHAPTER 4

# Family:
## One Important Developmental Context

In this chapter, respondents' family backgrounds were examined as a developmental context. Respondents were asked to describe their family relationships during childhood and adolescence. They described each of their parents' employment status, level of caring and personal support, alcohol or drug use patterns, involvement in criminal activities, monitoring and social control behaviors, and views on the respondent's illegal activities. Respondents spoke openly about the dysfunction and tragedy in their families. In most cases, their matter-of-fact descriptions of those devastating situations reflected cognitive dissonance as well as limited exposure to alternative models. One respondent's description of his family characterizes many among the sample:

> DARRELL: I am not going to say it's a Brady Bunch family or one of them happy families but it's a family where I could say anything goes. I don't really know how to describe my family.

Respondents were raised in a variety of family situations. Only 16.7 percent of the sample grew up in a two parent family, 61.7 percent were raised in female-headed households while 17.5 percent were raised by other family members including grandmothers, aunts, uncles, or siblings. The average family had 5.4 members with a mode of 4 members. Most of the respondents' families faced numerous hardships, losses, and economic instability and family members strongly influenced the outlooks of respondents. The characterizations of family life were generally dynamic; respondents often experienced changes in family life over their childhood and adolescent years.

## SINGLE-MOTHER HOUSEHOLDS

Single mothers raised the majority of youth in this study. Most of these young men stated that their mothers did the best job they could to raise their children with limited resources. Respondents most often reported positive, loving relationships with their mothers. Jeff made the following comments about his single mother:

JEFF: And for my mother, my mother has tried her best, you know, to, like, take care of me and raise me the right way. But you know, like I told you, she would just want me to stay home so she could just take care of me and not want me to do anything. My mother would just spoil me, she would. But I can't go with that, I like doing things for myself.

The majority of respondents felt that their mothers had a strong presence in their lives. Often single mothers were expected to fill the role of both mother and father for her children:

INT: Were you raised by both of your parents?
NICK: I was raised by my mother. My father left me when I was three years old. So my mother was basically my father too.
INT: Did you know him?
NICK: I heard what people told me about him. Like other family members, like my uncles and sometimes my moms would talk about him.
INT: When did you see him since he left?
NICK: I saw him when I was older, like as a teenager. We didn't really click 'cause he basically was a stranger to me.

Many young males were very close to their mothers, expressed their deep emotional bonds to mothers, and desire to do something positive to improve their mothers' lives. For some, the absence of the father made the relationship with their mother more important to them:

INT: Tell me about your family.
NORM: My family is cool, man. My mother (...) my father left when I was a baby. But my moms, she was always there for me. I'm a guy. Guys always close to they mothers. And my moms just raised me, man. So to me it's like I ain't got no father. That's it. And I still grew up tough and I ain't... I don't need my pops. If you ask me, I tell you the truth, I don't really need him. I stuck with my moms through thick and thin. She still there for me. Just trying to do my thing. Get this education, that's all. To educate myself, and get this money, that's it.

Several respondents lamented about loving their mothers despite the painful experiences they may have endured. Jamal explained:

INT: Can you tell me a little something about your mother?
JAMAL: Yeah, my mother, she, she's been strung out on drugs ever since I was in her motherfucking womb. I think that's why I'm so fucking crazy now.
INT: How's your relationship with her now?
JAMAL: I love my mother even though everything she done. I still love my mother, man. That's my mother. Right now, my mother is one of my family members out of the six that's incarcerated. So we can't do shit together but talk on the phone and write letters to each other.
INT: How long she been locked up?
JAMAL: She been locked up for the last year and a half.

The majority of single mothers (57.5%) referenced in this study were employed outside of the home. These workingwomen struggled to balance the demands of motherhood with economic concerns on their own. Jabari explained that his working mother could not watch over his activities:

INT: So how did your moms react when you get in trouble?
JABARI: When I was younger she used to beat me. But when I got like fifteen, fourteen she like 'fuck it.' She works all day, there was nothing she could do. She work all day. She couldn't keep me in the house all day. I had my own set of keys. When she got home I never be there.

Approximately 15% of single mothers described in this study had problems with substance abuse or addiction, 5.4% were involved in other criminal activity, and 1.4% had passed away, according to respondents. Some respondents had mothers with an active addiction. David explained:

INT: Your mother wasn't giving you money?
DAVID: Yeah 'cause she was on crack or whatever. She needed her drugs.
INT: How do you know your mother was on crack?
DAVID: 'cause I saw her do it.
INT: You saw her?
DAVID: Yeah.
INT: How that make you feel?

DAVID: I didn't want her doing it but I didn't have no choice. That's her life, so...

INT: Did it make you lose respect for her?

DAVID: Not until we moved back to the Bronx.

INT: And then what happened?

DAVID: Then she do some ol' crackhead shit. Like give me a few dollars, then I go to sleep and she sneaking in my room taking a hundred dollars. Yeah [after] that crackhead move I started losing respect, but that was still my moms.

Christian's mother was an alcoholic who was involved in prostitution. Although he claimed not to care, he clearly was upset while talking about his mother:

INT: Tell me about your mother.

CHRISTIAN: She's 49 years old. She's a fucking wino, always drinking. I'm trying to sleep, two, three o'clock in the morning she over there breaking shit, stabbing the walls with rusty screwdrivers. Threatening to kill my father. That's why I grew up to be the way I am, because of that shit, man. Her not showing me no love. I just turned into an evil motherfucker. Now my moms, she fucking selling her ass.

INT: What you mean, selling her ass?

CHRISTIAN: In a whorehouse. I don't give a fuck. All my friends hit on her. That's her decision. She want to sell her ass, to be sucking the next nigga's dick, let her do her fucking thing. I'm living my life.

In the next example, LJ's mother died of cancer after a life of alcoholism, leaving LJ on his own after her death. LJ explained:

INT: You don't live with your moms, right?

LJ: Nah man, my moms died. She was an alcoholic, man. She found out she had cancer. She just started getting sick, she started going to therapy, you know. She just died. She died in '92. I was taking care of my moms and giving her what she wanted. She used to drink a lot, man, that's how she died ,yo. She drank so much she didn't know she had cancer.

INT: Damn, son, I'm sorry. What about your pops?

LJ: Nah man, I never even met my pops. Nigga probably died for all I know. I don't give a fuck either.

Another young man described being on his own after both of his parents were killed. He speculated that their deaths were related to his involvement in the drug business. Andres explained

INT: How was it growing up?
ANDRES: I don't know, my moms, she was wilding, my father outside selling drugs, they both passed away already. I don't know, I'm just by myself now.
INT: And your parents passed away?
ANDRES: Yeah.
INT: Why? What happened, could you tell me a little about that?
ANDRES: They got shot.
INT: Your mother and your father got shot?
ANDRES: Yeah, they was both together coming home for supermarket.
INT: And when did this incident, incident occur?
ANDRES: Two years ago.
INT: Where?
ANDRES: Right on my corner.
INT: In your neighborhood?
ANDRES: Yeah.
INT: Over what?
ANDRES: I don't know, I guess they wanted me and they had to get to who I love most.
INT: What you have problems up there in your neighborhood?
ANDRES: Yeah I got problems. Right now I be walking the streets I have to watch my back.
INT: How you feel about what happened to your parents?
ANDRES: I feel bad, but I figure you got to go sometime.
INT: And ever since your parents left, I mean, what you've been doing?
ANDRES: I got the apartment, my welfare, but I got to sell drugs to make money. I feel, I don't know really, I feel bad but I've got to do my thing, I've got to survive by myself.

## TWO-PARENT FAMILIES

Of all of the family situations described by respondents, two-parent families generally provided the greatest stability both economically and emotionally. Among the 20 two-parent families, 71 percent of fathers and 60 percent of mothers were legally employed. In one example, Andres explained:

> ANDRES: My father was a hard-working man, he did everything he could just like my mother. Came home, put the food on the table, put a roof over my head. I ain't have no complaints about him.

A few respondents described their fathers as positive hard-working men who were the sole providers for their families. For example Rodney described his father:

> RODNEY: Yeah, he was always there. He was a person who worked hard, took care of his children. He went out there and bust his ass.

Several respondents believed that their parents were good providers but were not available to them because they worked long hours. In the following example, Cal claims he looked to the street "for love" because his parents were not around very often:

> CAL: So that's why I grew up in the streets. I grew up as looking for somebody to love me in the streets. You know my mother was always working, my father used to be doing his thing. So I was by myself. I'm here looking for some love, I ain't got nobody to give me love so I went to the streets to find love.

According to another respondent, the demands of his father's job kept him away from the home:

> INT: So what about your father?
> AVERY: My father, he wasn't around much. He works too much. He's a truck driver, he had to be at this place like Sunday mornings and got back the next Monday. So I really hardly got time to see him.

A few respondents reported that they experienced violence at the hands of siblings while their parents were away at work. One respondent described a situation from which child welfare officials eventually removed him:

> PABLO: My moms and pops used to go to work and my sisters and brothers would beat me up. I was born around

violence. I wasn't a violent person unless, you know, I felt my life was in danger. But I got separated from my moms and pops, you know. The system took me away from them at 12.

A few respondents described two-parent households that were disrupted by illness and death:

MARC: When I was little my moms was like always working and shit, maintaining everything. My father, he had his own business so he was the one taking me to school, dressing me, saw all my shit, all that type stuff. But my moms, weekends I would see her 'cause she's off and she'd drag us to church. My moms is my mother. My moms is my world.

INT: And your father?

MARC: When I was little things was much more simpler. It was all about going to the park, shit like that. He died when I was 10. He was real strict with me.

INT: So what he died of?

MARC: He had some shit called Hodgkin's disease in his liver.

Although the presence of two parents often is beneficial, two-parent families still are vulnerable to the problems endemic in these neighborhoods. Among the two-parent families describe in this study, 54% of fathers and 28% of mothers struggled with substance abuse and/or addiction during the respondents' upbringing. In addition, 43% of fathers were involved in criminal activities. Abuse of alcohol and drugs including crack, powder cocaine, heroin, and PCP had a major destructive influence on many respondents' families. Although a few respondents admitted having their own substance abuse problems, most were distressed over their family members' problems. In some cases, both parents had drug and alcohol problems that affected respondents profoundly:

INT: What was it like coming up?

JOSE: First of all, I was growing up my parents were involved in drugs and shit. I seen all that, man. Well that's the way they were. A lotta shit happen to me because of that. Yeah man, too much shit. Just too much drama. Everybody in my family been locked up before. So I'm used to it already, man. It's all I heard, you know.

INT: Did anyone use drugs in the family?
JOSE: Hell yeah, man. That's all up in the family. To me, I
think that's in everybody's family. You always got one fiend.

Although the scenario described above was not unique,
respondents more often reported that their family members disapproved
of their lifestyles and taught them good values:

STEVE: My mother and father told me drugs is bad but I did
what I wanted to do regardless. I still did what satisfied
myself. When I was brought up I didn't have too much money
in my lifetime. I got stuff, I got clothes and everything but I
felt I needed more, I wanted more than what they was giving
so I had to go out there and get more. So I had to go out there
and do what I had to do myself. What my mother and father
was giving me wasn't enough for me, I wanted more. So I got
a Fila suit one day, I wanted something else the next day.
They give me five dollars this day, I wanted twenty-five the
next day.
INT: Why is that, you think?
STEVE: It all about you felt like you ain't getting this much
and you wanna go out there and get more. So I'ma go and do
what I gotta do to get more, you know. If I'm working,
hustling, or whatever. That's how I get down.

Travis explained how his father's drug use broke up his parents'
marriage after 18 years of stability:

INT: Was you raised by both your parents?
TRAVIS: Ah, yes, until 18 years.
INT: And then what?
TRAVIS: And then, um, he was messing with that shit, crack,
and my moms kicked him out. So he in Puerto Rico.
INT: How was your pops when you young?
TRAVIS: My pops is all right, don't get me wrong, though he
started fucking with that drug shit, but my [pops] was all right,
he used to always hit me off [give him things he wanted] and
shit. He was a father ,you know. My pops was a father. I'm
happy when I was older I could understand it and shit. 'Oh
that's drugs,' I understand that he fell victim to the drugs.

## OTHER FAMILY SITUATIONS

Many respondents had been raised by other members of their immediate family such as grandmothers, aunts, or siblings during long periods of their childhood and adolescent years. In most of these cases, grandmothers took care of respondents after the parents had died or lost custody due to personal problems. Relative to the rest of the sample, these respondents grew up in the most unstable environments. Six examples are provided below:

INT: Did you grow up with your mother and father?

DIEGO: I grew up with my mother and father until I was like eight. And we got separated.

INT: How? Why?

DIEGO: Over fights and you know, my moms, they wasn't taking care of themselves too good so I went to foster care up to around 11. I went to my grandmother's until 14, and then I went to [my] uncle and now I'm 16 and I'm in a group home.

CAL: I live with [my] aunt. My moms passed away.

INT: I'm sorry about that.

CAL: And my pops, I don't know my pops. That's my family right there. I lost my moms when I was, what, two or three years old. My grandma raised me.

INT: Can you tell me about your family?

JOEL: My family, I live with my grandmother right now. My mother is a lost case. She uses drugs, whatever. I have an older brother, a younger brother, and a little sister. She was there for us, but you know, she just flipped so, you know, she is in her own little world. My grandmother is taking care of us right now. My father was never there for me at all. So it's not like I got a mother and father. The only one I have is my grandmother.

INT: At what age did your grandma take custody of you?

JOEL: My grandmother lived in the same building ever since I was born but it's been, like, 11 years that I been with my grandmother. My momma sees us whenever she wants. She ain't bad or nothing, she just got a drug problem and she be with her friends and shit. I guess her friends are more important than her daughter and her sons. So my grandmother let her know she is welcome to come see us or whatever, but she really don't care much about us. Anyway, that's the story about my family.

INT: Did your parents split up?
LARRY: Yeah, 'cause my mother was a alcoholic. She used to drink. She used to leave the house and go out and drink. And once the building caught on fire. 'cause she wasn't there. We almost died and ...we was in a foster home for a while. They took us away when we was small. They put us in different foster homes.
INT: How long was you at the foster home?
LARRY: Like for two years. My [step]father come and took me out though, 'cause my mother always in a bar drinking and shit.
INT: Do you see her now?
LARRY: She lives with us now.

BRYAN: Yeah, it was all right, my father was doing his thing, he was dealing with drugs. He had half of Hunts Point locked down back in fucking '80s, '85 and shit. Then my father died and separated from my moms. My moms started hanging out and telling my sister to take care of us, and that's when BCW came and took my brothers and all that shit, that weekend I stood in my grandmother's house.
INT: Yeah.
BRYAN: Yeah, they ain't snatch me 'cause my grandmother took custody of me. And [my mother] went to Puerto Rico.

INT: Why was you in foster care?
ALONZO: 'cause my mother was on drugs and she gave us to them 'cause she was smoked out. She gave all us up to my grandmother and my aunt.
INT: So did you mom stop? Go to rehab or something?
ALONZO: Yeah. She had stopped on her own, she started going to church. From then on she was just done.

A few respondents were placed in foster care or group homes. One respondent was given up for adoption by his parents; he had problems in his adopted family and ended up in a group home at age 16:

INT: So where are your parents now?

DAMONE: I don't know where the fuck they are. I don't give a fuck about them. They gave me up for adoption kid, why should I give a fuck about them? Excuse my language, but I don't even know who they are. Then my adopted parents put me in there [group home]. They gave me up 'cause I was so bad and doing bad shit. They just sent me to that home shit.
INT: How did these people treat you when you was with them?
DAMONE: They treated me alright but I just didn't like it. Go home early and have to take their shit, curfew and all that shit. I was getting locked up and they wasn't having it. My life was already fucked up.

## RELATIONSHIPS WITH FATHERS
Fathers are "present" in the lives of only 51 of 119 respondents in our sample. Seventeen respondents reported their fathers were deceased, 30 had fathers with serious drug or alcohol abuse problems, and 36 had fathers who were involved in the drug business or other criminal activity. Of those young men raised in a female-headed household, 59% had no relationship with their birth fathers. Thirty respondents reported at least some type of relationship with their fathers. Among these fathers, 50% worked legally, 73% are involved in some type of illegal activity, 50% had drug or alcohol abuse problems, and 9.7% had been killed in recent years.

Many fathers had been deeply involved in the illegal drug trade and died as a result of their involvement with criminal activity. Several respondents offered powerful descriptions of their father's violent deaths. One young man states:

INT: What about your pops?
ERIC: My pops passed on.
INT: Sorry.
ERIC: Yeah, he passed last September. He sell drugs. I didn't know that. I used to kind of think, well, where he gets all this money if he don't go to work. Well, you little, you don't question much. You the kid, go to school, got the best, don't question.
INT: No doubt.
ERIC: Nah, no complaints. He got shot up. Last September it happened. He was going to sell 25 kilos of coke and they

blasted him. He had a [Lincoln] Town Car. Dress in suits and shit. Money is like a drug, you know.

In the case presented above, Eric's father was a vivid example of the allure as well as the deadly consequences of drug business. Note how he highlighted the symbolic representation of "success" in the drug business as illustrated by his father's choice of automobile and clothing. Rasheed lost his father in a similar manner:

INT: Was you raised by both parents?
RASHEED: My father was killed when I was eight.
INT: Damn, I'm sorry. If you don't mind me asking, what happened?
RASHEED: He was shot in a drive-by. Gang shit.
INT: How did that affect you?
RASHEED: It made me more aware about death, 'cause before that you hear about people dying and you would say nah, I never had that experience.
INT: Did you ever find out why it happened?
RASHEED: It was a hit on him. It was a hit.

The young men find ways to come to terms with losing their fathers through difficult situations like drug addiction, homicide, and suicide. Derrick had to come to terms with his father's recent suicide:

INT: What happened to your pops?
DERRICK: Pops passed away.
INT: When?
DERRICK: Four years ago.
INT: Sorry about that. From what? If you wanna talk about it.
DERRICK: Alright. It's not really based on nothing. It's just that he felt that he was going through too much pressure and he took his own life. Hung himself.
INT: How that made you feel?
DERRICK: I'm saying at that time, I didn't feel anything, really. It was all inside me, but after a while I got used to expressing myself so I eventually got over it. After I started talking to people about it. Counselor, my moms or something help me out.

Travis lost his father to drug use at an age when Travis felt he could understand and come to terms with the loss. He explained:

TRAVIS: My pops, my pops is all right don't get me wrong, though [he] started fucking with that drug shit. But my pops is all right he use to always hit me off [give me money] and shit. He was a father you know I'm saying, my pops was a father. You know I'm happy [it happened] when I was older you know when I could understand it and shit. 'Oh that's drugs I understand that he fell victim to the drug you know.'
INT: True that.
TRAVIS: If I was younger and that woulda happened I would not [have] understood it.

Some fathers had been incarcerated for most of the respondents' lives. Some respondents stayed in contact and others did not. Felton described a relationship with his father who was incarcerated for 17 years:

FELTON: I was raised with just a mother.
INT: Just moms?
FELTON: Yeah, my pops was locked down.
INT: For what?
FELTON: Like, 17 joints. I was mad young. Like one.
INT: But you spoke to him while he was in jail?
FELTON: Yeah, I was going to see him when I was younger. When I was like six, seven, I was going back and forth to see him. My moms was taking me to go see him. So that was kinda cool.
INT: What was he locked up for?
FELTON: Bodied a nigga back in the days. Murder and shit.
INT: So when did he come home?
FELTON: Beginning of '94.
INT: What does he do now?
FELTON: He chill. He's Muslim. Me and my father, we cool.

Clarence's father was described as living a "life of crime." The father's criminal lifestyle and frequent incarceration left Clarence feeling as if he did not have a father in his life. He explained:

INT: So, um, what did your father get locked up for, do you ever remember hearing about it?

CLARENCE: He did some ol' stick up in a bar and he got caught.

INT: How much time did he do?

CLARENCE: Um, I think about four years, he did a armed robbery. After that he lead a life of crime. He was in and out of jail.

INT: Oh word, how did that make you feel knowing your pops was locked down and shit.

CLARENCE: I'm saying, I didn't have a father.

Father-son relationships can change considerably over time. In many of the interview discussions respondents reported longing for a strong bond with a father figure. In recent years, Clarence's father reformed himself, re-established contact with his son, and attempted to help his son change his life:

CLARENCE: And another role model that I look up to now and I kind of love and I'm sad that I ain't have him all my life was my pops, too. 'Cause he turned around, he took his life and maybe about five years ago he put himself in a program. He put himself in and when he came out, he came out a new man. Now he got a little job, he's a counselor. He has a little more, he got a little car. He can do for me now. Even though it may be a little too late in my life to show me what to do, but he kind of showed me not to give up hope. No matter how much time passed. And he even tell me to this day that he regrets that it took him so long to get to where he's at now.

INT: Yeah. Respect him for changing man.

CLARENCE: We do. He kind of hooked me up into coming down here today. 'Cause he sees that I'm kind of tired of the street, the path in front of me. He tried to help me about two years ago but I was like 'psst, man, forget this, pops I'm living the fast life. I got money, girls, I'm chilling.' But now I kind of, see, I matured a little more. I really don't want that test, all it leads to is either jail or death.

Some respondents felt that their father's choices to be involved in criminal activity put the family and marriage in jeopardy and lead the end of numerous relationships. Drug use and selling was a common reason for the breakup of relationships between the respondents' parents, as Sony explained:

INT: So you was raised by your moms and pops, or just... ?
SONY: Yeah. My moms and pops 'til I was eight. My father was selling drugs and all that, you know. But he was doing his thing, giving us money. But he fell victim to what he was selling.
INT: He started using it?
SONY: Yeah. So my moms couldn't take it. So she was like, 'nah, I can't go down like that.' She seen him falling off, so she tried to help him. He couldn't help himself, so she had to take the bounce [leave].
INT: Yeah. How did that affect you as a kid? You knew he was doing it?
SONY: Yeah, I knew what he was doing. 'Cause, see, he was doing it in the house. I was young, I used to just see money as a little kid. Always.
INT: Did you ever see guns or whatever?
SONY: Yeah. He had a whole fucking suitcase of guns. One time I went under the bed and found that suitcase of guns.
INT: How old was you?
SONY: I was like seven, eight. 'cause I used to just go in the closet, where he had his money. He used to have a whole lot. Mad dough.
INT: Where he used to hustle? Around the way?
SONY: Yeah, he used to just hit people off and he was selling around the way too.
INT: Yeah.
SONY: People used to knock on the door. He used to come hit them off, you know.
INT: Yeah, so he put your house in jeopardy like that?
SONY: Yeah.

Just asking the questions about fathers invoked a great deal of emotion in our respondents. The interviewers frequently had a difficult time with this topic. Once the respondents started talking about their feelings of being deprived and abandoned by their fathers the interviewers showed compassion and allowed them to vent their feelings. In many cases, respondents knew neither the identity nor location of their birth father. Several respondents grew visibly angry when asked about their fathers:

INT: Alright, tell me about your father.

GEORGE: That –I don't wanna talk about him. [stated with anger in his voice]

INT: Was your pops around much when you was growing up?

GARY: No.

INT: What kind of things you all used to do together?

GARY: It's kind of hard for us to do things together when he wasn't there. Ain't that right, what the fuck did you ask me that dumb ass questions for?

INT: Calm down, calm down money. Chill out for a second.

INT: Tell me about your pops. What kind of things you all used to do together?

BEN: I really can't remember, man. Fuck that nigga. I don't like my pops no more.

INT: Can you tell me about your father?

ARMANDO: I haven't seen that motherfucker since I was five.

INT: And that's it?

ARMANDO: Yeah, that bastard.

INT: Did your pops have a job when you was growing up?

TIM: Nah man that faggot ass. He nah. I don't like talking about him. For real.

INT: Alright.

TIM: I be wanting to blast that nigga sometimes. That nigga get paid $800.00 every Friday yo. And don't give me shit. He got another girl that he live with now. And she got a son and he take care of him more than me. When I use to go stay with him like a little weekend. He use to do his thing like he would send me to the movies. That shit was nothing. When my mother was really hurting sometimes. You know what I mean. Ask that nigga to help her help her pay half. Answer would be 'No.'

Many respondents felt that their family experiences influenced the decisions they made to get involved with the drug business and other illegal activities. Economic deprivation also was cited as a factor in becoming involved in illegal activities. Several respondents described recurrent source of criminal modeling by their fathers and other males in the neighborhood. Examples were provided by Patrick, Rasheed, Cal, and Max :

INT: Anybody in your family use drugs or sell?

PATRICK: My father, he snort cocaine.

INT: Is it a problem?

PATRICK: It is like he got a habit 'cause he been doing it for so long. I got people in my family sell drugs.

INT: How does that affect the family?

PATRICK: When I was younger, my father showed me all the drugs that he was fucking with. And it was like, when I get old enough I could fuck with them. If he would have stayed with my mother my life would have been better, even if he was fucking with drugs, because he explained it to us like a man would. So it was like me and my brother was thinking about fucking with it. It was like 'oh, all right daddy said we get older if we want to, we can do it too.' My father was a hustler, but he was very intelligent.

RASHEED: It was all right, my father used to deal in guns and drugs and shit. A lot of that shit was going on. I just didn't want to see that shit. First you dealing with the guns, then I remember seeing the big bullets. His stash used to be on the floorboard underneath the heavy dresser. We had to move the dresser over to the left, I remember the reason I remember that stuff [is that] I knew what kind of bullets he had. Big long pointy bullets, nasty big crazy shit, right next to cases of guns, always drugs inside that bow.

CAL: That's when my father was doing his thing. You know, it's like, living in a house where my father was doing his thing, I'm growing up, I see it like it's cool. I be down, I see all the money, I see the money 'cause all that money is getting me my clothes or my toys or whatever. But when I started growing up and getting older, you know I used to see that wasn't tight cool. Somebody coulda came in there and try to stick my father up. Kill everybody while we was living there. We had a little stash, he had money, all that. So you don't know who's who. People used to knock and I coulda opened that door and got shot. When I older, going to school, you know, I used to think of it as like that.

INT:  How about your pops?
MAX: My father, he's an all right person.  He is a big time
drug dealer too.  He sell cocaine.
INT:  Who taught you how to sell drugs?  Was it your father
or your friends?

MAX: My friends taught me, but my father gave me the idea.
'Cause we always seen him selling drugs.  And seeing him
with so much money I wanted the same thing.

## VIOLENCE IN THE HOME

For many respondents violence was common within the home
environment including spousal or intimate partner abuse, child abuse,
sibling fighting, fighting between other adults living in the household,
and drug-related attacks on the home.[9]  Regardless of the source of
violence these experiences seemed to have a lasting affect on the types
of relationships the young men had with family members for many
years to follow.  In first example, Steve changed his opinion of his
father when the father started using physical violence to control his
behavior.  He linked the early experiences of being beaten and thrown
out of the house as being evidence that his father did not like him.  He
explained:

INT: When you was coming up like, you was growing up, you
ever had like any role models?
STEVE: Not really, 'cause when I was younger, I thought my
father was my role model, but then he started beating on me
and all that, you know what I mean?
INT:  Yeah.  How umm, how your pops doing now?
STEVE: Well last time I heard my sister told me.....
INT:  You speak to him?
STEVE: Nah I don't speak to my pops.  I ain't speak to my
pops for two years.
INT:  Since he kicked you out?
STEVE: I spoke to him after that, but I ain't speak to my
father for like two years now.
INT:  Why what happened with that?

---

[9] These questions were added to the protocol mid-way through the
study.  As a result not all respondents provided information on this
topic.

STEVE: Cause he don't like me.

INT: Why?

STEVE: I don't know, I'm his name sake, I don't know why he don't like me, 'cause I, I was the one that was gonna do my own, my brother was going by the rules, I was gonna do what I wanted.

Another respondent reported getting into physical fights with his mother and sisters including several incidents that resulted in injury. At first Alonzo reported that he never hit his mother but then goes on to describe violent situation in which his sisters would get involved to protect his mother. Clearly, Alonzo was concerned about impression management when he was answering this question. It appears that Alonzo did not want the interviewer to think that he hit his mother. He minimized the seriousness of the physical violence despite the use of knives and the need for stitches on two separate occasions.

ALONZO: I got thirty-something stitches and then I started having arguments with my moms and shit, we used to get into little fights...

INT: Why?

ALONZO: I ain't never hit her, well I did hit her but... Then it was me and my sisters, they used to be protecting my moms. When we used to fight they used to get their little knives and shit. And then one time I went to grab the knife and I cut my hand, from, cut my whole hand. I had to get a hundred and something stitches.

INT: So, so, that was the only time you and your mother got into something like that?

ALONZO: Nah. A few times.

Some respondents told vivid stories of patterns of domestic abuse, occasional violent episodes, and verbal abuse between parents or other adults in their households as they were growing up. Again, we see evidence that youth felt that the violence modeled in their home environment influenced the way that they handled conflict in their current lives.

INT: And how often did you see your pops hit your moms?

JOEL: Too often. I think that's... I think him hitting my moms is what s... got me started. 'Cause I saw him hit my moms and it made me build up hatred of home. Instead of taking it out at home I couldn't take it out. I figured so I take it out on other people. Like at school that's how I get into problems   and that's how it started to me.

SHAREEF: But I had a step pops and my step pops use to fuck my moms up and shit cause he use to get drunk and just beat my moms down.

Another young man, Rod, was exposed to his father's violence against his mother as well as his father's involvement in street violence.

> INT:   So when you was coming up, you ever experience violence?
> ROD: Yeah. I saw somebody get beat up. I saw my pops beat up my moms and I couldn't do nothing. I hated my pops for that.
> INT:   Oh.
> ROD: That's it, I saw drugs and a lotta guns 'cause of my pops. I never saw him shoot nobody. I saw him beat up people. That's it.
> INT:   Um, like for what?
> ROD: Like, I think only drugs, probably, something like that.
> INT:   Oh, your pops hustle?
> ROD: Oh yeah.
> INT:   And guns?
> ROD: Oh yeah. I seen guns pass around.

In many of the reports of domestic violence the young men felt compelled to do something to stop the violence toward their mother. One respondent described using a pen to stab his father during a severely dramatic violent attack on his mother when he was nine years old. According to his account, Kyle's actions allowed his mother to temporarily get away from the abuse.

> INT:   Did your moms and your pops ever fought with each other?
> KYLE: Yeah.
> INT:   A lot?
> KYLE: Nah, only once when I was younger,  , I stabbed my pops with a pen.
> INT:   The day you stabbed your pops with a pen?

KYLE: Right cause he was fucking my moms up. Shit is real son, yo he was fucking my moms up. He had her under the bed, she was crawling under the bed trying to get away from a nigga. Nigga was grabbing her and pulling her out son, punching her in her head and all that. I was 9 at the time, I got a pen son, I stabbed the nigga right in his leg son. He let go of my moms son, she burned him with some water and shit, we ran.

The next example reveals that in certain situations, especially when the abuser was a step-father or live-in boyfriend, the children got involved in protecting their mothers. The story also demonstrates how Ramond attempted to make sense of the chain of events in his life by linking them causally. Specifically, he felt his father's withdrawal from the family was linked to his mom getting involved with an abusive man. He also explained how the step-father was a destructive force on his older brothers.

RAMOND: Yes, after my step-pop, after my father left my mom, my mom started messing with this guy like maybe sixteen years ago. I was little. I was younger, you know what I am saying. And he started abusing my mom, hitting her every time he got drunk and shit like that. And I think my father was part of that, because if he would have never left my mom, my mom wouldn't never messed with him, you know what I am saying. And believe it or not, man, my step-father was the one that fucked up my big brother's life, you know what I am saying. He use to send my big brother to rob for him.
INT: Was this recent?
RAMOND: No, man. Like eight years ago, no, like nine, ten years ago. He was hitting on my moms. And we all came at the same time and jumped him and fucked him and threw him out of the house.
INT: Never came back?
RAMOND: He never came back. Not my big brother, my older brother bigger than me. [He] hit him with a four by four in the head and dragged him out of the house and stuff like that, fucked him up. The cops came and we explained to them. My mom had a black eye. She was crying, scared. She couldn't sleep for days. She was thinking he was going to

come back and kill us or something, because he always use to threaten her.

INT: She was glad he was gone?

RAMOND: She was glad he was gone, but she was also scared. Because he use to threaten her. 'The day you leave me, or the day you call the cops on me, or the day this or that, then I am going to kill you. I am going to come back and kill you.' He use to always tell her that.

INT: Did he do that in front of you?

RAMOND: He use to like wait for us to go to sleep, but the noise use to wake us up, you know what I am saying. And back then my big brother was locked up.

The way that Ray describes the abuse that his father perpetrated against his step-mother in this next example is especially troubling. It appears that Ray did not feel the father's abusive behavior was wrong. He thought the situation was humorous. As he explained it to the interviewer he was laughing and somewhat embarrassed by his laughter. The interviewer questioned him on why he thought the situation was funny and Ray seemed content to justify his position because the woman was not his real mother and she was a bad cook.

INT: Did your parents ever you know fight with each other in front of you?

RAY: yeah they use to have a lot of my father and my step mother use to fight. Yo that nigga use to fucking come home. Yo cause she didn't know how to cook to good and shit. She use to fucking burn the rice still. So he use to come home heated. Cause he use to be mad hungry. He used to come home slap in Pancho. He use to fucking beat her ass cause of that shit.

INT: Serious?

RAY: I use to be hearing that shit man. It's funny but it's not really funny, you know.

INT: Why is it funny like what?

RAY: He bitch slapped her yo. (LAUGHING) and he use to gave her punches in the back and all that. Coonck coonck hear that nigga punching and all that shit, kid.

INT: This was your step-mother right? With your real father?

RAY: Yeah.

INT: What he used to come home late?

RAY: Yeah and expect food to be there. And the food use to be there but it use to be burnt. She didn't know how to cook to good. It's funny man. It's kind of funny.

INT: So what he used to come in and just hit her like what? Come in and check the food?

RAY: He use to come come in side open the pots slam the fucking pots slam those shit you hear those shit bang bang. Slamming the pots throwing the rice all over the place. (LAUGHING) Yo and fucking go to the room and start blabbing about the hen. Saying why you didn't cook ha ha ah bam and start smacking her & punching her & all that shit yo.

INT: How, like what?

RAY: With the back of his hand, bow, bitch smack her.

INT: But I'm saying like like he use to like did he ever hit her so bad that he had to hurt her or how?

RAY: He used to give her black eyes like.

INT: Black eyes? But nobody called the cops or nothing like?

RAY: Nah.

INT: Oh um so how often did you pops hit your moms like how long did this go?

RAY: I think years like 2 years. Years, I know it was years. He used to be hitting her ass.

INT: And what what she used to do when your father you father use to hit her?

RAY: She was down on the ground. My father is a big man. She couldn't do nothing. She was a little lady, a little pretty lady. She could not do nothing. She could have not done nothing. He was a big fucking man.

## PARENTAL OR FAMILY BASED SOCIAL CONTROL

Respondents described a variety of levels of social control within the context of their own families. A variety of family structures existed among the sample, the most common experience was being raised by a single mother without a consistent father figure in the home. There was a diverse range of family based social control among the sample. Most respondents described a semi-formal set of rules during their childhood that included staying inside the house (not getting involved with the "fast life" on the street). Most respondents reported a mixture of following and breaking the household rules that were established for them. Regardless of the amount of social control within the family, respondents consistently reported a move toward autonomy or independence from the family rules between the ages of 12 and 16. A small number of respondents reported having little or no parental control throughout their lives. Disobeying or ignoring the rules, was a common theme among the young men in both neighborhoods.

The first two examples illustrate the point that parents (mostly mothers) did attempt to establish and maintain rules but often those regulations were overlooked.

INT:  Some parents have rules for their teenagers and young adults while others don't. Did your parents have rules for you when you were growing up?
TYSON: Not many.
INT:  Of all the rules you had when you was younger, which ones did you break and which ones did you follow?
TYSON: Curfew I broke and which one did I follow. Basically, not too many rules?
INT:  So why you always broke your curfew and your rules?
TYSON: Cause I always had my own way of doing things.
INT:  What type of rules did your parents, have in the household that you had to follow. You know as far as curfew, the people you hung out with, going to school.
LUIS: I ain't have no rules. They let me live. But they ain't have no choice. I always wanted to do my own thing. I use to always just be out. Break out in the middle of night, be out and just go. Chill whatever.

Many respondents understood that their parents did not condone their behavior yet they had limited success in controlling it. In the next example despite Pablo's efforts to conceal his drug use his family became aware of his behavior. According to Pablo, once his mother discovered the truth she had a talk with him about being safe in his marijuana use. The story demonstrates how one mother struggled to define rules of behavior and deal with the decisions that her son made independently about smoking marijuana.

INT:  So so how she found out that you was smoking?
PABLO: My pops really found out. He started asking question, 'you smoking weed?' I was like 'nah,' he said 'you

sure don't lie to me because I used to smoke weed to, I know the deal.' I was like 'nah nah nah.' At one time I had came to the house to the with my eyes mad red, I was just like... My mother ask me 'you smoke? Your Father told me that you smoking.' I was like 'you know what I ain't even going to lie to y'all I'm smoking, I ain't smoking nothing else but weed.' I explain to her she was like 'I don't like you doing that but if you going to do it make sure you be safe when you do it. Don't smoke with everybody,' she was just explaining. They don't want me doing it but was gonna do it regardless.

Other families had a tighter reign on their youth especially when the boy was younger. Respondents explained that most parents did not want their kids hanging out on the streets after dark or for extended periods of time.

INT: When you was growing up did your moms set aside rules for you, your moms or your pops have rules or regulations?
JAVIER: Not really my mother, my pops really. My pops was always the one beating me, my pops was always the one setting me ground rules. My moms was more laid back.
INT: What type of rules, like curfew?
JAVIER: Yeah see, my mother set down curfew, my mother set down like 11 o'clock curfew when I was younger, she wasn't too strict on curfew 'cause she knew I liked to hang out until whatever. My pops, see, he just made sure when I was younger, younger, like 9, he used to tell me to come in, it'd be like 7:30, 8 o'clock. shit like that.
INT: Alright. Did your parents or did your mother or your father have any rules for you about like the time you spent have to be in at night?
RAUL: I used to be in my house every day. When I hit twelve, that's when I hit the streets. That's when I started hustling, smoke weed, drink 40, that's when I used to be buck wild.
INT: Did she got any rules for you to come home at a certain time at night?
RAUL: Yeah, ten o'clock.
INT: Did you follow that rule?

RAUL: Nah cause my father didn't have a chance to give me curfew and shit, he passed away at that time.
INT: So your mother didn't have a curfew?
RAUL: Yeah, ten o'clock those days. And I used to be like eleven o'clock, twelve o'clock come back and she'd be mad.

The example below shows that family members can exert control over teens by establishing firm rules and sticking to them. Jorge learned through experience that there were consequences for disrespecting his aunt and uncle's household rules. He explained:

INT: Do your aunt and uncle have rules for you at home?
JORGE: Yeah.
INT: What sort of rules?
JORGE: Those rules are don't come, you gotta come in the house by 10 o'clock. 10 o'clock in the latest or if not, if not my aunt she has, she put the chain on the door.
INT: Yeah?
JORGE: And once that chain is on the door, you gonna you end up gonna have to take the bus back down to your mother's house, to my mother's house.
INT: Yeah. You don't like to do that?
JORGE: Nah, I don't wanna do that so I just respect that rule.
INT: Yeah. You respect it, you don't break it?
JORGE: Nah I don't break it. I respect that rule cause it happened, it happened to me once. I did it once already, tried coming in at 12:30 but, you know, she wasn't hearing it, you know, that chain was on the door. The chain was on the door. She don't want me to smoke in the house, that's disrespectful, smoking. They won't let me smoke no reefer in the house or nothin' like that or drink or anything in the house.

Also, some mothers are able to affect their son's behavior by firmly establishing how concerned they were about the young man's safety and well-being. In the next example, the young man tried to keep his mother informed of his whereabouts so that she would not worry about him. Although he admitted that he did not always follow the household rules he reported being motivated to prevent his mother from worrying about him.

MIQUEL: Yeah I got a curfew. It don't matter how old I am I always got a curfew.

INT: What time is that?

MIQUEL: I got I gotta be home before before ten.

INT: Ten? Do you follow that rule?

MIQUEL: Yeah I follow that rule.

INT: Never break it?

MIQUEL: Sometimes but if I have an excuse, I I call my mother and I tell her about it cause she's she's the type of person who would worry about it.

INT: How about rules against hanging out with certain people?

MIQUEL: Yeah they tell me about that and I sometime I don't listen and then when I when I when things happen. I be like damn, I should have listened to my mother, should have listened to her.

Defiance of authority is a common behavior in adolescence. Specific manifestations of youthful defiance or rebellion vary with the social position of the family and the community. Many young men growing up female-headed households did not view their mothers as legit sources of authority. In fact, many respondents felt that as they got older (physically mature) their mothers had no power to enforce household rules and therefore they could do as they pleased. Like all children, they often tested the boundaries and resolve of their caretakers. The absence of a male figure appears to have made controlling adolescents behavior more difficult. Orlando explained his views on this issue:

ORLANDO: Whether she didn't or she did I didn't give a fuck it was my choice. I was the one who was growing up. She wasn't going to be there every time I was going out to be a man. It was my choice to face the world by myself whether she was there or not. I did everything my parents told me not to. I tried every drug in this world.

INT: Rules against getting high?

ORLANDO: Getting high not cause they told me not to do it and I still did it and once I did it I not chose to it. So I tried it. Yes I did I tried it. I didn't like it. So it was my choice whether I kept doin' it or not.

INT: Of all the rules your parents had for you, when you were younger. Which ones did you follow and which ones did you break?

COBY: I broke every single one of them.

INT: Why?

COBY: And I didn't. Huh? Why cause that's what I chose to do. As I got a little older I guess I got more streetwise.

INT: Hm. When, okay, was there a certain age when like you totally stopped following anything they said like any rules they?

COBY: Yeah, when I when I reached the age of thirteen. I thought that I was a grown man by then. You know?

INT: What did you start doing like at age of thirteen?

COBY: I started I started hanging out with the wrong people.

INT: Hm.

COBY: People who was influence with drugs. People who steal cars. People who you know, who do all the bad things.

INT: In the Neighborhood?

COBY: But I thought it was cool.

Disobeying household rules is described by one young man as an expression of his anger at his mother in specific situations. Pedro describes being mad as a legitimate excuse to violate the household rules.

INT: Some parents have rules for their teenagers and young adults while other parents don't have any rules. Did or do your parents have definite rules for you about let's say being the time being out at night?

PEDRO: Yeah.

INT: What's the rule?

PEDRO: I gotta be in by like more like 10 or 11.

INT: Like 10 or 11?

PEDRO: Yeah.

INT: Do you follow that rule or do you break that rule?

PEDRO: I follow the rule sometimes.

INT: When when do you not follow it?

PEDRO: Like if they get me mad or something.

INT: What would you do if they get you mad?

PEDRO: I won't come home for the night.

INT: You stay out all night?
PEDRO: Yeah.
INT: What happens in the morning?
PEDRO: I come home and I hear it start yelling this.
INT: And what age you started doing that breaking the rules?
PEDRO: Couple of years ago.
INT: You mean like thirteen?
PEDRO: Yeah like going on 14.
INT: Alright. You think your parents approve of most of the things that you do now as a young adult?
PEDRO: Nah.
INT: What don't they like the most?
PEDRO: The way the way I be acting in the streets.
INT: How is that?
PEDRO: Like somebody disrespect me and like I just want to fight all the time.

Additional evidence of attempts to gain autonomy and grown up status were gleaned from questions about whether or not youth shared similar opinions to their parents. Many respondents felt that they had similar opinions and views of the world as their parent(s) while others clearly did not. In some cases, respondents describe a generation gap that is translated into a lack of understanding by the older generation. These respondents frequently reported feeling that their parents do not comprehend the difficulties they face growing up today. Hector explained:

INT: Are you opinions about most things similar to the opinions of your parents (moms/pops) or are they different? How are they similar how are the different? Give examples?
HECTOR: Well they totally different. Straight up. Cause they grew up in it wasn't as bad as it is now man. They ain't had to worry about the stuff we worry about. They still living back then back back in the old days. They think the same rules apply. They apply a little bit but not all way man. You know cause things is changed. It's a lot more drastic out here in the streets.
INT: Right.
HECTOR: That old stuff will get you half way there. But this new shit is a game you know that man.

Two respondents explained being in similar positions:

> ETHAN: I started breakin 'em really when I was around
> sixteen years old about two years ago.
> INT: Yeah.
> ETHAN: When I thought I was gettin' grown and stuff.
> INT: Do you think your moms approve of most things that you
> do now as a young adult?
> ETHAN: Hmmmm, nah she don't.  She wants me to do right.
> You know? And sometimes I don't want to do right.
> INT: Do you think do you think that your parents now approve
> of the most of the things that you do?
> LaSHAWN: They approve? I don't I don't really know if they
> approve. It's just they know that, I'm my own man now. So
> it's like.... I do what I want now.

Respondents also emphasize a gender gap between themselves and
their mothers who are often the only parent present in their lives.
Although most respondents describe a relatively close relationship their
mothers they also report keeping information and problems away from
their mothers because "she is not a man." Many respondents report a
strong disapprove of their illegal activities and involvement in the street
world.  Javier explained:

> INT:  Do you usually talk to your moms about your personal
> problems, stuff like that?
> JAVIER: Depends on what problems, if it's a little to personal
> I'll talk to my boys instead of my moms.  My moms wouldn't
> understand if it was like a man thing...

Parents tolerate a wide variety of behaviors that their sons are
involved in. In the neighborhood context, fighting is often promoted or
at least approved of as necessary.  Felippe explained:

> INT: Did your mother know about stuff you were into,
> violence, fighting, or hustling?  Did you hustle when your
> mother was around?
> FELIPPE: Nah.  She knew I was fighting a lot but she always
> told me if I need to, if I have to fight, fight.

Some behaviors may be seen as age appropriate by parents.  But,
as the next example illustrates, the actions of an older adolescent may

put the younger siblings in jeopardy. According to Justin, his mother was less upset about his gun ownership than she was worried about the risks it posed to the younger children in the household. Many of the social control situations that mothers confronted may be difficult to manage because of the potential dangers introduced by their adolescent sons. In the example below, Justin described his mother establishing more stringent rules for his younger siblings after he suffered a serious injury due to violence. Justin explained:

JUSTIN: Nah. She does my mother my mother didn't start started seein' like stuff like this until I grew up. So now when she sees my little brothers she's like, I don't want you hangin' around with this because she has seen it for me already, so she be putting rules to them now. Cause now, she woke up, like I don't know. All this experience that happened to me, all this stuff that happened to me, she like it woke her mind up more so now she knows about good and bad now.

INT: How about does she have any rules about you using violence? You ever keep any guns in the house?

JUSTIN: Yeah. Back in the days I used to keep mad guns in my house and she used to be like, she was the type of person that she always used to go to her mom's house. She used to be lonely. So I used to bring mad niggas to my house. I be like, yo I got this hooky jam at my house yo. So niggers used to bring mad ghats (guns) and shit. I used to hide em in the closet. One time my mother was cleaning the closet and she found two ghats. She started barkin' at me. She was like yo, why you got two guns? Imagine if Toby and Randy would have found it, they

INT: Your little brothers?

JUSTIN: Yeah. So that day she was buggin' me. She told me she didn't want nobody in the house this, this, and that. I was like damn alright momma.

INT: You have parties after that again?

JUSTIN: Nah, from that day I never had I couldn't bring 'em cause from that day on she never used to give me the keys or nothing. She never used to trust me no more.

**YOUNG MEN AS FATHERS**

Many respondents were well on their way to repeating the patterns of their own families of origin. Forty-five of 96 respondents reported having a child or children of their own at the time of the interview. Fifteen of those respondents reported living with the mother of his child. Some respondents stated that having kids of their own provided an opportunity to give and receive love that they missed. Almost every father reported "taking care" of his child or children although few described formal child support or custodial care. One example explained how his inability to provide for his child reduced his desirability to the mother of his child. He explained:

> INT: So umm how old is your kid right now?
> JOSE: Damn, my kid is gonna be two years old man.
> INT: Ah kid, how 'bout you still with the mother?
> JOSE: Nah she don't, she don't want to know nothing about me, man. She cares for me and shit like that but what the fuck am I doing for the kid, Bee. I ain't doing shit man. What the fuck is ten dollars gonna do Bee for a kid, that you gonna give her. What the fuck Bee? Fucking food Bee cost like twenty dollars kid.

Many young men reported feeling stressed about their perceived inability to provide a proper home, material possessions, and family life for their children. The hopes and dreams these fathers held for their children's futures rarely matched the realities of their lives. One young man explained:

> INT: Who's taking care of you right now? You taking care of yourself or....?
> JOSE: Nah Bee. My moms is taking care of me you know I'm saying. But I feel bad for that bullshit 'cause I got a kid and shit you know I'm saying. I'm supposed to be the one taking care of that shit, not fucking welfare but fuck it, you know welfare is here fuck it, let them take care of it man.

In the majority of cases, the child was in the care of the mother and conflict with the child's mother frequently was cited as the reason that respondents had drifted away from their children. A few young men were exceptions to this general pattern especially when the child's mother was addicted to drugs or unable to handle her parental responsibilities. Dennis described his custody arrangements:

INT: Does he live with you?
DENNIS: He lives with me, yeah.
INT: You have custody?
DENNIS: Yeah.
INT: Where's the mother?
DENNIS: The mother gave him to me. She didn't give him to me, but she let me, like her moms let her, threw her out of her house and shit. She lives in her cousin's house. So I told her let me, leave my son with me. I'll take care of him better. And she see him on weekends and shit.
INT: How's your relationship with her?
DENNIS: She is my baby's mother. Yeah, we cool. We don't fight. She just messed up on drugs and stuff.

Most young fathers felt they were doing a better job at caring for their children than their own fathers had done. Being a "good father," or at least projecting that image, seemed to be an important part of young fathers' personal identities. One respondent explained:

INT: What do you hope for yourself in the future?
AARON: To work and show my daughter, it's basically about my daughter. When she get older she could be like my pops did this, my pops did that. Instead of being like my pops was locked up or my pops got killed in the drug business.

For some respondents fatherhood put their own father's behavior in a light new. The difficulties of maintaining contact with children in situations in which the relationship with the mother of the children is precarious caused one young man to reason that his father may have faced similar problems. He explained:

INT: So um was you and your pops close?
SHAREEF: Nah. I never got to know him. He was never there for me. I respect him as a man. Truthfully I don't really know what really went on 'cause I have a daughter myself and my baby moms is rejecting me from being a father with my daughter. So you know maybe my moms did that too.

Some respondents also expressed concerns over concealing their criminal activities from their children. Their own experiences, however, suggest that children figure it out eventually.

The descriptions provided above show that family life for our respondents was dysfunctional, maladaptive, unhealthy, and complicated by a variety of issues. As the evidence suggests, this generation of young men was hit hard by the crack epidemic of the eighties. Many of the young men were second- or third-generation drug dealers with few, if any, alternative role models in their lives. The father-son relationships (or lack thereof) had a huge impact on how the young men conceptualized their experiences and their role in the world. The role models present in the families described in this chapter demonstrate the need for additional sources of social support, modeling, and social capital. The decent vs. street family orientation (articulated by Anderson 1994; 1998), though a useful conceptual framework, may be too simplistic in that many of our respondents would have been classified as hybrids or on a continuum between 'street' and 'decent.' For example, some 20 respondents who were deeply involved in the street life also described strong and decent family systems.

The quotes presented in this chapter show how family serves as an important developmental context for protecting against or promoting violent behaviors. As youth strive for independence and autonomy household conflict is evitable. Maintaining household rules becomes more problematic as youth age into early adulthood yet continued to reside in the family home. The struggle to exert social control on teenagers and young adults can be understood as a tug-of-war with the streets. The depictions of family-based social control and adolescent defiance are clearly reminiscent of Anderson's (1990) description of this process among so-called "decent" families. One clear message is that these adolescents and young adults know the difference from right and wrong, have some degree of parental influence in establishing behavioral norms, and push for autonomy in the mid-teenage years. By the late teenage years these young men were nearly impossible for mothers to control despite their best intentions. There were no stark differences across race/ethnicity, neighborhood, or age with regard to family-based social control.

# CHAPTER 5

# Peers, Social Networks, And Other Affiliations

In the criminological literature, adolescent peer culture often is blamed for "creating" criminal or deviant behavior. This section explores the nature of peer relationships by summarizing respondents' descriptions of their "bonds" to peers, frequently referred to as "peeps," "boys," "family," or "brothers." Recurring themes include: solidarity, respect, and trust. The types of activities that youth enjoy together shape friendship bonds. Belonging to a clique or street-corner group fulfills a variety of needs for many young men, including protection, income generation, adventure, companionship, love, identity formation, partying, and the social construction of violent events. This section focuses specifically on the protection afforded by friendships that are described as part of the peer group process. Many of the violent events, both gun and non-gun, described were embedded in group processes. The majority of youth in this study were not members of formal youth gangs. Although much of the violent behavior described occurred with other youth this activity was not part of an organized youth gang structure. The study neighborhoods are not areas where youth gangs are prominent. These very basic descriptions further explicate the social context of violence among urban male youth.

The majority of our respondents were closely associated to one or, more typically, several young males who live in the same or surrounding blocks. As one respondent explained "your block is where the love is at." Friendships or associations develop out of geographic proximity, common interests and values, and joint experiences over several years' time. Neighborhood-based group solidarity seems to be especially important throughout the teenage years and early twenties. The majority of our sample belonged to tightly knit peer groups and described their social relations accordingly.[10] Some reported being part of smaller networks including dyads and triads. Others reported being on the fringe of larger peer networks and a few respondents described

---

[10] The chain referral sampling strategy used in this study would obviously skew the sample toward individuals who are embedded in social networks. There is some heterogeneity on this dimension; however, the majority of respondents were affiliated with a neighborhood-based group of similarly situated youths.

themselves as independents or going "solo." As some members of the sample got older, they report more diversity in their associations, including less large-group membership and more frequent associations beyond the immediate neighborhood.

These social relationships were described as dynamic with varying degrees of closeness and distance over time. Many aspects of these associations were positive and meet specific human needs for the respondents. Other aspects were negative, and were recognized as such by the sample. Elements of these associations are described below, focusing primarily on the tightly knit peer group.

## KNOWING AND UNDERSTANDING

Respondents talked about understanding, familiarity, and joint participation from their peers. Sharing common experiences was seen as an important element of friendship. One respondent explained: "We do a lotta things together, me and my homeboy, we did everything together. I mean dirt... dirt and all that. Good stuff, we did good deeds together. Bad stuff, all that." It seems that "insiders" who have been through the same experiences are more supportive, accepting, and easier to deal with. Another respondent explained how "knowing" was important:

> INT: Are you pretty tight with your friends?
> GREG: Yeah.
> INT: Why?
> GREG: Because we grew up together. We grew up together...and everybody, everybody in my clique, in my crew, we all know each other. We knew each other from mad small, we could always motherfucking bring up something ...the next nigga probably wouldn't know about...

Some of the bonds of friendship were described as extremely strong, more like family relationships. Another respondent described what happens in his tightly knit peer group: "Yeah, I would say that most of the people I consider [other] friends is more like family now ...we don't even consider each friends no more." Growing up together and sharing experiences cemented many relationships among young males. One respondent reported an example of the lengths to which friends should go to for each other:

INT: How would you describe your friendships... with guys in your neighborhood?

TONI: Um [long pause] I can't really describe it for you. You don't... nobody's really your friend until... you know? Until some shit go down. Then you know that that mean it's bad. When a nigga die for you, that's what a friend is to me.

Many of the relationships are described as lifelong bonds affecting individual behavior. One respondent explained that his behavior changes when he was with his friends:

JOEL: Yeah, sometimes yeah, 'cause you know when you with your friend you think you all big and bad and bold.

INT: Then when you by yourself?

JOEL: Then when you by yourself, you just act to yourself. It's not you trying to be bad and everything in front of your friends it's that you know they just get you hyped and they want you to do shit. But you know I don't get down like that, that's not my style.

In this context, breaking away from a tight-knit group would be difficult unless there was a good reason for it:

INT: So y'all... y'all street family, y'all close?

RUBEN: Yeah we close, anything go down major we talk about it. If there's something we could all do together as a whole, we talk about it. Anything that's basic, and then even then there's nothing to do we just talking around, playing a little basketball or something.

INT: Most of the people that you... that you talking about, y'all grew up together?

RUBEN: Yeah... since little, and we try to stay together. Some of us break off, but then come back later on with something. That's good, though, as long as they went to do something.

## STRUGGLING TOGETHER

The chaotic nature of life in the inner city was often cited as a reason for a strengthening of friendships. Respondents frequently described their relationships with peers as deepening over the years.

INT: So do you still describe your relationship activities or, you know, degrees of closeness with your friends in your neighborhood?

CAL: Oh yeah, yeah. We really close ...I grew up with my peoples since day one, you know. I like ...I just grew up my peoples since I was like six years old ...so I been around for a while doing my thing. ...There's, there's other peoples that been around longer than me, you know, but they, we, we definitely got love for each other 'cause we understand each other to the certain ...most deepest extent, you know. We... know about each other's problems, you know, we know what everybody's thinking, we know what's going on. We... know how to fill the difficult time, we stay by each other, you know, it's real. Whatever, don't matter how many fights we have, whatever, you know we still gonna be next to each other, you know, so it's real.

Acts of mutual assistance were considered to be evidence of the strength of peer group attachments. Respondents reported pooling resources, including money, work opportunities, guns, clothes, food, drugs, alcohol, and cars.

INT: Are you pretty tight with your friends?

DONNELL: Yeah, you could say that. Because we all basically from the same 'hood and we basically all going through the same circumstances out here. You know, nobody's really different, no matter if you live in a private house or a project. That doesn't differentiate to who is richer or who's poorer. It's like we all grow up through the same situation, so nobody's really different. So that's what makes everybody just click. Most of the time everybody looks out for each other, you know. If one don't have, the other will have. It's like, if I'm going to a party and I know I got extra gear in the crib, of course I'm going to give my man a little something because I wouldn't want any—because if he don't got it, I wouldn't want him to go to the party looking, you know, one way and I'm another way. Of course, I wouldn't like my man to go looking a certain way. So that's what makes most of us closer, because we're able to look out for each other like that.

Donnell explained that owning and maintaining certain material possessions (e.g., a car, gun, and a girl): was important for fitting in with his crowd. Having the right clothes and jewelry also elevated (or equalized): social status in the group. Although the excerpt presented above suggests that group members may pull together to provide for each other or as one respondent put it "see each other live" some adolescents did this while others never did. For teenagers combining or pooling resources facilitated establishing independence from parents and other adults. As one respondent described, peers played an important role in that process:

> INT: So um, do you have friends?
> RUBEN: I got street family that's mad big, large, we big, and we stick together.
> INT: A street family? And what... Do y'all work, so some of y'all work... or what?
> RUBEN: Most of us work, put in for the street and then a lot of ...a lot of people that don't work just hustle and it's like, we try to work together and if there's a job opening we go for it but hardly [ever] it be, it's not enough jobs for all of us. We got to do something 'cause if we stay in the house living under your mother and stuff she ain't gonna try to see you there all the time, so she gonna tell you to get out and do something with yourself or whatever.

## MUTUAL RESPECT AND PROTECTION

One common link between youth seemed to be mutual respect and defense of other clique members. Getting respect is very important to the young men in our sample. Personal identities typically were shaped between ages 8 to 14 years when boys won or lost the battle for respect in their peer networks. As described by Anderson (1994; 1999): and in Chapter 9, the quest for respect is an integral part of the male experience in inner-city neighborhoods. Displays of respect were central to maintaining close friendships. As one respondent explained, "We have mutual respect for one another. Those that don't respect me, I don't hang around."

Repeatedly, peers were described as "helping out in a time of need," whatever the need may be:

> INT: You all help each other out and stuff like that?

DJ: Yeah. If they get into beef, we'll help, everybody participate in it. Everybody know everybody, so everybody look out for everybody.

Another respondent explained how friends "go all out for each other":

BRANDON: Say, like, if my man get into some beef, I'm going all out with you for the simple fact, you went all out with me. But I ain't going go out if you gonna go start beef with somebody else. We gonna have to do something. But like I said, if you my man I'm gonna get busy with you, for the simple fact you my man, I been down with you for years.

To many respondents, close friends on the street were considered good influences because they offer protection. Both the previous example and the next illustrated the reciprocal nature of these relationships:

INT: Do you think your close friends are a good influence on you?
JESS: Yeah.
INT: Why?
JESS: 'Cause we always stick together and everything that happen to me, happen to him. You know he always [got my] back. He always back me up.

For the most part, the peer network was one social context in which adolescents were safe to lower their guard to a certain extent. According to the sample, different rules applied when handling conflicts with your friends compared to handling conflicts with everybody else. Serious intra-group fighting was extremely rare. One respondent described the existence of different violence thresholds within the peer network:

INT: Y'all don't never get into any, like, no drama with each other, right?
SONY: ...Basketball games or something... you get fouled or something, you know what I mean, real hard... 'Cause we play rough with each other, you know what I mean, wrestling or something. Sometimes it get real... Sometimes... you know what I mean... Everybody just having fun.

INT: Where it would come up to a fist fight? Y'all never tried
to hurt each other?
SONY: Yeah, so we just say, All right. Never, no guns.
INT: Never, no guns?
SONY: Never, no guns! Nah. It...we don't never take it to the
violence with each other... 'cause you know, we grew up with
each other, you know what I mean.

Within the closed environment of peer relations, young males found
safety that rarely existed outside the group.

Group solidarity seems, at least in part, to develop out of a need for
protection against threats from outside the neighborhood, primarily
from other groups of youths. Fighting between groups of corner boys
or neighborhood rivals has long been documented in the literature (See
Short and Strodbeck, 1968; Anderson, 1999; Sullivan, 1989). Peer
groups play an important role in promoting gun acquisition, carrying,
and use. In numerous violent events, one or several members of a
clique were armed in situations where violence would erupt. Peer
involvement in violent events and group decision-making processes are
explored in Chapter 8.

Respondents described a variety of situations in which group unity
was high and other times in which there was considerable
fragmentation and conflict. Respondents generally were reluctant to
talk badly about their close friends and often glossed over problematic
situations within the peer group, suggesting that it would be
disrespectful to do otherwise.

## PARTYING, CRIME, & HAVING FUN TOGETHER

The majority of the activities in which respondents reported engaging
with friends were described as: "what any teenager would do now."
Ninety-five percent of the sample reported that "hanging out" with
peers involved frequent drinking or drug use (primarily marijuana, beer
or malt liquor). Jamal indicated that drug use in the context of the peer
group made the experience more pleasurable:

INT: What kinds of things do you and your friends do
together? Give me some examples.
JAMAL: We get high together, man. Ain't nothing like getting
high together, everybody feeling the same way, everybody

smoking a lot of blunts, everybody drinking, feeling like thugs.

The young men reported extensive partying with peers on weekends including going to clubs and house parties. Peers like to hang out together to talk about girls, reminisce about the "good ol' days," try to get girls, cut school, eat, play sports, listen to music, DJ and mix music, see movies, go skating, get money, play fight (slap boxing), and play dominos, pool, cards, and dice. They also described frequent criminal activities within the group context, including selling and using drugs, other hustles or con games, stealing cars, shoplifting, stick-ups or robberies, assaulting low-status individuals or strangers, and shooting guns.

For the most part, respondents reported considering themselves to be independent thinkers. Only about a quarter of the sample reported having done something just to fit in with his peers, usually around ages 10 to 14. Drug and alcohol use was the most frequently cited activity for which respondents felt pressure to join their friends followed by violent and other criminal activity. Outsiders who enter the neighborhood scene later in adolescence most often had to use violence "not really to fit in, but to let others know what [they were] was capable of..." Of those who reported never having made a decision to fit in with a crowd most cited personally wanting to participate in illegal activities as their reason for involvement. One respondent explained an experience he had when he was trying to earn the respect of a peer:

> AUSTIN: I did do something to be down with somebody one time. I pulled a gun on somebody else, to be down with my man and shit. He's like, 'yo, you know, [you haven't] pulled out a gun on nobody.' I did, but he, he ain't seen me do it. So... we got a competition, he was like yeah, all right, all right, so we going to stick this person up, we just did it.
> INT: How old was, how old was you?
> AUSTIN: I was like seventeen.

## BEING ON THE FRINGE OF PEER NETWORKS
Several respondents described moving toward the fringe or creating distance in friendships after experiencing violations of trust and respect. Others explained how peer groups splintered at different points in time as young men approach adulthood. Some respondents

maintained loose associations with peers but did not regularly associate with them; one respondent is wary of activities his friends engage in and chooses to "stay to the side":

INT: Are you tight with your friends?
BRANDON: I'm tight with them, but I don't... there's a lot of shit been going on, so I try to just stay to the side.
INT: How many friends would you consider, like, your tight friends, like you really close, like family, whatever...
BRANDON: I don't consider nobody like that, nobody.

Another respondent described the situation as a bit of a struggle between needing to be a part of the clique and needing to leave the group behind:

MALIK: Well, half of them I grew up with, and when I'm growing up with some of them, others became they own man, wanted to do they own thing, so they don't really be cool with people in the neighborhood no more. It's like they start to see things for theyself, and just, like, they don't wanna be associated with nobody in the neighborhood, they feel it just bring them down.
INT: Yeah.
MALIK: But a lot of guys won't [be] cool with you, you know, real—real thick—real thick like that, and it ain't just because we just together, because we see eye-to-eye on certain things. And when you see eye-to-eye on certain things it's good to stick together 'cause in the long run you never know, the person may be there for you–
INT: Yeah
MALIK:--help you out in the future.

A few respondents described situations in which they had only one or two close friends, preferring to stay on the fringe of larger networks. Being new to the neighborhood seems to have something to do with seeking a smaller affiliation, as one respondent explained:

INT: Do most of your friends live in your neighborhood?
LUKE: My old neighborhood. ...I don't got no friends over there in the East. ...you don't know who the fuck to trust over there, somebody rob you. Everybody's getting down over there. ...Tell you the true I want to get a partner, somebody

who cool, we make money together, we go hang out, you know how people got partners from jobs and shit. They go out, they go to clubs, they might go to a little club at night but then they both cool, they both got money, they ain't bums. They got something going for themselves. I want friends like that.

As expected, recent arrivals to a neighborhood seemed to have a more difficult time developing attachments and trust for others in the new neighborhood. One respondent described how he made his way as a newcomer:

CALVIN: Yep, when I first moved to East New York, I didn't know too many people, so I had to blend in.
INT: What did you do to blend in?
CALVIN: Started drinking and smoking and I picked a fight with... I wouldn't call him the smallest person but, you know, the person that was least respected in the neighborhood.

Most youth who had moved during early adolescence or later maintained closer ties with their old neighborhood friends and were more likely to see their new environments as threatening and unsafe.

A small number of respondents reported that even if they were affiliated with a group, they preferred to handle their business on their own:

INT: You never tried to go look for other friends that you can trust?
ARLO: Yo, I never, it's, that's not my style. It's not like that's how you grew up. Nobody in the neighborhood like that...
INT: So, when you got problems none of your friends like help you, talk to you or nothing?
ARLO: Nah. No, there was no such thing.

## DEATH, INCARCERATION, AND LOSS OF PEERS

The majority of our sample reported losing a close friend or family member to some type of violent death. Death was described as a very "real" part of life in the neighborhood. Expectations about one's own death as well as the death of one's friends were very high. During the interviews, many respondents had difficulty discussing experience with close friends who had died on the streets. Approximately 35 of 125 respondents made actual references or acknowledgments to loved ones who had died, including "rest in peace" and "God bless the dead." The impact of death on peer attachments was intense as two examples below illustrate:

INT: Lost a close friend?
LEO: A few close friends. A lot of close friends.
INT: Like who, like?
LEO: Well I lost my friend, a lot of friends, wow, I lost too many names, like I lost, like, 10 friends in the past four years. In the same neighborhood, 184th and Morris.
INT: So, um, what were those guys and how was their life?
LEO: Well they all got killed through their selling drugs or robbing people. ...They robbed people and the people came back and retaliated.

INT: You ever had any friends of yours that been murdered and shit?
FELTON: Yeah, my man that lived in the building across from me.
INT: Word.
FELTON: Yeah.
INT: What happen with that, tell me?
FELTON: Him and this kid that lived next door from me. My other man. It was them three. It was his birthday. ...Went to a restaurant to eat before they went out. And some kid ran up on them in the restaurant and shot [him]...
INT: How it made you feel and shit?
FELTON: It made me feel like, ah, a part of me died too. It's like a part of me left too. I ain't gonna never...I I remember how he, how he looked, know what I'm saying. But I just can't, it's like, I ain't gonna never see him again. It's like he just went away on a trip. And I ain't gonna never see him again, know what I'm saying?
INT: Yeah.
FELTON: That's how I'm trying to think of it. He alright.
INT: Yeah.
FELTON: 'Cause I know he all right now. In a better place right now.

Young men also described the "cycle" of incarceration as an additional sense of loss. They clearly missed seeing their friends who were locked up, especially those in state facilities that were too far away to make frequent visits. The frequent movement in and out of the criminal justice system takes a toll on friendships, as one respondent described:

> INT: So now you chilling and shit, so your other boys, they out there?
> RASHEED: Most of them is getting locked. ...Like half of them got locked up already, now it's like a circle, kid, niggas come home, some niggas go up, some niggas come home. ...I didn't get to see my man yet, I came home and [he] got locked up.
> INT: It is a cycle, man, going in a circle.
> RASHEED: You got to jump out of the cycle, you [either] end up in a cell or in a coffin.

> INT: Why...you think that now everybody changing and shit?
> SONY: 'Cause ...it's too many people getting locked up. You got Pataki, you know. You got... you got a whole... lot of people that they...they just trying to get rid of you, you know. So it's... it's over for them drugs, you know what I mean. 'Cause as soon as you step on the block, police harassing you. You getting locked up. They...They...they not playing no games no more. If they got to put a force to wrestle you, to get you up out the streets, they gonna do it. So everybody on parole. Trying to hold your head, 'cause if they go back up north, no telling when they gonna come back down. Everybody got kids.

This chapter has explored many aspects of peer social networks and their relations to violence that was available in the narratives collected. Friendship and group affiliation had a strong influence on attitudes, perceptions, behaviors, and life experiences. Respondents' interactions with friends revealed that most young men had close "tight" bonds with a small group of "peeps" but a general mistrust of their peers as a whole. Both the positive and negative aspects of those relationships were described in an effort to situate the violent events described in Chapters 7 and 8 in a specific socio-cultural context. In Chapter 9, additional linkages between peer relationships and violence will be drawn out to refine the conceptual framework for studying violent events.

# CHAPTER 6

# Limited Opportunities:
## Education and Employment Experiences

Given the low level of educational achievement and lack successful employment experiences of respondents in this study it is unlikely that these youth will make a successful transition to mainstream adult social roles without some type of remediation or intervention. Making money and having enough resources to purchase basic necessities that are not provided in the house and luxury items that bring status within the adolescent culture drive many of the choices that these young men made. Most of these youth were deeply involved in illegal activities, especially drug selling: their views of legitimate work and educational attainment reflect either feelings that those avenues were out of reach or that the criminal lifestyle was preferable. Alienation from mainstream opportunities runs high in this context while long-term planning and gradual advancement were rarely observed.

## SCHOOL EXPERIENCES
Respondents were asked about their school experiences in terms of level of achievement, good and bad points about school, and their educational aspirations, if any. Of the 113 respondents who described their school experiences, 37 were actively enrolled at the time of the interview. Most of the respondents who were still enrolled in school reported sporadic attendance, had earned only a small number of credits relative to the number of years enrolled, and had disciplinary problems while in school. Jamal explained:

> INT: Are you in school now?
> JAMAL: Yeah, well, I go school when I feel like it. Right now I['ve] been in the 10th grade for two years. I'm supposed to done graduate already.

Twenty-four respondents had either graduated from high school or successfully completed a GED curriculum; of those, seven had attended at least one semester of college. Of the nine individuals who received a GED, six had prepared for and passed the examination while incarcerated on Rikers Island or in a state prison. Young males who quit school tended to do so around age 14. Also, older respondents had more favorable opinions toward school and the value of education, and generally reported greater success with school than did younger respondents. This disparity perhaps is attributable to the perspective older respondents gained in their time away from the educational system.

Respondents age 16 to 19 tended to focus on the need to make money in the short term. Cutting school, and eventually dropping out altogether, was described as a necessary step to get money to live day to day. The money earned through hustling most often was used for clothes, jewelry, drugs, alcohol, and entertainment. Respondents frequently cited their parents' inability to provide the latest fashion and other material possessions as part of the pathway to illegal activity. Peer pressure, coupled with the internalized relative deprivation, seemed to make the choice to abandon school easier for young males such as these.

Although the educational achievement levels generally were low for the sample as a whole, respondents from the South Bronx were much less likely to have graduated from high school, completed the GED, or enrolled in college. In fact, only four individuals (10%) obtained a high school diploma or GED, while 53.5% of respondents from the South Bronx dropped out of school. Judging from these data, young men from the South Bronx were much less likely to have plans to continue their education in the future than young men from East New York.

## Cutting School, Dropping Out, and Drifting Away
For the majority of the sample, school-related problems began in junior high school. Many respondents described difficulties with course work, school structure, dealing with authority, conflicts with other students, and disciplinary actions taken against them. When asked "what could have made the school experience better for you?" the majority of respondents said that their problems resulted from their own behavior (e.g., cutting school, not doing the work, and causing trouble in school). One young man explained:

> TYRONE: Yeah, if I would of just stopped smoking marijuana, would have never got with that, or if I just stopped messing with the wrong people when I was in school, and I would have been all right. I would have been somewhere right now.

Many respondents reflected back on the point at which things "went wrong" with their education. This failure usually occurred at about age 14. Many respondents described situations in which they had been pushed out of school because of their inadequate performance, absenteeism (or poor attendance), or disciplinary problems. One respondent described his difficulty in trying to overcome academic problems within the public school system as frustrating, confusing, and discouraging. Eventually he gave up on school as a result of what appears to be a misunderstanding:

INT: So, um, how far did you go in your education?

JEROME: Um, ...ninth grade, tenth grade.

INT: Tenth grade? And you dropped out?

JEROME: Yeah.

INT: Why?

JEROME: 'Cause, um,... I used to go to Tailgate. I was doing bad there. I didn't have no credits so they told me, all right that they was going to send me to a alternative high school until I could build up my credits.

INT: Yeah.

JEROME: 'Cause I only had... what one credit, one and a half credit from there. They transferred me to this school McDonald Prep and, um, I stayed there for one year. And outta that one year they was only giving me half a credit for every class I pass and, um, I was doing good there. I went back to, um Colgate to show them, you know, to show and prove that I was doing good. I want to go back to school. I told them I want to go back to school. They told me nah, they don't want me back. I went to a couple of schools they said they didn't even want to take the kids from alternative high schools, so I just stopped. I just didn't go no more.

INT: Why you didn't just stay in the alternative high school and complete it there?

JEROME: At the time I was only fifteen, when they sent me to the alternative high school.

INT: Ah.

JEROME: And they only give you half a credit for every class that you pass. Half a credit, that wasn't good for me, that wasn't nothing. I would have to stay there for, like, five or six years to finish everything.

INT: They must have... they didn't explain it to you right.
JEROME: No, they didn't.

Another respondent explained that he was not allowed to return to school after being incarcerated:

PATRICK: I couldn't get back in school 'cause I got locked
up. They didn't want me. I couldn't get back in. They told
me I was out too long and all this bullshit. That was July
'95 and I didn't get back in school yet but I'm gonna. I'm
definitely going back to school this year.

Many respondents reported engaging in violence at school. One individual was kicked out of numerous schools for various acts of violence before determining that school was "wasting my time:"

JESS: When I was in the seventh grade I got kicked out for
telling the teacher I was going to hit her with a chair. So
she got scared, she kicked me out of school. She send me to
another school. About a day later I got thrown out 'cause I
was so violent. I burned the hallway. Tried to set a fire in
the hallway. I got thrown out of school. Then I kept getting
arrested for trespassing in the school. I never went to class.
Kept on going to school and getting kicked out. I was in
and out, in and out, getting kicked out. So I was wasting
my time going to school. I was just, you know, crazy
motherfucker. I should've been called retarded, 'cause I
was very retarded. I never made it to high school.

School environments were described as chaotic and violent. Respondents tended to focus on the social aspects of school, including hanging out with friends, girls, smoking marijuana (weed) at school, victimizing "punks" or "herbs," disrespecting teachers, and participating in physical education classes. Although admittedly contributing to the problem, the young men felt that the lack of personal safety in the school environment was a big issue. Reportedly, the schools provided a marketplace for drugs, weapons, and stolen goods:

KURTIS: Ain't nothing you could do with the schools now.
They are still going to do what they want to do, in most

cases selling [drugs] or whatever in the school or just cutting and fighting. You ain't going to change it.

School also provided a stage for violent performances and reputation building. One respondent explained that he "threw a piece of paper at a teacher in school to gain, like, a couple of confidants to run behind me." Another respondent explained that violence could erupt out of routine interactions at school:

INT: What didn't you like about school?

AARON: I didn't like the passing in the hallway, every time you passed [someone] in the hallway everybody get loud and fights break out because somebody walk too close to somebody and stuff like that.

The respondents characterized schools as dangerous places in which violence was likely to occur. In fact, about 10% of the violent events occurred in the school environment.

## EMPLOYMENT EXPERIENCES

Like their experiences with school, respondents described a bleak picture of their employment histories and future prospects. Although most respondents defined "work" as any type of activity that generates money, their participation in the formal economy was limited at best. Respondents reported that most males under 25 years old in their neighborhoods were not employed legally. About 20 percent of the sample had no legitimate work experiences to report.

Several respondents described a societal stigma that limits their prospects for employment. Respondents tended to view the workplace as a hostile setting for young African American and Latino males. Like the stories Wilson (1986) and others documented in Chicago, young men in New York reported experiencing racism and classism in the job search process (Wilson, 1996). The interviews suggested that these young men lack many of the job networking and presentation skills that would make them stand out as a good job candidate. Generally, low levels of effort, closed doors, rejection, and unsatisfactory opportunities characterized their job-hunting processes. For many respondents, programs linked with the criminal justice system (probation and Friends of Island Academy) introduced them to job opportunities, training, and information about jobs. The process of securing employment was described as extremely difficult and oftentimes fruitless. Some individuals took an active role in the search process while others were more passive.

Respondents held many traditional views about work including: the desire to achieve the American dream, to be a male good provider for one's family, and to achieve success by working one's way up the ladder. Most respondents, like most Americans, aspired to reach a middle class standard of living –the career, house, wife and kids, car, and more. The middle class ideal was the norm and what was "proper":

> INT: So, what do you hope for the future?  What do you want for yourself?
> JP: I want -- my own crib, I want to have a big ass job that pays some dough.
> INT: Yeah.
> JP: I want go -- I wanna be with my girl and shit like that. I just wanna be proper. I just wanna be set for future, you know what I mean?
> INT: Yeah.  So what kind of job you're looking for? JP: Me, I'm looking for stock or anything you can get available, mailroom.....
> INT: True.  So what do you hope for the future?
> JP: Having my own business, and having a nice house behind a ocean or river with a big bunch of rocks.

Many youth had strong desires to be a good provider.  Respondents talked about having the means to buy material possessions (their "gear" --clothing, jewelry, drugs, food, etc.) as a positive aspect of getting older and being a man.  Most respondents desired independence from their mothers or other family members.  Those respondents who had children expressed a strong desire to take care of their families financially.  Within these descriptions one also hears a tone of regret and fantasy.  In the first example below Fast Freddy was recently released from jail and reflected on the good feeling he got from working in the past and providing for his girlfriend and kids.  His current jobless status was troubling to him and he desired to get back to work quickly:

> INT: ...Now it is time to go to work.
> FAST FREDDY: That's why I'm trying to look for a job now. 'Cause I was working before. It feels good yo, when

you work and you come home, tired on a Friday or when ever you get paid. Before you come home you go and buy something for the kid, little outfit, outfit for your girl. Then you go out to eat and shit. That's why I want to get a job now man, 'cause now I got my kid and I know there's a lot of things I see that I want to buy. I just don't want my girl to buy it, I feel like a bum and shit. Like she is doing everything and I'm not doing nothing you know for my baby. So you know how people talk, that's why I want to look hard for a job . Try to support my kid. There's not a lot of guys out here that do that. I love my kid and I'm going to be there for my kid.

The respondent felt concerned that he was not fulfilling his male role especially when he explained that "I just don't want my girl to buy it, I feel like a bum and shit."

The next example shows how one young man justified taking the risks of illegal activities by emphasizing his ability to provide for his children through what he made in the drug business. The interviewer was tried to point out that the impact of his incarceration may be worse for his kids in the long run, however Red held strongly to his own position:

INT: I'm saying a couple of years and you might be taken away from your kids. [If you don't get locked down]

RED: In a couple of years they might take me away from my kids, but they ain't in there, I put myself in there, that's the choice I wanted to take.

INT: True. But what about them? As they growing up, you know, they want they daddy.

RED: True, but that's why I said I can't blame them, it's me, it's what I wanted to do, it's something I chose to do. I mean, I love my kids, but I need money in order to feed them and put clothes on they back, you know, so I gotta do what I gotta do, long as I know, if I go to jail, if I go to jail for putting clothes on they back I'll feel good about myself, you know what I mean?

INT: But if you in jail for a whole year you can't put clothes on they back.

RED: Then that would be my loss, it be my fault 'cause I
know, at least I know I was trying to provide for them.
INT: Oh, true.
RED: I was trying to provide for them.

## Types of Job/Work

Respondents' jobs were typically described as low-paying unskilled
positions of short duration in areas such as construction, maintenance,
security, mail delivery/messenger services, office support, retail
(record, clothing, hardware, or food), day care, barbering, and
landscaping work. Only about 20% of these young men had been
employed in jobs that lasted longer than six months.

Summer youth work was the most common type of employment
experience for respondents. Some reported positive experiences with
summer youth jobs and had continued in the same position for several
summers. Interestingly, many of the summer youth job placements had
been with the New York City Police Department or in local hospitals
where boys ages 14 to 16 years old did filing and other miscellaneous
tasks. Despite the widespread popularity of these programs, the
youngest members of the sample, those 14 to 17 years old reported
fewer experiences with this type of employment in 1995 and 1996.
Many respondents hypothesized that recent budget cuts in youth
programs resulted in the apparent lack of job opportunities for urban
youth.

Respondents viewed the construction business as a good field that
paid well and was available to those without training or special skills.

INT: You ain't got no job opportunities for you now?
GABINO: Nah. Well, I'm trying right now. I want to get into
the construction business, know what I'm saying. They pay
good. You know, 30 bucks an hour, 20 bucks an hour.
INT: Yeah.
GABINO: That's a high paying job, construction.

Although they thought paid well, construction work was described as
sporadic and hard to get when the economy was weak.

INT: So did you ever have a job?
BO: Yeah, not all of us, had little commercial jobs like
construction, painting, delivering eggs.
INT: What was your first job?

BO: I used to pack bags when I was like, what, 11? ten. That's when my moms and pops was still alive and get my little $20 and shit. I wasn't doing, I ain't have nothing to spend on so I always liked to get money. The last real job I had was, like, one of them construction jobs, painting and shit like that. That's a few months ago, but it's a temp job, you know those little side jobs with a couple of apartments, that shit is gone, that's it, no more work.

**Keeping a Job**
The length of time respondents reported keeping a job varied from one day to three years. Respondents left paying jobs for a variety of reasons; more frequently, paying jobs left them. The examples below illustrate important obstacles the young men faced with regard to job retention. Many respondents said they were resistant to the traditional 9-to-5 hours of legal employment:

JAMAL: I told you, I love selling fucking drugs. I can't see myself waking up 8:00 in the morning to go to work to sit behind a fucking desk all day when I can stand outside of a building and make some lost motherfucker sell my drugs for me and make my pockets big.

Most respondents felt that there were few opportunities available to make a living wage. One respondent described his struggle to make ends meet while working a low-paying job. To compensate he tried to work more hours but was unable to keep the pace going; eventually, he got into trouble with his manager:

CLARENCE: I used to work for a supermarket.
INT: Oh, true? Right here in Brooklyn?
CLARENCE: Yeah. I mean, towards a while it got, like, it got pretty tense because it's like my manager was, like, always barking on me and stuff like that. It was, like, the job itself was only paying $4.25 and I was living on my own so I was paying my rent and taking care of myself, you understand, so I needed to pay bills. I needed, like, half of the money so, like, I could clean clothes in the week, you know....
INT: Yeah.....
CLARENCE: Plus enough to pay my rent, you know, to pay for any other bills. Take care of my son, because I do have an

18 month-old son now, you know. He's 18 months right now. Back then he was like 16, like 15, 14 months going round there and I was taking care of him too, you know. ...I just needed to have money stretch out, and $4.25 an hour wasn't making it for me.

INT: Yeah.

CLARENCE: So I had to, like, struggle ...I had to work 16 hours a day sometimes. You know, I would get out, I would get out pretty late, so I would get into work the next day, like, pretty late and my manager was always getting on my case. It came to a point I just ended up quitting.

One respondent decried the infrequent paydays of legitimate employment as opposed to the daily cash that accompanies the drug trade:

STEVE: A week, it's too long for me to get paid.

INT: [Laughs] For real, man.

STEVE: Too long.

INT: What, every week?

STEVE: Every week too long, man. I want money every day in my pocket, every day. I want money everyday, like every single day I want money in my pocket, I would like at least to have a buck-fifty to two hundred in my pocket every day. I'm saying by hustling you can do that.

INT: Yeah, but, you ain't, well, carpentry, man, that's a good line of work, you can, you can get paid.

STEVE: It [carpentry schooling] take a lot of time too.

Another respondent who lost his job after failing to call in sick during a legitimate illness viewed the experience as a lesson in responsibility:

DAVID: I got laid off at a fast food restaurant 'cause I fucked up in there.

INT: What happen with that?

DAVID: I'm saying 'cause I didn't get the phone number. I got paid I took two days off 'cause I was sick, legitimately sick but I didn't have the number so I came back there. And he did what he had to do. He said he gave my spot to some other nigga.... I'm saying it was only right 'cause when you working somewhere you supposed to know.

A few respondents quit legal jobs due to the costs associated with commuting and being on the job. Several respondents lost jobs because of conflicts with bosses or co-workers in the workplace. These respondents described their difficulty with authority figures as a major reason for losing jobs. In some cases, the conflicts escalated to serious violence. One 17 year-old explained:

INT: Ever have a job?
ERIC: Yeah. I worked good jobs. ...I worked, worked for three different retail stores.
INT: What happened, why didn't you maintain that?
ERIC: My boss, every single boss I had was an asshole. That's it. Never had a good boss, except one time. So, never had a cool boss. Not the type of person to sit there. One time, me and my co-worker take lunch. I need my paycheck. I want the check now. [I try to] get it for lunch, so you [I] can cash it. I see my paycheck in his hand, and he say 'Nah.' So, I was gonna fuck him up, I want my check. I got my check, cashed the check. [laughs]. I got back upstairs and he upset. So, [we fought]...

Another respondent repeatedly got into fights in variety of workplace settings:

INT: You ever worked before?
LJ: Yeah, I worked before, but I just get into fights. I can't take, I can't take orders.
INT: You never had no jobs?
LJ: I had jobs before, but not for long. For a few days.
INT: Could you remember your first job?
LJ: My first job, construction, man.
INT: You was working in construction?
LJ: Yeah, man.
INT: How long you did that for?
LJ: For like a month. You can't even last in that shit, got into a fight. Try to hit a nigga with a sledgehammer.
INT: You tried to hit somebody with a sledgehammer?
LJ: Yeah, man.

One respondent reported getting fired over a dispute after he failed to complete a task at work. According to Desmond, his manager used a racial slur and he responded by assaulting the manager:

> DESMOND: I worked first at a popular fast food restaurant got fired from there for punching the manager in the eye.
> INT: Can you tell me a little about that work at a popular fast food restaurant?
> DESMOND: It was all right, it was just some shit that they never showed me, and one day they asked me to go to it and didn't know where to go so I didn't go, so I didn't do nothing, I did whatever I had to do and then.
> INT: Was this before selling drugs or after?
> DESMOND: While.
> INT: Oh while selling drugs so you was getting money out there?
> DESMOND: I was getting clean money and dirty money.
> INT: So what happen?
> DESMOND: Well, that day the manager told me to leave and then he called me a spic, and this is a white guy and you know we take that very seriously, so I punch him in the face.
> INT: The manager, so what happened with that?
> DESMOND: He terminated me, he got me signed out it not work in no popular fast food restaurant anywhere, I'm terminated from all foundations.
> INT: So what happened afterwards you punched the man?
> DESMOND: Nothing, I left and just kept on selling, I just didn't work.

In several cases, respondents had been either fired or had their hours reduced during slow periods. During these times, many respondents quit their jobs to pursue other activities:

> INT: You ever had a job before?
> ROD: Yeah.
> INT: What? Doing what?
> ROD: Um...restocking in the supermarket. Reshelving. And then when the, um, customer is done, when they leave with the shopping cart, I'd just take it back and put it where it belongs.
> INT: Oh. How long you had that job?
> ROD: Hmm. Probably like a year. Yeah.

INT: Why...How you lost it?
ROD: They...My Pops wanted me to quit anyway. He wanted me to stop so I could go to school. And then they had me working, like, one day a week 'cause it was getting so slow and that's it.

**The Drug Business**
Most youth worked in some capacity in the illegal economy; 84% of the sample reported being involved in the drug business during the previous two years. Work in the illegal economy generally was the dominant means of support for the sample. Employment in the drug business was readily available, more lucrative, produced almost instant payment, and allowed a flexible structure with few time and physical constraints. The examples below illustrate the appeal of drug work for young males. Sid and Chet explained:

INT: You would rather sell drugs or work?
SID: I sold drugs.
INT: You would rather sell drugs than work?
SID: I rather, no. I rather work. Really, but I'm saying though, I like selling. If work ain't there, I rather sell drugs.
INT: Oh.
SID: 'Cause I like quick money, you know, I like money in my pockets everyday... I don't like walking around with two dollars or a dollar or something, I like walking around with like a 100, 300 dollars in my pockets.
INT: You ever have a legit job?
SID: No, I worked once or twice legit, people that try to give me, they be like 'come on leave drugs and all that.' But it's not the same from bringing $400, $500 a night to your house and bringing $300 a week it's not the same. It gets harder.

INT: So, like, how was that for you, like your first experience with that selling drugs?
CHET: Oh. Because after this, while I was doing that I had other friends that was just trying to do the right thing too 'cause they had good families and all that. And they family wasn't having that --hanging out in the street, so after school they would work in McDonald's and little supermarket jobs. And they was getting they little peanuts, they had they little

gear and all that but... my mother's a single parent and the little money she would get she would have to pay for bills.

INT: Yeah.

CHET: So I couldn't, she ain't have no money really to buy me $80 sneakers and the little $30 pants and, I couldn't have as much gear as I wanted so I had to find a way to get my own. My moms wanted me to get a job but I kind, I was kind of, 'Nah.' [I] kind of seen the way this crowd was looking, fast it [looked] much easier I wanted to do it. And you know, shortest period of time, who could make the most.

INT: Umm.

CHET: They having to go to work for eight hours... a day.. And only making maybe $25 that for the little eight hours, it don't work.

INT: Umm..

CHET: When I could be out here making my own hours and hustle when I want to and make all the money I want to.

INT: Yeah.

CHET: But in a way it kind of spoiled me and ruined me.. It kind of made it harder for me to. respect the little bit of money that, if I did have a job, the little money that they give me, it would be hard for me to have respect for that money 'cause yo, that ain't nothing. I could go over there and really...

INT: You lost the value of money.

CHET: Like it's nothing. I could spend $25 dollars on a cab. Where if you work for it, you would save it. You probably be like 'Nah. I'm gonna save this," but being that you was just like boom [snaps fingers]. Hell yeah...

INT: What about work? Nobody work, guys don't work? Guys your age?

CHET: Nobody around here on this side. The people I be with, they work, but they sell drugs. That's what they call work.

INT: So, um, like, on the level of 1 to 10, how many guys in your neighborhood work or go to school?

CHET: Nobody. Like nobody.

INT: Why is that?

CHET: 'Cause people want to be out here making that fast money in drugs.

INT: But what about a job or school?
CHET: I don't even know.
INT: You think it's hard to get a job?
CHET: I don't know. I ain't never try that.

Some respondents, who worked mostly legal jobs, supplemented their income with money from the drug business or robberies. In the next example, Nick viewed himself as mostly working legally except in times of financial need. He explained:

INT: So, you working now?
NICK: Yeah, I'm now working the midnight shift in a mail company. I'm doing that now. 'Cause I used to hustle but it got too drastic for me so I'm trying to chill right now. I see a lot of brothers getting locked up. It ain't right like it was in the '80s and shit.
INT: How long you been working at your job?
NICK: I guess six month, seven months.
INT: So now you don't do none of that no more?
NICK: Yeah, yeah, I still do it on occasion when I need the money. If I need the money really bad, I'll either stick up somebody or hustle and shit. I'm thinking about hustling rock now, know what I'm saying. You know, buy some weights and shit, cook it up and sell it. 'Cause, you know, the job is good for me but it's not paying the bills.
INT: You can't get a better one?
NICK: I can't get a better one now, know what I'm saying, 'cause I'm not really motivated, I just want to get it over with. I'm tired, man, I'm getting tired of this resistance, man. You know a lot of things I feel that I done and shit, you know, it's not getting me nowhere. It's getting me depressed and shit. I don't know what to do no more. The way the living standards is in the '90s it's so different now, man. You got to be so fast-paced. You got to have money. That's the thing to do, have money, money, money, that's the way to live. And I don't have enough of it so I got to do what I got to do.

For others who sell drugs, a part-time job served as a front or cover to their families and the police:

INT: Do most guys in your neighborhood work?

GABINO: Some of them work, but that's just a front. So when they doing their real shit, which is selling drugs. What they do, like, they, um, do they work legit, for they could, um, you know, cover up on illegal activities.

INT: Do most of the guys do the same thing, work legit to cover up they criminal backgrounds?

GABINO: Some of the, some of the juveniles and some of the older guys, you know. The big, they call them the "bigger niggas," some of them have jobs so they can do what they really do. You know, in case the cops, you know, they have money on them, cops roll up, 'where you got this money?' There's a pay stub right here. Pull out the pay stub and shit, you know and say 'you work, with you C company, this is my rent money.

This chapter has shown that the urban males in our study lived primarily outside of mainstream avenues of success. With most legitimate avenues compromised, drug selling and other illegal activities become the most predictable option for these youth. Youth experience isolation as a result of their nonappearance in educational and employment institutions. School and employment failure shapes our respondents hopes for the future, personal identities, and indirectly their violent behaviors. In the final section of the book, the focus shifts from individual-level factors to the violent events that those individuals participated in. When examining the narratives of violent events it is important to keep the respondents' structural and cultural positions in mind. An event level analysis focuses primarily on human agency, that is, how actors make decisions in specific situations—bounded or limited by structural factors.

# CHAPTER 7

# Decision Making In Violent Events:
## An Examination of Sparks and Other Motivational Factors

Prior research on violent events has shown that violence reflects a variety of motivational and situational concerns. Little information is available on violent events where adolescent and young adult males are main participants. The descriptive analysis of violent situations is presented in two chapters. I present a characterization of the sample of 306 violent events described by respondents. The descriptive results are presented in tables 7-1 to 7-4 in this chapter and tables 8-1 through 8-8 in chapter 8. The event data are coded on 13 different dimensions including:

> type of weapon present;
> type of weapon use;
> who was armed;
> role of the respondent;
> role of the opponent;
> relationship between combatants;
> role of the other parties present, including: the respondent's associates, the opponent's companions, and neutral bystanders;
> a classification of collective decision making in violent events (co-offending);
> reason or spark of the event;
> location or context;
> role of alcohol and/or drug use in the event;
> role of the police; and
> an analysis of outcomes of the violent event including injuries and conflict resolution.

The data are presented by each of these domains in an effort to illustrate the heterogeneity of violent situations among adolescents. The detailed examples provided often illustrate more than one theme requiring multiple references to specific event descriptions across domains. Because weapon type is centrally important to the research questions of this study, all categories are examined across type of weapon. The focus of this chapter is an examination of the "motives" or "sparks" for violent conflict among adolescent males. Respondents described a variety of reasons to engage in violent situations.

Chapter 9 explores a variety of situational factors, including context, the relationship between combatants, the role of third parties, alcohol and/or drug use, the role of the police, injuries sustained, outcomes, and aftermaths. The interactional process by which an interaction escalates toward a violent outcome is important. The developmental literature would suggest that the violence process may be different during this period, reflecting immature decision making by younger actors and other contingencies (Slaby, 1997; Slaby & Roedell, 1982; Steinberg & Avenevoli, 2000).

## TYPE OF WEAPON AND WEAPON USE IN VIOLENT EVENTS

Respondents were asked to describe violent events with guns, knives, and other weapons that were either "completed" or "defused." They also were asked to describe fights without weapons. In total, respondents described 151 gun events, 37 knife events, 14 including other weapons, and 111 events with no weapon (just hands). Events were classified by type of weapon according to whether or not a weapon was part of the interaction between actors. For example, if any person in the situation had a gun, the event would be classified as a gun event. Weapons could have been brought into the situation by the respondent, the respondent's companions, the opponent, or the opponent's companions. Each of these situations was coded for level of lethality. TABLE 7-1 presents the lethality level by type of weapon used.

### Gun Events

Research on gun violence tends to confound gun carrying with gun use. To overcome this problem, each gun event was classified by different types of gun 'use.' Respondents reported having guns in 102 violent events, opponents having a gun in 88 situations, respondents' companions having guns in 69 events, and opponents' companions having guns in 35 situations. Of the 151 gun events, guns were used to threaten 23% (n=34), to beat 7% (n=10), and to shoot or shoot at someone 71% (n=107) of the time.

**TABLE 7-1. Intersection of Type of Weapon by Level of Lethality (N=306)***

|                      | Total n (%) | Gun n (%)  | Other Weapon n (%) | No Weapon n (%) |
| -------------------- | ----------- | ---------- | ------------------ | --------------- |
| **Level of Lethality:** |          |            |                    |                 |
| Threaten             | 68 (22.7)   | 34 (22.5)  | 13 (25.5)          | 22 (19.8)       |
| Used (Fire or Stab)  | 138 (46.2)  | 107 (70.9) | 29 (56.9)          | - (-)           |
| Beat                 | 93 (31.1)   | 10 ( 6.6)  | 9 (17.6)           | 89 (80.2)       |
| Missing              | 7           | 0          | 0                  | 0               |
| Total Valid          | 299         | 151        | 51                 | 111             |

*Data were missing on different domains. Percentages are for valid cases only.

As shown in TABLE 7-2, there were 55 gun situations in which both the respondent and his opponent had guns. During 40 of these events the respondent had the assistance of friends who were also armed with guns whereas the respondent faced his opponent alone in 15 incidents. Twenty-one of the events were "shootouts" between the respondent's crew and the opponent's crew.

Respondents held an unarmed opponent at gunpoint in 43 situations. In 18 of those situations, the respondent's companions also were armed, and the respondent was armed and alone in 25 situations against an unarmed opponent. Respondents described 3 situations in which they were armed with a gun while their opponent had a knife.

Respondents described 31 situations of being unarmed when facing an opponent with a gun. In 10 of those incidents, the opponents had armed friends backing them up. In a small number of cases, an event became a gun situation because of the actions of other parties. Respondents' companions brought guns in 10 situations, while the opponent's companions brought 3 situations to the gun level.

Respondents described both offensive and defensive moves in gun events. For example, 70 gun events were initiated by respondents (both

**TABLE 7-2. Intersection of Level of Lethality of Gun Events by Who Was Armed (N=151)\***

Type of Gun Use

|  | Total<br>n (%) | Threat<br>n (%) | Fired<br>n (%) | Beat<br>n (%) |
|---|---|---|---|---|
| **Armed Actor:** | | | | |
| Respondent Armed Total | 99 (65.6) | 19 (55.9) | 75 (70.1) | 5(50.0) |
| R. Armed Vs. Unarmed O. | 43 (28.5) | 12 (35.3) | 26 (24.3) | 5(50.0) |
| R. & Coms vs. Unarmed O. | 18 (16.8) | 6 (17.6) | 10 ( 9.3) | 2(20.0) |
| R. Armed & Solo vs Unarmed O. | 25 (23.4) | 6 (17.6) | 16 (15.0) | 3(30.0) |
| | | | | |
| Respondent vs. Opponent Both Armed | 55 (36.4) | 6 (17.6) | 49 (45.8) | 0 (0.0) |
| R. & C. vs. O. | 40 (37.4) | 4 (11.8) | 36 (33.6) | 0 (0.0) |
| R. Armed & Solo vs. Armed O. | 15 (14.0) | 2 ( 5.9) | 13 (12.1) | 0 (0.0) |
| | | | | |
| Respondent's Team vs. Opponent's Team<br>(Crew on Crew) | 21 (13.9) | 0 (0.0) | 21 (19.6) | 0 (0.0) |
| | | | | |
| Opponent Armed Total | 86 (57.0) | 15 (44.1) | 69 (64.5) | 2(20.0) |
| O. Armed vs. Unarmed | 31 (20.5) | 9 (26.5) | 20 (18.7) | 2(20.0) |
| O. & His C. Armed vs. Unarm. R. | 10 ( 6.6) | 1 ( 2.9) | 8 ( 7.5) | 1(10.0) |
| O. Armed. & Solo vs. Unarm. R. | 21 (13.9) | 8 (23.5) | 12 (11.2) | 1(10.0) |
| | | | | |
| Total | 151 | 34 | 107 | 10 |

\*Data were missing on different domains. Percentages are for valid cases only.

alone and as a group) while 63 events were started by an opponent. According to our analysis of the data, the 'options' available when armed with a gun included pulling out (to threaten), shooting in the air (to threaten), pistol whipping, shooting to injure, shooting to kill, attempting to shoot (failure), and drive-by shootings. The 'options' available when confronted with an armed opponent included stalling or talking one's way out of the situation (with no retaliation), stalling or talking one's way out of the situation (with planned retaliation), negotiating another type of violence (disarming), pulling out a gun and facing off (no shooting), having a shootout, friends pulling out guns and forcing the opponent to back down (overpowering arms), and fleeing the situation to escape harm.  Respondents decided which action to take based upon their prior knowledge of an opponent's willingness or ability to use violence (or their on-the-spot impression of the opponent), the respondent's assessment of his own ability to outperform the opponent, the likelihood that other parties would get involved to aid either party if needed, the level of anger/emotion during the event by both parties, and the respondent's assessment of risks and benefits to his social identity by using or avoiding violence.  Guns clearly tip the scales of power in favor of the person who is armed.

**Knife Events**
Knives were used in 37 (or 12%) of the violent events described by the sample.  For the knife events, combatants had knives in six situations, the respondent alone was armed with a knife in 11 situations, and the opponent alone was armed with a knife in 13 situations.  The respondent's and opponent's friends each introduced knives to three additional situations.  As shown in TABLE 7-1, knives were used to threaten 31% (n=11) of cases and to stab or cut an adversary 69% (n=24) of the time.

**Other Weapon Events**
Events in which other weapons (e.g., bottles, broken glass, bats, rocks, sticks, pencils, bricks, and forks) were used were less common among our sample.  In these types of situations, the actor(s) typically picked up an available object and used it as a weapon against an unarmed opponent.  The respondent fought his opponent in seven situations with some other weapon.  The respondent was unarmed in 5 situations in which his opponent had this type of weapon.

**Events with No Weapons**
Violent situations in which no weapons were used occurred in 111 of the 306 events described.  In these situations, the unarmed respondent fought an unarmed opponent.  In addition, if either party's friends were present and involved, they also did not use any type of weapon.  The majority of these conflicts resulted in a physical fight; however 15 events were resolved before the situation escalated to violence.

## REASONS OR SPARKS: RESPONDENTS' DEFINITIONS OF THE SITUATION

The sparks or causes of violent events reflect a variety of issues and concerns for the actor(s) that were both situational and normative. The early moments in a potentially violent situation were important in allowing the actor(s) to make sense out of the situations and define the situation as serious or not. The reasons or justifications respondents offered for the violent events include both motivational and interactional domains; the two were often impossible to disentangle. Respondents described a number of reasons or sparks for conflict including: challenges to identity/status, jealousy/competition over females, self-defense, robbery, drug business transactions, revenge/retaliation, defense of others, rumors, territory/neighborhood honor, money/debts, unfair play (e.g., sports and gambling situations), misunderstandings, and fun or recreation. Descriptive statistics for the sample of events are presented, followed by an examination of the detailed narratives of the most common contingencies within each type of event. The excerpts provide a glimpse into the content and context of these violent events. Some of the events were used to illustrate multiple domains; in these cases, the event descriptions are presented in sections throughout the chapter. As shown in TABLE 7-3, many violent events involved more than one reason or spark.

Existing data on offender motivations often make broad claims about the overlapping existence of several motivational factors. A correlation matrix of the different types of motivations is presented below to illustrate the degree to which respondents' motives did or did not overlap. The data show that violent events among adolescent males in these two neighborhoods reflect a wide variety of issues and contextual dynamics. As shown in Table 7-4, some economically motivated violent events were significantly correlated with each other; specifically, drug business transactions correlate with events coded as igniting over neighborhood or turf concerns and the repayment of debts. Both drug business violence and robberies were negatively correlated with events erupting out of identity or status concerns or over females. The results suggest at minimum two separate motivational trajectories. Consistent with prior research, robberies and violence associated with the drug business were significantly correlated with guns as the weapon of choice.

## Challenges to Social Identity or Status

This section comprises narrative reconstructions of violent events classified as erupting out of some type of challenge or test to one's social identity or status. These events could be called 'character contests,' strategies of 'impression management' and/or 'face saving' situations. An event was coded as sparking out of identity or respect concerns if either the opponent or respondent felt 'dissed,' challenged, or 'played.' These situations typically involve the denial of personal status or identity manifested through insults, ridicule, bump, slight, ice grill (hard looks), lack of proper acknowledgment, cheating, deception, domination, cunning, unwarranted threats, or unprovoked physical attack. One hundred twenty-nine situations (67% of the total) reflected identity or status concerns, according to respondents.

**TABLE 7-3.** Intersection of Type of Weapon by Spark or Reason for Event (N=306)*

| | Total n (%) | Gun n (%) | Other Weapon n (%) | No Weapon n (%) |
|---|---|---|---|---|
| **Spark or Reason for Event:** | | | | |
| Identity/Status | 129 (42.2) | 61 (41.2) | 21 (41.2) | 48 (43.2) |
| Girl | 94 (30.7) | 38 (25.7) | 20 (39.2) | 39 (35.1) |
| Self-Defense | 67 (21.9) | 30 (20.3) | 17 (33.3) | 20 (18.0) |
| Robbery | 61 (19.9) | 42 (28.4) | 8 (15.7) | 10 ( 9.0) |
| Drug Business | 53 (17.3) | 40 (27.0) | 3 ( 5.9) | 9 ( 8.1) |
| Revenge | 53 (17.3) | 32 (21.6) | 9 (17.6) | 13 (11.7) |
| Defense of Others | 34 (11.1) | 16 (10.8) | 8 (15.7) | 10 ( 9.0) |
| Rumors | 18 ( 5.9) | 7 ( 4.7) | 3 ( 5.9) | 8 ( 7.2) |
| Territory (non-drug) | 16 ( 5.2) | 10 ( 6.8) | 3 ( 5.9) | 3 ( 2.7) |
| Money or Debt | 16 ( 5.2) | 12 ( 8.1) | 1 ( 2.0) | 3 ( 2.7) |
| Unfair Play | 15 ( 4.9) | 9 ( 6.1) | 3 ( 5.9) | 13 (11.7) |
| Misunderstanding | 5 ( 1.6) | 0 ( 0.0) | 1 ( 2.0) | 4 ( 3.6) |
| No Reason | 5 ( 1.6) | 3 ( 2.0) | 0 ( 0.0) | 2 ( 1.8) |
| Fun or Recreation | 4 ( 1.3) | 3 ( 2.0) | 0 ( 0.0) | 1 ( 0.9) |

*Data were missing on different domains. Percentages are for valid cases only. Reflects multiple sparks per event.

**TABLE 7-4. Correlation Matrix Spark or Reason for Event & Weapon Type**

| | 1 | 2 | 3 | 4 | 5 | 6 | 7 | 8 | 9 | 10 | 11 | 12 | 13 | 14 | 15 |
|---|---|---|---|---|---|---|---|---|---|---|---|---|---|---|---|
| 1 Identity/Status | 1.00 | .02 | .09 | -.19** | -.13** | .06 | -.09 | .07 | -.05 | -.08 | .00 | -.02 | .04 | -.06 | .02 |
| 2 Girl | | 1.00 | -.01 | -.20** | -.21** | -.08 | .08 | .04 | -.09 | -.13* | -.10 | -.10 | .09 | -.01 | .08 |
| 3 Self-Defense | | | 1.00 | .02 | -.05 | -.05 | .04 | .04 | .02 | -.09 | -.11 | -.03 | .05 | .11 | -.07 |
| 4 Robbery | | | | 1.00 | .07 | -.04 | -.13* | -.13* | -.08 | .03 | -.10 | .20** | -.04 | -.03 | -.18** |
| 5 Drug Business | | | | | 1.00 | -.07 | -.08 | -.00 | .16** | .16** | -.02 | .24** | -.14* | -.02 | -.16** |
| 6 Revenge | | | | | | 1.00 | .09 | -.04 | -.03 | .01 | .11 | .10 | .07 | -.10 | -.11 |
| 7 Defense of Others | | | | | | | 1.00 | .04 | -.08 | -.04 | -.11 | -.01 | .00 | .07 | -.03 |
| 8 Rumors | | | | | | | | 1.00 | -.06 | -.06 | -.03 | -.05 | -.01 | .01 | .04 |
| 9 Territory (non-drug) | | | | | | | | | 1.00 | .01 | -.02 | .06 | .01 | .02 | -.08 |
| 10 Money or Debt | | | | | | | | | | 1.00 | -.02 | .09 | -.09 | .02 | -.05 |
| 11 Unfair Play | | | | | | | | | | | 1.00 | -.06 | -.08 | .05 | .09 |
| 12 Gun | | | | | | | | | | | | 1.00 | -.36** | -.18** | -.72** |
| 13 Knife | | | | | | | | | | | | | 1.00 | -.08 | -.23** |
| 14 Other Weapon | | | | | | | | | | | | | | 1.00 | -.16** |
| 15 No Weapon | | | | | | | | | | | | | | | 1.00 |

* Significance level of .05
** Significance level of .01

Personal Attacks

Respondents described a variety of situations in which non-verbal communication between two or more parties resulted in violent conflict. These situations most often involved a direct challenge to the rights of each individual over defining and controlling both the situation and space. In some cases, the initial exchange was simply an attempt at defining a situation, what Luckenbill called the 'naming' stage. As illustrated by the examples below, many factors affect situational definitions in potential conflict situations.

Several examples show how violent events can erupt out of what respondents call 'ice grills,' 'icing,' 'grilling,' 'hard profiling,' or 'staredowns.' This form of communication between strangers within certain age-demographic groups is common on the street. In some situations, a look may be targeted at an individual with the goal of discovering more about his intentions in the setting. In other cases, ice grills were aggressive attempts to defend against any potential threat anticipated by the presence of a stranger in the neighborhood. These gestures speak loudly in a variety of settings to ward off attacks and identify situations in which attacks may be successful.

In the first example, the opponent was ice grilling Jon and he became angry to the point of thinking about getting his gun. Jon interprets the opponent's ice grill as an extremely hostile threat and anticipates the opponent's return to the scene with a gun. This conflict may have escalated further if a mutual friend had not intervened:

INT: Tell me what happen.
JON: We went to the spot to buy weed. So this dude came up start ice grilling me.
INT: What caused the beef?
JON: He was grilling [me]. Then he ran up straight to the block. He went for his gun and I was gonna go for mine but my man came over. My man right there, [we] use to go to school with each other. So we just dead that, squashed it.
INT: What made you decide not to hurt your opponent?
JON: 'Cause he my man's peoples.

Looking back on the situation, the respondent felt that "if I had a gun and was by myself I probably woulda shot him." The ice grill was perceived as a serious personal insult. Jon was only willing to drop his grievance with the opponent because of his relationship with the third party.

Taunting and ice grills (hard stares) between young men were common features of violent events. One such event occurred during a baseball game in jail. Rashard "iced" his opponent for making a "slick comment" and paid for his transgression against this powerful individual with a physical injury.

> INT: Alright. Try to remember....three or four times in the past, in the past year or two, ...that you got into fights with people. I want you to describe the scene so I could picture it...
>
> RASHARD: The fight, the main fact I can remember is when I got jumped and I had to get 140 stitches across my eye. Right at the bottom. And the situation was... it started on a baseball field where someone said a slick comment towards me and I turned around and I iced him and that person was well known ...basically he ran [in] the building and he got all his peoples that was on my unit, my wing [in jail], to take care of his business, so when he was there, I was fighting at least eight people, guys who was doing 18 to life, lifers and there was not no skinny, you know, they wasn't no skinny puny people. They've been there, they've been working out... it was a rough battle.
>
> INT: How the fight had started?
>
> RASHARD: I already told you how it started, it started because...
>
> INT: I mean like in your unit, how did they approach you?
>
> RASHARD: They approach me, they approached the way, you know, handled their business, they just said, 'pardon me may I speak to you,' and once I came inside that room then, we got it on.

### Outsider Status and Identity Uncertainty

One central theme in identity- or status-related violent events is that identity challenges resulting in violent events were more often between strangers. The examples presented below illustrate how these conflicts unfold in a variety of situations.

In the setting where these occurred bumping into someone represents a personal attack. One respondent, Antoine reacted to a bump by swinging at his opponent. While this seemingly spontaneous conflict could have resulted in a physical fight without weapons, the opponent chose instead to get his gun. Antoine explained the situation:

INT: Can you tell me about a gun event that you was involved in? I want you to tell me what happened, what it was over, everything.

ANTOINE: I was walking through the projects one day. I was going to a party. It's not around my 'hood, [I] ain't know nobody around there. And this kid bumped me. And I swung at him. Then he ran to go get his people. And he came back and he shot at me twice.

INT: Um, was there some type of argument before the gun got involved?

ANTOINE: Nah just when he bumped me and I swung at him.

INT: Why you swung at him for?

ANTOINE: 'Cause he bump me and then he look back like he was going to do something. So I swung.

INT: What he say?

ANTOINE: 'What's the fuck wrong with you, man?'

INT: What was it about this situation that made it necessary to handle it the way you did?

ANTOINE: They way he talk to me. And he never knew me before.

INT: Who made the first move toward violence?

ANTOINE: Actually, I did.

INT: You swung at him?

ANTOINE: Yeah.

INT: What did he do after that?

ANTOINE: He ran to get his gun.

INT: Was anybody else around?

ANTOINE: His peoples.

INT: What kind of stuff was they sayin'?

ANTOINE: 'Kill that nigga.'

INT: How did you feel about what his friends was sayin? Were you afraid?

ANTOINE: I was. Man with a gun, shooting.

The other individuals in the situation clearly were against Antoine and verbally encouraged the opponent's gun use. The event escalated to a gun incident quickly and Antoine fled the scene without injury. Two factors made the respondent's presence in that neighborhood problematic: he was vulnerable to attack because of his outsider status and he did not have a gun.

In the example below, Chuckie was confronted by a member of a rival crew while walking with a female through a park. The unarmed opponent, known to Chuckie as "Big Willy," lived in a nearby neighborhood. The opponent initiated the violence by hitting Chuckie and continuing to attack him. Chuckie reacted by pulling out a gun from his pocket and shooting the opponent in the leg. He explained:

> INT: Can you tell me what happened and describe the situation, how it happened and what it was over?
> CHUCKIE: Alright, in the park a crew named Deceps [Deceptacons] came. This kid smack me, he smack me in front of a female, and you know you can't have things like that. I was about 17 at the time and I had a lil' two-five in my pocket.
> INT: Alright, what happened next and how did it turn to a gun situation?
> CHUCKIE: Well, first of all, I knew it was on for the simple fact is, every time he got close I backed up, he got closer. Every time I backed off he came closer. I knew it was gonna turn into a gun situation for the simple fact I know what I had on me, and I kept sayin', you know, the next time I back up, I'm not movin' no more, and then he come messin' me, whatever he do, if he don't knock me out, I'll shoot him. That was on my mind. You know and after he did it, I jumped back at him but I ain't swing. My mind was tellin' me 'why swing when you can just hit this Nigga off right there and get outta there,' you know. So, I took a couple shots at him, hit him in the bottom of his legs...

In this description, Chuckie's anticipation of the opponent's actions influenced his own action. In the heat of the situation, he concluded that his opponent's failure to disable him equaled an opportunity for a defensive move against the attacker. According to this account, Chuckie believed he had been pushed to a point where gun violence was necessary and easier.

Another respondent became involved in a gun conflict when his opponent bumped him in a party. Scot was high and refused to accept the apology of the opponent. The event unfolded in the following way:

> INT: Alright, let's talk about the gun event. What happened? Can you describe the situation? And how did it happen, what

started it?

SCOT: It's like I said before, you know, just me and my man was just jiving and bugging out, dancing and shit, you know, drinking, smoking. Shit, some niggas just wanted to try to play you and shit, make us look stupid. So, you know, [they] pulled out the gun and started shooting in the fucking house and shit, everybody screaming and shit. Me and the niggas shot back at them. They shot my man twice. So then after that, like, everybody just started screaming and running, so we, like, just started shooting.

INT: Was there some kind of argument before the guns was used?

SCOT: Nah. Yeah, of course, you know, of course, you know.

INT: So tell me, like, everything that was said.

SCOT: All right, like me and my man, right, we was dancing and shit, smoking, all that, drunk like a motherfucker, you know? So like one punk, you know, like, bumped my man and shit, you know. So, you know, they came out arguing and shit, you know, pussy and this and that, you know. So we was like, all right, so then I went up to my man, I was like 'what's the deal and shit,' he was like 'I don't know, somebody just trying to play you.' So I just started shooting at them, you know? Fuck it. We was high and shit, so I was like, 'I'ma shoot these motherfuckers', so that's that...

As the example below illustrates, individuals may react to bumps or "hard profiling" in a less confrontational way. In this case, the "bumpee" waited to attack the "bumper" when he least expected it. The respondent accepted this experience as punishment for his foolish behavior:

JEROME: I got shot over here [showing interviewer the scar]... I got stabbed twice in my back, too.

INT: For what?

JEROME: Bullshitting. I got fucked up one day and I just when I first started out. I just thought I was the man.

INT: How old were you?

JEROME: Um. Fifteen. Um, yeah, about 15.

INT: And you got stabbed twice in your back?

JEROME: It's 'cause... we went to this party and sometimes I thought I was the man 'cause I smoked weed so I thought I was the man. So I used to act like a fool, profile, I use to profile hard. Going into parties, rock my shoulders, bumping people. And after the party was over I got jumped and I got stabbed twice.

INT: You got stabbed twice?

JEROME: Yeah.

INT: By somebody in the party that you bumped?

JEROME: Yeah. I don't even know who stabbed me. I just know I got jumped and somebody stabbed me.

INT: You was leaving the party and some guy just ran up on you?

JEROME: Yeah. I wasn't by myself, though. Everybody that was with me ran. Everybody that was with me ran.

INT: What they stabbed you with, a knife?

JEROME: Nah. I guess it was an ice pick.

In the next example, JP immediately sensed the opponent's hostile stance toward him as soon as he entered a party. Again, JP was an outsider to the neighborhood and put himself in a risky situation by attending the party. In this case, however, he brought his gun. He explained:

INT: You wasn't scared or nothing?

JP: Nah I wasn't scared I was thinking about murdering the nigga. Nigga came up to my face talking shit.

INT So that night, so, how did Y'all get into that beef? JP: We went in the party...we walked up in the party.

INT: Who started it?

JP: Ain't nobody really start it. As soon as I walked in the party niggas was looking at me hard.

INT: True.

JP: So I tried to ignore that... So I started with this chick in there, kid. Niggas was looking at me wrong from when I first stepped in the party. Niggas was playing themselves. Talking about 'look at the new faces up in here,' 'Cause I ain't from around there.

INT: So what, true true. Who made first moves out there?

JP: When we was in the party, I made the first move. I told money 'let's go outside.' He came up to me, so I told him 'let's go outside.' It was in a small-ass little apartment. A little room. With the lights off. All his peoples were there.

But I wasn't sweating it 'cause I had my gun on me.
INT: True. You know if money was strapped?
JP: Nah, he wasn't strapped. 'Cause when he went outside, he went back... he ran back inside when I pulled out. He ran back inside.
INT: You don't know if he had a joint in there?
JP: Yeah. He musta have a joint inside there. Yeah. I'm saying. It was his party.

Accusations: Attacks of Honor

Many violent events result from situations in which one or more individuals make accusations or claims to the other for some wrong that supposedly has been committed. The accused typically responds with a hostile reaction that almost always pushes the dispute toward violence. These exchanges could be classified as attempts at obtaining justice, or as what Donald Black (1983; 1993) has called "self-help." In the following example, the accusations angered David and his denial of the claim fueled a physical fight between the two parties.

INT: What was y'all fighting for, y'all money? Drugs?
DAVID: The nigga came home talking some bullshit, talking about this drug king and his girlfriend or whatever. He can't find his girlfriend or whatever. [That] we killed her or whatever, some bullshit. It was over bullshit.
INT: It was... it was bullshit.
DAVID: Yeah. It ain't nothing to die for.
INT: I mean, when you think about it now.
DAVID: Yeah. I think about it now and psss..... It's like you saying, 'it was bullshit,' that ain't nothing to die for, man. Not for bullshit, man. Word up! I'd die for my moms, my kids, that's it. I ain't dying for no words, man.

The description above recounts only the middle event in a series of related exchanges that resulted in several deaths, illustrating the serious consequences of accusations.

Hostility was a common response to accusations of stealing or dishonesty. False accusations in front of others were often taken extremely personally and were usually denied. Being accused was typically perceived as a personal threat or attack on one's name or personal honor. Among our sample, accusations often instigated confrontations that eventually became violent.

INT: Tell me what happened, describe the situation so I could picture it, how it happened, what it was over.

DEAN: I remember I got in a fight at school. 'Cause me and my man, we was cutting and shit. And somebody coat got stolen out they locker. The kid approached me and he was like 'I heard you got my coat.' I told him I didn't have it. So he started getting loud and shit. So I snuffed that nigga. So he went and told his peoples and then they came back and they tried to jump us. My man was there so we just was fighting. We got beat up and all, but we got him back.

INT: Was there a specific point you realized you was going to have to get violent?

DEAN: Yeah. 'Cause I was like 'I ain't got your coat' and he stood up in my face trying to yell and shit. So I was 'yo man back the fuck up,' you know, and the nigga was still talking shit, so I was like, all right, we going to have to brawl. We going to have to do this shit.

Respondents explained that the way in which an individual makes a claim or accusation influences the response. Depending on the situation, there is a "right" way and a "wrong" way to express a grievance. Fighting or other violence was an important part of defining these contests.

## Material Attacks

Identity attacks often include taking another's possessions as a statement of dominance or control. Respondents described situations in which they had taken the possessions of others, or vice versa, and many described the battles that were waged to keep possessions. These material attacks reflected attempts to identify, maintain, and degrade social identity. Three examples are provided below. In the first example, Clarence defended himself and his cousins against a personal and material attack that occurred as they sat on the stoop of a tattoo parlor in another neighborhood. In the following example, note how the introduction of a pistol dramatically changed the balance of power.

INT: So tell me about the time you had to pistol-whip somebody?

CLARENCE: Oh. We went downstairs. We was chilling in front of the place. It was kind of hot upstairs, we was getting bored. So we wanted to go outside. So we just stepped outside and sat right outside on the stoop. And, I don't know, for one reason or another there was, like, four black kids walking on the block. We were talking amongst ourselves, we not paying attention to them. They a little older than us too, so we like, yo, they ain't acknowledging us, we ain't acknowledging them. We carrying on our conversation. And so me and my cousin in front of one stoop and about, like, two feet over there's another stoop and my man was sitting there, and he had on a little New York Knickerbocker hat, a little phat hat that just came out. The first two set of kids walk by and they was just kind of looking, but I kind of ignored them 'cause I was talking to my cousin. But my man, he's a little guy too so he wasn't looking for no trouble or nothing like that, but he ain't going to let nobody disrespect him neither. So the first two walked by. They ain't even look at nobody. The second two that's walking behind them, they just looking and, you know, carrying they little conversation too. They walked by me and my cousin and as they passing my friend they just, one of them snatched his hat off his head, and put it on his head. He was like 'what, money, what you want to do for this?' So my man kind of stepped up and he was like 'yo, what's up, man, I ain't trying to have that,' and kind of snatched it back, he got a chance to grab it back and my cousin had stepped up too. It was four of them and it was like three of us, so we was like 'damn, whatever, whatever. They going to have to leave us here on the floor, leave all of us here. So they was like 'what?' and then the other two that was in the front turned around they was like, 'oh, what's up, man, y'all niggas want to do these niggas or what?' They tried to treat us like we was herbs. So that's kind of like, I kind of felt funny.

The respondent reported that "they tried to treat us like we was herbs;" felt disrespected and became angry. As Clarence continued the story he described pulling a gun out to protect his friend from the opponents' threats. The gun gave him the ability to counter-challenge his opponents' personal and material attack.

CLARENCE: For one reason or another, my aunt just happen to be coming down the steps and at that point, soon as she open the door I just grabbed straight for the purse and I pulled the joint out and I was like 'yo, man, what y'all niggas want to do now?'

INT: Umm.

CLARENCE: And the first two, they was like 'yo,' and they started taking off, and the other two, they was like yo they didn't know whether to run or if I was going to bust or not. So I got kind of close to him where I could swing on him and I swung on him with the joint boom. And I hit him in his head and that was it. He had to step after that. Then after that I turned around and it was kind of like a cop car coming down the block, and I'm glad my aunt grab the joint again and she put it back in her purse and she went upstairs.

The next incident, which occurred in jail, was a common experience for an individual new to a facility. The young man explained what happened:

INT: I want you to tell me about what happen. What it was over, what started it, everything.

WALT: Well, it was when I was in jail, in the sprung. And shit, as I went in my bucket and I was missing something I had in my bucket, you know, and I saw another kid with it on. So, you know, I went and I asked him if it was mine. He told me no. So then I didn't stress it for that day, but he kept going around telling everybody he had my shit. So then one of his boys told me 'yo, my boy said if you wanted it back to go in the bathroom.' So I went in the bathroom.

INT: Which sprungs (a unit within the jail)?

WALT: Sprung two. I went in the bathroom and there were mad heads there, so I thought I was going to get jumped. So the kid gave me the fair one. He rocked me and shit, but I got mines, 'cause I earned it back and shit. And that's it.

INT: How did the situation end?

WALT: Well, after the fight he came up to me and he told me that since I went out for mines that if I want my shit that I could have it, but that you just don't play him close and he won't play me close. And we just left it like that.

In the previous example, the act that "he kept going around telling everybody he had my shit," suggests the theft was motivated by an effort to establish dominance, or at least to test Walt's resolve, rather than a material acquisition.

In the subsequent example, a respondent ignored the risk of injury and fought an opponent who was armed with a knife. The respondent described his efforts to keep his bike:

INT: So, what happened? Tell me from the beginning.

DANIEL: We was riding the bike and he wanted to fight so I was like, 'for what?' and he was like 'cause I wanted your bike and you didn't want to give it to me.' So I was like, 'nah, I couldn't give it to you. It's not yours.' So he started fighting me.

INT: So how did the knife get involved?

DANIEL: He pulled it out and I was like, 'you really want to kill me?' He was like, 'yeah, give me your bike.' So I was like, 'well then, let's throw the hands if, you know, you got the knife.' He was like 'nah, nah,' and so he started swinging with the knife and I picked up a bottle and we started fighting, and I hit with the bottle and he cut me and dropped the knife, and we started fighting with the hands.

INT: So how did this situation end?

DANIEL: We started fighting and he didn't get to take my bike and he left. It ended—he left. He was like, 'I'll catch you next time.'

INT: He told you?

DANIEL: Yeah. I was like, yeah whatever.

In the next example, DeShawn took ownership of his former friend's dog and refused to return the dog after keeping him for several weeks. The grievance stemmed in part from DeShawn's ability to claim rights to the dog. In the situation, the actors fought for the right of ownership over the dog:

INT: I want you to tell me what happened, what it was over, everything.

DeSHAWN: I had a fair one right across the street at my house. Last year. Are talking about recently?

INT: Last year, yeah, recently?

DeSHAWN: Recently, um, this boy... I had a fight right in front of my building. 'Cause I had this... he had his dog. So he had no home, so I was like 'I'll take it.' The dog's name was Homicide. I trained that dog to be mean, to chase cats, fight when I wanted him to fight. Shit when I wanna make him shit. I did all that. I could put him on the corner and walk around the block or go to park somewhere, he'd be right there when I come home.

INT: What you all had the fight for?

DeSHAWN: Over that dog. He was like 'yo, why you took my dog?' I was like 'no I didn't take your dog. You gave your dog..' [I] took it and I trained it, and I ain't giving that shit back, 'cause I wasted like two-three hundred off that dog, for the shots, everything. Come on, I had that dog for everything.

INT: Who made the first move towards violence?

DeSHAWN: He did. He wanted to smack-box me, and I didn't want to just smack-box. And he swung on me, and I like... he smacked me, so I punched him in his jaw. Then ...I keep on punching him.

INT: What was you trying to accomplish when you hit him?

DeSHAWN: To stop playing with me. I wasn't playing with you, so don't play with me.

INT: What was the outcome of the fight? After the fight did anything change about where you hung out at?

DeSHAWN: I had to watch my back cause he come back for me.

INT: After the fight did you do anything extra to protect yourself?

DeSHAWN: Yeah.

INT: What?

DeSHAWN: Carry my gun.

INT: What sort of relationship did you have with the guy after the fight?

DeSHAWN: Me and him still ain't friends to this day.

## COMPETITION OVER GIRLS, SOCIAL IDENTITY, AND VIOLENT EVENTS

Social interaction among adolescent males reflects a growing interest and preoccupation with sexuality and heterosexual companionship (Collins and Repinski, 1994; Brown, Mory, and Kinney, 1994; Eder, 1995; Gilligan, 1982). Violence is one of many strategies used by young males to create and sustain relationships with females in a context where competition is perceived as intense. "Girls" were cited as the subject of violent disputes in 94 of the 306 incidents described by our respondents. These situations typically resulted from sexual competition (both maintenance and acquisition), the protection of a girl's honor or reputation, the defense of a female after physical victimization, the spread of rumors and the escalation of disputes through gossip, and the amplification of impression management in the presence of a *relevant* female. Like toughness, relations with females may provide males with opportunities for developing valued social identities.

Competition over females involves a number of interesting social processes reflecting both a normative system and violations of those rules. The competition for females often reflects multiple definitions of a situation, including: those of a young man who perceives himself as having a particular girl, those of another young man who wants a particular girl, those of a female (who may or may not consider herself to be in a relationship with a particular male), and those observers who may make public judgments and pronouncements. Conflicting definitions of a female's relationship status often result in violent encounters among competitors.

The social world and attendant status-conferring of dating and sexual behavior among young males is highly competitive, and potentially dangerous. Respondents characterized the implicit rules of dating game as such: don't look at, talk to, talk about, befriend, touch, have sex with, or attempt to have sex with another man's girl. Although the young males in the sample understood these norms, they were frequently violated when the opportunity presented itself.

Respondents generally avoided selecting potential "mates" from among those females who were in relationships with members of the respondent's own social networks. Girls who were not part of this social network were considered "fair game" for competition. It is evident that respect (in this case, applied to the rules of dating competition) is granted almost exclusively to members of one's social network. Violations of dating competition among members of the same social network frequently were characterized as a reason for serious violence among associates and the dissolution of long-lasting male friendships. Some disputes resulted from the ambiguity associated with determining exactly *when and how* a female became one man's girl. Meanings attached to "dating" situations and female "commitment" typically were defined by males, who often internalize definitions of monogamous relations with females (regardless of females' definitions of the relationship and often despite outward evidence to the contrary).

Violence stems from sexual competition in two ways: defending existing relationships and challenging others for the right to new relationships with females. Once an individual has an established relationship or has made clear his intentions to pursue such a relationship, respondents described the need to defend that status at any cost. It seems that the rules of competition for females depend on whether one is defending a relationship or seeking a new one.

**Sexual Competition**
Respondents described many scenarios in which rule violations regarding relationships with females resulted in violence. The escalation of these situations seems to follow certain patterns, including the identification of an advance on one's girlfriend by another man, the lack of a respectful account to the "boyfriend," and physical rebuttal without a verbal account by the opponent. The example below illustrates the "don't talk to my girl" rule.

INT: Tell me one that you remember the most?
LJ:   One time I was chillin', we was chillin', me and my companions on the fucking corner, ...chillin,' talking to fucking girls. Next thing you know, nigga fucking roll up in a fucking Lexus, and niggas said 'yo, you niggas talking to the fucking wrong bitches. These bitches are trouble, kid.' So we ain't pay no attention, we just keep on talking to bitches, them bitches looked good. We wanted to hit the bitches up.
INT: True.
LJ:   So we keep on talking to them ...and their fucking men came... and them niggas just started fucking talking shit, kid. So we just pulled out, and they pulled out. Niggas started running and shit, so we just did some crazy shit. Shot and shit...and the cops came and we all broke out, man.

The next example illustrates the "don't touch" rule and what happens when one party does not properly account for his actions. The respondent interpreted the touching of his girl as disrespect and asked the opponent for acknowledgment of his transgression, instead he was challenged to step outside to fight for the girl. The event unfolded into a shooting, as described by James:

JAMES:  Yeah, man, we was at a party, man. This cat started throwing his arm around ...this girl I was with and everything.

He was trying to rub up against her.....
INT: What, he was trying to dance with her?
JAMES: Yeah, man, but she didn't wanna dance with him,
and he was rubbing up. He was drunk and shit. Boom, I tell
him, you know how you be trying to avoid shit? I tell him
'you know I'm with her, don't disrespect me like than, man,'
and he was like 'what son, what what? Let's take this outside,
son, what you want!' I'm like 'say no more, say no more.'
Everybody go outside, and once I walk out, bong, he snuffed
me. He caught me. I wasn't really dazed. I was upset though.
Boom, my man passes me the .380 and shit, the chrome.
Bong, I hit him with the butt of it. I pistol-whipped him, right
in his head. Then he snuffs me. So then, um, his man is going
to get him something. I don't know what it was look like it
was a revolver. His man hit 'em off, right when he hitting him
off, bong. I blazed him, I hit 'em two times. I caught him
right there, on his back, his stomach and his back, his stomach
first. Then he turned around and I caught him in the back.
Then I bounced. I got caught half an hour later.

The next example illustrates what happens when a guy befriended
another man's girlfriend with the intention of winning her away from
the other man. Friendship was used to cloak ulterior motives. The
respondent who explained this event was pulled into the conflict to
assist his brother, who had become friendly with another man's
girlfriend. He explained:

INT: What? Tell me about that what happen?
JEROME: All right um. One time my brother, he was
messing with this girl in the projects. ....She had a man and
um, every time her man used to go there, it's like my brother
used to give him this dirty look. ...And one time the dude just
got sick and tired of it and um, pssst, screamed on my brother.
My brother shut up and he didn't say nothing.
INT: Alright. Where they was when he screamed on him?
JEROME: They was in the projects. At the girl house.
INT: And he was there? Your brother was with the girl?
JEROME: Yeah. Her man came, yeah. 'Cause they act... let
me tell you. Her girl, I mean Duke girl, always told him that
'nah, we just friends, we been friends for a while,' after that it
was dead. My brother used to give him this dirty looks. He

not supposed to, he supposed to be some DL (down low) nigga, but my brother wanted more from her, you know, cause she used to tell him that she wanted more from him, too. So my brother was trying to get her to leave him and come to him. So the dude, um, I guess he was [not] trying to hear it. Like a week later or two, a week later or two he flipped on him. He flipped on him and, um, then...

INT: You all beat him up?

JEROME: Yeah.

INT: Why?

JEROME: I guess 'cause of what he said. My brother never went out, kid. I was upset. I was just upset at the fact that, um, that he played, that Duke played my brother and shit. I wasn't thinking about that he had probable cause or nothing.

INT: Yeah. You was just rolling with your brother?

JEROME: Yeah. I was just down with my brother. I was just down for my brother.

More of this event is described below showing how females can play an important role in facilitating and escalating conflict through talk and playing one male off another. The young men in this situation believed that the girlfriend had told her boyfriend where to find the competing male even though the girlfriend denied doing so. The respondent continued the story:

JEROME: And we just flipped him. And then I guess his girl, I guess his girl had told her man where we stayed at and where we live at, and niggas started coming around looking and asking for us and stuff, but nobody wasn't saying nothing.

INT: The kid was coming to your neighborhood?

JEROME: Yeah. They used to come into our projects. They used to come I mean come like, pss, two cars deep. Two cars, I don't know, that's not much heads, but still, they used to come in two cars deep. My brother had told anytime the next time we see those dudes to call him. And then they came around again, the same car. This time... they use to just come around searching, they ask like one or two, three times and then they stopped asking. They just was with the searching just in case they see us. My brother had told my man 'the next time you see the car, call me.' We had called my brother...

INT: How that made you feel, knowing that now these guys

are looking for you?

JEROME: I was scared. I was scared to death. I was scared out my sock. I was scared to death. And um, my brother, he was scared too but he wasn't showing it. Me, I used to look at every corner. Them niggas probably got guns, want to take me out or something. And I use a gun so I knew you could die. Die. So um, my brother had two guns. He had a four-fifth (.45 caliber) and a three eighty in the house. So um, my man had called me one day saying that he saw the car, 'the car right there, the car right there, oh shit.' We ran upstairs and we got our ghats. So they was still riding around the block, so we just started shooting at the car and shit.

INT: How about those guys? What they do, drive off?

JEROME: Yeah. They drove off. And didn't never come back ever since.

INT: So um, after that, that was it?

JEROME: Yeah. After that, that was it. My brother, pss. Afterwards, the next time he saw the girl, he smacked her and told her why, what she doing telling people where he live at, and she talking about she didn't tell nobody nothing. He told her to tell her man 'fuck it, if he want it just keep bringing it,' talking shit out his mouth.

INT: Who, your brother?

JEROME: Yeah, he be talking shit out his mouth. He keep telling the girl 'yo, tell that nigga to come back. They never came back...

Several respondents blamed females for these types of confrontations. Females were expected to be monogamous in relationships, while males were not. One respondent explained how he had recently handled a situation like this:

DONNELL: Well, recently, this guy stepped to me about being with his girl and shit like that. You know, he came at me on a aggressive tip, like 'I heard you been fucking with my chick and the whole nine.' So, you know, I'm not a nigga to fight over a broad. And obviously he was a nigga that wasn't used to having many girls and shit. That's why he was ready to fight for this one. So I had to school the nigga, I was like, 'yo, don't ever step to another man over a girl. Because nine times out of ten, it's the girl's fault. You know, if the girl doesn't mind, then it doesn't matter. That's something that you got to step to your girl over.' And that's what I let the nigga know. It's mind over matter. If your girl don't mind, it don't matter. Half the time, like the saying goes, your bitch chose me. Fight your broad, don't fight me. I'll leave the chick alone if that's the case, I mean, if you stressing them like that. But that's not my bag, you know? I have to let him know that, so that shit is squashed. He respected me more, being a man, to let him know. You know, he was a young nigga so, that was that.

Parties, clubs, and other social settings where members of different social cliques intermingle often were hotbeds of violence. Competition over the attention of females frequently was cited as a source of this conflict. Respondents described how public gatherings were integral to gaining and maintaining male-female relationships. Males who already have girlfriends perceive these situations as opportunities to show off their girlfriends and have a good time; those without girlfriends perceive parties or clubs as locations for picking up or hitting on women. As respondents explained, females at clubs and parties were fair game:

INT: What was they saying when the beef went down?
JORDAN: My man...one man was talking to... dancing with this girl, and he was like, 'nigga it's a party, niggas is dancing with everybody, I didn't know that was your girl. Don't bring your girl to a party if you don't want a nigga dancing with her.'
INT: So what you was telling that kid?
JP: Nah, I'm saying I just explained ...the girl was in the party, so we was just dancing. He wanna act [hard], come out his face, talking 'bout that's his girl. I'm saying straight up and down I don't care if that's your girl. She's was in the party, she looking good, that's about it.

According to respondents, many neighborhood or territorial disputes also were connected closely with females. Many respondents described frequenting other projects or parts of the neighborhood to pursue female romantic interests. They were generally not welcome by the young men who live there. Of course, this was considered an outward display of disrespect toward the male residents of these areas.

Many conflicts erupted between different groups whose "interests" were at stake:

> NICK: We was walking through there and shit. Actually, one of my peoples went up to see a girl, that's mostly what beefs come from too. Girls and shit. Niggas do the weirdest things for girls. But we went up there. He told us 'wait outside' and shit. We had some weed and shit. We was smokin', mindin' our own business and shit. Then the niggas from the other side come up and ask mad questions, 'who this?' you know, like 'who the fuck are you?' And I'm like, you know, 'who the fuck are YOU!?' and shit. What the hell are you, what's the problem, man, we just chillin'. So, you know, we started with the lip and shit. And one thing led to another and we was fightin' and everybody started pullin' out and we started bustin' each other, and I think nobody got hit. One person got hit from the Brownsville side, 'cause my man hit him up against the chest. I didn't get hit. So it was a lot of gunplay and shit. And we started blastin', not really paying.... When people blast I don't think they really aimin' at anyone, you know, a blast is just a blast. A lot of stray bullets be going everywhere, you know. I'm glad we got out of that situation.

### Projecting the Right Image in Front of your Girlfriend

Identity attacks in front of one's girl also were sources of conflict. The presence of females increased the stakes of impression management and shows of disrespect by other men. As illustrated in the example below, the display of disrespect may have been an intentional effort to make Diego look bad in front of his girlfriend. He explained:

> DIEGO: 'Cause they see I got a fly chick, they call me a faggot or pretty boy, pretty boy loose. Nigga tried to put me down one day when I was with this chick, so I pulled out on him.
> INT: So, you was with the chick, you pulled out on him?
> DIEGO: Yeah. He tried to play me in front of a shorty.
> INT: Why he tried to play you though, son?
> DIEGO: This nigga was jealous, man.
> INT: Oh, jealousy?
> DIEGO: Jealousy. Jealous ones envy all the time, that why a lot of shit be happening, 'cause jealousy. They see you got

this, they ain't got it, they want and they wanna do something about it.

INT: So, was it good for the girl when you pulled out?

DIEGO:  Nah, she was kind of scared, but I had to calm her down. After all that I ain't never seen Duke again.

In the next example, a respondent pulled out a gun on a guy in part to save face in front of his girl and to protect her from harm:

BRYAN:  Well, one time I was up in my girl's projects, and some dude came up to me and said I stole his car and I was like 'I ain't steal your car.'  He was like 'yeah, it was you, somebody pointed you out.'  I was like 'look the first thing I don't steal in the Bronx, second thing is I got a car, I got everything I need in my car.'  Why would I wanna steal his? So he came up to me and told me he had a fucking knife at that time I used to carry the gun in my car 'cause, like I said, I did the carjacking, you know.  I used to walk everything on me, prepared just in case I might see a car I like. And umm, I reached under my seat and put the gun dead up in his face, you know.  I'm in the middle of the housing projects. I wasn't thinking.

INT: So why do you think you did what you did?

BRYAN:  You know, I hate the way he approached me. I said he try to step to me with a knife.  I was like 'aw, shit,' I was like 'here I go again with fights.'  'Cause you know, he disrespected me.  I'm chillin there with my girl, I got beef. Take me alone, but he gonna take me when I'm with my girl. I look at it like this, I got my own personal beef, I don't need nobody else getting hurt.

INT: What was happening with you that day?

BRYAN:  I just went to pick her up, keeping myself busy, thinking about a cool date, and he comes up to me with his hand on a fucking knife, like I was supposed to run or something. C'mon, I got a fully loaded in my car. I wasn't stressing it, I wasn't stressing nothing. I looked at it like this: if you get shot up by me you just get shot up. I wasn't hesitating back then 'cause I always looked at shit like this. You do what you gotta do.

INT: How long did the dispute between you and that dude went on, you know, after you pulled out on him?

BRYAN: After that, umm, nothing. He was saying 'oh, I know where you live at,' this and that... I felt that was a personal threat against me, ...trying to scare me. But ...as soon as I pulled out, he... man... I haven't seen him since.

## Protecting Her Reputation

According to many respondents, a young man is supposed to fight for the honor of his girlfriend whenever necessary, because her image reflected directly on his own status among peers. When one individual ridiculed or insulted another man's girl, it was taken as a disrespect of him and became a source of conflict. The next example illustrates this process.

INT: Why you got beef with him?
BRYCE: 'Cause I told some stupid shit. I told this girl to take off the wig.
INT: You told a girl to take her wig off?
BRYCE: [Laughing] Yeah. Then he came in my face riffing, and I was like ah-ight, I'ma see you again. So I saw him walking, started just shooting at him. Hit a little kid in his leg.
INT: You hit a little kid in the leg?
BRYCE: Yeah, the kid, like, thirteen.

The confrontation described below started over a comment about a girl and escalated into a knife event between multiple participants. The respondent's 17–year-old friend did not like the way a stranger on the train was talking about his female companions. He explained:

ROBERT: This Muslim man was selling incense on a train, and my man was on the train with his girl and another girl. So the Muslim man was going through the car and he's like, 'oh , you a pimp.' My man was like—the nigga big, that's why I don't think my man didn't nothin' by himself. So my man is like, 'fuck you talking about, that's my fucking girl, you trying to call my girl a whore? What the fuck wrong with you, man?'

After this first confrontation, the friend relayed the story to his clique and they went back to find the man, who frequently sold incense on the subway.

## Defending and Retaliating for Females

Several respondents described situations in which females were involved in their own violent conflicts and young men became involved when a female had been victimized. The following example shows how several males were drawn into the situation to obtain justice for their man's girlfriend after she had been robbed and injured by other females. He explained:

INT: So how did they rob her?

JAMAL: What happen, it was three ...I'ma tell you her story. Her story was, three morenas came up to her—morena is black, black females. And they... They just took the earrings from her. They just took them, man. Snatched them off her ear and left the rip mark in her ear. They didn't even bother to tell her to take it off, they just ripped the shit off.

INT: So she went back to your neighborhood crying?

JAMAL: She went back after she came out the hospital. They robbed her for her earrings, so we were going back there with my man and shit, with his girl.

INT: Alright. The girl and the guy was from your block?

JAMAL: Yeah, the girl and the guy was from my block. They robbed my man—my family member, they robbed his girl.

INT: What she was doing, she was walking out there?

JAMAL: Yeah, she was walking through, and since my family member has money, he bought her these awesome earrings and these black bitches robbed her. So we went back to get these black bitches. Not to hurt them, 'cause I don't hurt females. Just to go tell them we wanted the earrings back or the money back. The females' mans fronted on us. They started busting (shooting) at us, so we said fuck that, man. We busted back.

INT: So how many were y'all like?

JAMAL: It was eight of us, man.

INT: All right, so what went down when y'all went back?

JAMAL: When we back, we went back with intentions to either get the earrings back or hell would have to break loose and I don't care.

INT: So was this in the nighttime, the evening?

JAMAL: Yeah, yeah, we went back approximately 12 o'clock,

yeah, 12 to 1 o'clock. After we got our crew together.

INT: So it wasn't nobody out there really, right?

JAMAL: There was really nobody out there. But them kids that started busting at us.

INT: How many were there about?

JAMAL: It was, I think, I seen, from what I seen—I was under the car, but I took a peek. I seen three kids. I seen three of them.

INT: Alright, so what went down after that?

JAMAL: After that, after they shot at us and we shot at them, we left, man. We went back to our block and to tell you the truth, we ain't never go back to do nothing. My man bought his girl some more earrings the following day. She couldn't put them in because her ear was ripped, so she stitched her ears up and that was it.

INT: ...What was going through your mind?

JAMAL: What was going through my mind? Well, a little bit of fear and anger. Fear and anger. Anger because I don't like the way they robbed us and fear because I didn't know what was going to be ahead of me when I got there. I didn't know what was coming... fear, 'cause I didn't know what was going to be in front of me. I tell you I can't tell the future, man. I'm not a gypsy, man. But I was scared. I had fear and anger.

Another respondent described a situation in a club where he was working as a doorman. In this situation, Donnell got involved in a physical fight between a man and his girlfriend. The respondent attempted to protect the girl, but was eventually arrested for assault when the opponent and his girlfriend pressed charges against him.

DONNELL: I worked in a club, and this kid was beating up on this girl, you know. So I went to jump in to break up the fight. So at that time, you know, he swung at me. He ended up wanting to fight me, swung at me. I swung back, caught him in the jaw about two or three times, you know. Dropped him on the floor, pulled out my gun and I pistol-whipped him. Then I kicked the shit out of him and left him there.

In sum, young women play a significant role in the social construction of violent events among this sample of inner-city adolescent and young adult males. These roles reflect certain social processes that have been observed in a variety of other settings (see for example, Eder, 1995; Kinney, 1990; Schwendinger and Schwendinger, 1985; Horrowitz and Schwartz, 1974; Majors and Billson, 1992; Hagedorn, 1997; Oliver, 1994; Polk, 1994; Campbell, 1993; Kruttschnitt, 1995; Bourgois, 1996; Connor, 1995). The violent events stemming from competition over females provide more evidence that, for most of the respondents, hegemonic masculinity guides behavior.

## SELF-DEFENSE

An event was coded "self-defense" if the respondent reported that the main reason for using violence in the situation was to protect his own safety and health. Self-defense was cited as the main reason for respondents' involvement in 67 incidents (approximately 22%). In the following example, Bryce was attacked and pistol-whipped by an older brother of an individual with whom he had problems in the past. Bryce attempted to defend himself but instead was beaten. He described the impetus for the initial attack on the opponent's younger brother as stemming from an attack on his reputation:

> INT: Any accidents?
> BRYCE: Yeah I got pistol-whipped.
> INT: Word?
> BRYCE: In East New York a month ago.
> INT: For what?
> BRYCE: Beef.
> INT: Word. What happened?
> BRYCE: Riding to my girl house and these grown men from the back of the projects. I'm riding [a bicycle] and I see a car slowed up in front of me, so I didn't pay it no attention, and I just see a grown man jump out a car and cock back his gun. I tried to ride off. He chase me and just pulled me and just started pistol-whipping me in my face and I was all right and I went back through there.
> INT: Why, you got beef with them?
> BRYCE: I got beef with his little brother 'cause at a party, his little brother was shooting at us and I went back through there and was shooting at them and almost hit his aunt.
> INT: When was that?
> BRYCE: This was, like, two months ago.
> INT: Over—what it was over?

BRYCE: Beef. Dumb beef like I don't like that nigga, he think he get busy, or he a faggot, this and that.

INT: But why y'all try to shoot each other over shit like that?

BRYCE: 'Cause I felt disrespected. He going around telling everybody that I'm a faggot. ...Yeah. But I know I'm not, but I just ain't like it going around telling everybody.

INT: So his older brother, he caught you?

BRYCE: Yeah.

INT: So now, so what you did after that?

BRYCE: Well, I could keep going back through there but they don't never be out there.

BRYCE: This was like in afternoon, like at four o'clock.

Similarly, events in which the respondent believed he was drawn into a conflict to assist or defend others were classified as "defense of others" events. In these situations, respondents were uninvolved until stepping in to fight for a friend or fight on behalf of a friend; in 34 situations, respondents came to the defense of others. The next story illustrates how individuals were drawn into conflicts to defend others. In this case, Jose aided his drunken friend outside a house party in a nearby neighborhood. Jose believed that his participation in the fight was necessary to protect an associate from his neighborhood:

JOSE: Past 'bout two years? Yeah, I got—yeah, man, I've gotten into four fights... Plus some hectic shit, man. One time I had this fight, man, I was with my man, and shit, he was out of it, but I was still there. Some nigga try to come up and shit, try to smack him around and just tell him 'oh, you don't belong around here.' Yo, fuck that. I got to defend my peoples from my neighborhood. I fought this nigga. He cut me in my fucking arm and shit. I still got that fucking scar there [shows interviewer]. Everytime I look at that shit I just wanna eat this nigga, B.

INT: So what started it, a bump? A looks?

JOSE: Nah. I'm saying it was with my man and shit. My man, I say, was drunk and shit. And he coming up to my man popping shit. Since I was there I gotta defend my man. He can't defend himself. So I took care of the shit. I just cuffed this motherfucker, B. And right there, you know I'm saying, just shot one on one right there.

INT: ...tell me when it first started? Did it start with the hands?

JOSE:  Yeah, it was with the hands... First of all, he was trying to play my man, so I came up to him, I snuffed him in his fucking face. Cuffed him there. He flew back and shit and I was, like, oh, that shit—he threw the hands up. I, like—he didn't take shit out on me. He just baw baw...My man was too fucked up. ....I was like, 'yo this is for me,' Baw, we fighting and shit. The nigga... he struck me. Like I say, he gave me a black eye and shit. But I cuffed him a few times, I caught him. I did.

INT: True true true.

JOSE:  That was a good fight, Bee.

Jose explained that even though he entered the fight to protect his friend, the event was ultimately about respect. His performance earned respect from his opponent and from other observers. He explained:

INT: So what you was saying when the beef was going down?

JOSE:  Yo, when the beef—at that time, kid, yo, you mind blanks out. You just go crazy, man. Especially me. I went crazy. I didn't give a fuck what was going to happen to me, B. I just want to get the shit done. To you it's all about respect. You gotta get your respect out here, man. Gotta get your respect. Is he gonna die, is he gonna say that shit? It's 'bout longevity, kid. How long you last. You know.

INT: Y'all fought with the hands or y'all was blazing at each other?

JOSE:  Nah, we fought with the hands. That's why I like this shit, B. Fought with the hands, yeah with this motherfucking Dominican that we fought hands and shit. Cab money gave—he caught me a few times and shit. I ain't gonna front. He gave me a nice black eye and shit, but fuck it. That's battle, kid. I caught him a few times too.

INT: Yeah.

JOSE:  He had his skills and shit like that, but I didn't go out like no pussy. Right now I look into his face, motherfucker got respect for me, I got respect for him. But if he ever try to play me again, yo, it's on again. Fuck it.

In the example below, Willie became actively involved in a fight to assist his brother. The argument preceding the fight involved both the respondent and his brother against the opponent; however the respondent left the scene. While he was upstairs, the opponent and the respondent's brother started fighting; when the respondent came back outside, he joined the fight:

> WILLIE: Alright. Boom, me and my brother was coming from my cousin crib. We entered the block, right, and there was this guy and this girl on my block, she had her boyfriend with her. So we walking and he looked at me, so I didn't pay it no mind. We walked, so I went in my house. I came back out, so I saw my brother try to fight him, so I told my brother to chill and I went to fight him. And it was over stupidness. It was over an argument with his girl.

## ROBBERY

The robbery category is fairly straightforward. An event was considered a robbery when violence or the threat of violence was used in order to get material goods from people. These situations have nothing to do with a conflict between the respondent and the victim. Sixty-one violent events were classified as robberies. The majority of robberies (42 of 61 events) involved gun use; respondents were perpetrators in 39 robbery situations and robbery victims in 22 situations.

Several examples of robberies are presented below. In the first example, Bryce and several friends used a gun to hold up people attending a party. According to Bryce, this robbery was unplanned and reflected a spontaneous decision. Bryce described himself as being the leader of the robbery:

> INT: So, um, you can't remember any other robberies after that?
> BRYCE: Um. This happen a week ago at party. We was just there chillin', then I saw chains on people neck that I wanted, and I had a gun on me and I was with my friends, so we just crashed the whole party and I just robbed everybody, taking chains and stuff' Money.
> INT: Just two of y'all?
> BRYCE: Nah, it was, like, bunch of us.
> INT: Word. Y'all had guns? How many of Y'all had guns?
> BRYCE: Nah. Only I just had a gun.
> INT: Oh, word. Anybody know it was you?

BRYCE: Nah. I didn't know the kid.

INT: Oh, y'all just went there?

BRYCE: Uh-huh.

INT: Cops came or whatever?

BRYCE: Everybody that was with me was beating up everybody in the street, people was getting robbed and I was just taking everything. No cops ain't come or nothing. I'm surprised.

In the next robbery situation, the offenders scouted out an appropriate target, then collaborated on the robbery, each handling their respective jobs in the situation. The respondent directly confronted the victim and maintained control over his actions; the victim complied with Nick's demands. As Nick's companions turned out the victim's pockets, another individual watched for police or other people who may have interrupted the robbery.

INT: Did you ever commit any other crime?

NICK: Yeah, I used to do stick-ups. I used to stick up people in there near the train. You know, I need the money.

INT: Tell me about that. A time you rob somebody or whatever.

NICK: One incident that me and some group of kids, like three of us, we went up to that area and we was under the train and we started watching people get off the train and shit, that's how we did it. So one time this man walked out, right, and shit, and we decided we was going to take him out. So we followed him for a few blocks, to see where he was going. We was, like, across the street, opposite him, but, like, a block down. But we had him in view. So he didn't notice that we was there. But he started going down this dark alley and so when we seen that we started to run up on him. So I had the gun, I came right close behind him and—I pulled my gun out and I said, yo, I came out real corny. I said, 'yo, can you have the time?' So he turns around and sees this gun in his face. He sucked [his teeth], he don't say shit. I told him to shut the fuck up. I didn't have to say no more after that. You know, I said, 'put your hands up and shut the fuck up, I'll kill you.'

INT: You took the money?

NICK: Yeah. Then my man runs up behind him, rips his pockets out, takes his wallet. I had this other guy, he was, like, the lookout. He's watching for cops or anybody trying to get to be a hero and shit. So, after we shake him down and take his shit, I told him to get on the floor. So once he got on the floor I kick him in the head. And we jet. [laughs] I guess he don't remember faces, 'cause I kicked him hard.

In the next example, Joshua was one of a group of six who held up a jewelry store. The robbery was planned ahead of time and Joshua was asked to join in. According to the respondent, the robbery went off as planned:

INT: Alright. You said that you used to stick up jewelry stores. Right?
JOSHUA: Yup.
INT: Can you tell me what happened from the very beginning?
JOSHUA: Well, my man called me up in the morning. One morning. So, he ... he told me what was going down. So, he gave me the address to be there... In the morning. So I went there. He give me his gun. He give me a little thirty-eight. So, I went back home and stashed it. So he called me back through ... he gave me a time to be there. He gave me, like, to the nighttime, to the evening, when they closed down. So, we went. I waited 'til that hour. So, I took the train downtown to the address he gave me. ...So all right. So we waited 'til the people closed down. It was like six of us. So we all had guns. So ...we was waiting to them... when people closed down. We had the plan. So, we went in there. Just got like ...like a handful of jewelry...
INT: So what y'all did to the man?
JOSHUA: My man just yoked the man. Put a gun in his face. Just ...he just say, 'Give me the money. Everything you got in the counter. Everything.' So my man—and this lady that was in the store, too. She was just scared ...scared like a motherfucker. ...my man had a gun pointing to her face. And then... as I was, um, taking all the jewelry that was in the back, just packing them shits up. I just ran out. The next morning, we had everything.
INT: So when y'all did this stickup, what y'all was telling the owner?
JOSHUA: Just to shut up. To stay the fuck down. And just

give me the loot that's in the counter. He was scared.

INT: What was the guy telling y'all? What was he saying? The owner?

JOSHUA: The owner? He just saying a lot of stuff. 'Why are we doing this?' You know, just talking nice shit. Cryin', too.

INT: How about the lady? What was she saying?

JOSHUA: She was screaming.

INT: Y'all didn't hit her?

JOSHUA: No, when she when she started screaming, we just had her up under... closed her mouth. She was biting my man. My man had his hand on her mouth. So, she was trying to fight him.

INT: So how y'all split the money? How much you had?

JOSHUA: I had $800 to spend, and two to just..

INT: How about in jewelry? How much you had?

JOSHUA: Nah, I didn't really took no jewelry. Money, yo.

INT: Just money?

JOSHUA: Just the money.

INT: Y'all wasn't worried about the cops or nothing?

JOSHUA: Yeah, we was worried about the cops. But we just—You have people looking out too.

INT: Outside?

JOSHUA: Yeah, outside.

## DRUG BUSINESS TRANSACTIONS

An event was classified as a drug business transaction if it took place in a drug spot or area, occurred as a direct result of the buying or selling of drugs, or occurred between workers in the drug business. Fifty-three violent events in the sample were attributed to some aspect of the drug business.

A variety of drug business-related gun events were described including disputes over turf and customers, product price, quantity and quality, shortages of drugs or money, retaliation for dishonest business practices, or protection from robberies during the course of drug selling. The situations included shootouts involving two or more parties, drive-bys, sniper attacks from rooftops or other distant locations, and setups. Below, one respondent described a gun event related to a business dispute over a crack-selling location:

INT: How did it happen and what started it?

RON: Well, what happened was this. On my block, right, the nigga's crack spot. Now—and let me tell you, my man got killed and this is basically why—let me tell you how [he] got killed. But what led up to it was, he had beef with the niggas from the crack spot and that's my man . And he fucked up the manager of the crack spot and he was like a monthly shit, he'll fuck him up and beat the shit out of him. So I guess the nigga from the crack spot was tired of getting his ass whooped, so one day they pulled out on him. And he was telling him 'just kill me, you motherfucker, kill me.' They didn't shoot him. So, I—so he started, the day—thing is, we could run to our roofs and shoot at them from down, you know, like they won't know who the hell is shooting at them. So my man did that. He went on his roof and he had a assault rifle, M16, so he was *pow, pow, pow, pow,* letting loose from the top of the roof and niggas was scattering all over. And they didn't know who did it. But I am sure [the guys from the crack spot] knew it was him. So then, like, about a week later, there is some new niggas at the crack spot. Some young nigga, mad young, he like 16 years old and he was up there with two other cats. It was me, my brother and my man, rest in peace, . He—we were walking to the corner because we were going to go to Weedgate and get some weed and all of a sudden the nigga stepped to him. Then I yell 'what's up man, you know, you dis nigga' and I ain't mentioning no names, but 'you dis nigga and they were like—and he was like, 'yeah why?' He was like, 'yo—that shit is over, son, that nigga got to chill with shit, you know, whatever. You know, like telling us 'either dead it or you are dead,' you know what I am saying. So my man says like 'what, what, stupid, son, this is my fucking block, man. Those niggas don't own shit, this is my block. So that moony pulled out, he pulled out a two-five on my man and it jammed. He aimed that shit at me, my brother, and him. It jammed and, you know, it didn't want to shoot. So my man snuffed him, boom, and he ran back up into the crack spot 'cause it was [a] house. So he ran up in there and then I thought the man was going to get his TEC [handgun], 'cause I know he got a (TEC). So he ran back to the house and came down with nothing. He stepped to him again. This time that kid bust open the door and came out with a nine and starting shooting pow, pow, pow and my man ran around a van. He caught him at the other side of the van and lit six shots into him, man, and he died in my arms that day, son. The man died in my arms, man. And to this day, man, niggas still be shooting at the niggas, but the niggas—because they fucked with some Morellos from my block, and the Morellos are crazy. Buckwild. Those niggas live, like, five or six them heads in the last three months. Five-O (police) always rolling around, so those niggas broke up. So his man dead right now. They don't even know who was shooting at them from like that. Those are my peeps. The Morellos are my peeps, because we all grew up together.

In the next example, conflict stemmed from an attempted take over of Patrick's drug spot while he was out of town. He described his feelings including his perceived need to retaliate for the transgression:

PATRICK: I got a little story. I got into some shit. I will run it to you real quick. When I had went away—my aunt was sick, I went down South with my cousin. God bless him, he dead right now. Me and him went down South to see my aunt. I came back—I had a spot, . My spots was making two, three G's a day. Each spot. I came home, niggas was telling me all they sold was 100 dollars. I had been gone 10 days, I'm like, 'yo, what is going on?' Niggas was telling me these niggas was in the store, tell my worker that they can't be out there hustling. So I stepped to the niggas, and the nigga was like 'yeah.' The nigga gabbed me, and that is the worstest thing he could do. And I went and got my joint and I came back. I put the shit in his mouth but it wouldn't go off, right. So I was like all right, cool. Then he went and told the cops on me. He was hustling, too. The cops was looking for me. Boom, he tell my little sister 'tell your brother I'm going to kill him.' So I was like all right, it was snowing and I told my father I'm going to sit out there. I hope it snow, 'cause I'm going to lay in that snow and when they open that store I'm going to murder them. Whatever, whatever happen. The next day came, I went down there and I took care of what I had to. I did what I had to do and you know the rest.

INT: Tell me about the guy that you did your thing with. Did you know him?

PATRICK: I'm saying—yeah I knew him. I didn't know him personally but I knew him from the store. I knew the guy that owned the store. Me and him was raised together, he was my man. And I told him 'yo, that nigga can't disrespect me, son. Before you all, even you all, even moved around, I been around here hustling.

INT: So he had a store and he was selling drugs in the store?

PATRICK: Yeah, they was selling in the store and we was selling on the corner.

INT: So he told your workers not to?

PATRICK: Yeah, and yo, was touching me, touching me. I don't like when nobody touching me, yo.

INT: So what did you know about him besides?

PATRICK: Yo, I'm saying the nigga was working in the store, but he was smoking crack and shit. Stupid motherfucker, talking shit. Always talking shit. And then what was so fucked up, the nigga wouldn't even buy they crack. He would come to me and buy my crack but tell my workers that they buy—he telling other people that is coming in the store they can't buy from me, but he buying from me.

INT: When you pulled the gun on him and put the gun in his mouth, what were you thinking at the time?

PATRICK: 'Word, son, I'm going to smoke this nigga.' I just turned on him and he was like 'oh, oh, oh, you going to shoot me' and I just clicked the gun and said 'shut up' but shit just didn't work. Shit had a double safety on it, but the shit didn't go off that time so whatever but I got him I took care of my business.

INT: Were you concerned about whether you would kill him or something and get locked up?

PATRICK: Nah, I wasn't thinking about that, I wasn't thinking about that because whatever happened cops didn't find out what I did. I wasn't never concerned, I wasn't afraid to kill, yo, because, you know why I wasn't afraid to kill? Because I'm saying I sat and analyzed killing. I know everybody done killed, from the smartest person in the world to the illiterate. Why? Because you done killed a roach or a bug. So everybody can kill.

INT: Were you concerned whether he had a gun that day, when you pulled out a gun and it didn't go off?

PATRICK: Yeah, I was concerned, actually, because I knew he did have guns, so I knew. That is why I want to take care of what I had to, because I knew you was going to try to smoke me.

## REVENGE OR RETALIATION

Events coded as being motivated by revenge or retaliation were precipitated by the outcome of a previous interaction with the opponent or his associates. These prior incidents typically were unsuccessful, incomplete, or unsatisfactory to the respondent, resulting in the "need" for additional violence. Respondents often were drawn into these situations as "torch- takers" or "avengers" seeking justice for wrongs committed against the individual and/or his group. Unlike the self-defense code, this domain includes both parties' involvement in revenge. Fifty-three events were sparked out of issues of revenge or retaliation.

The first example shows how an individual may rally the support of a peer to increase the chances of successful retaliation. In this case, initial transgression was the theft of a pair of sneakers:

INT: Tell me about a gun event, the last gun event that you did. Tell me what happened. Describe the situation—how it happened and what it was over.

THEO: The last gun event—that was probably when I got robbed for my sneakers. I called my cousin and shit. And then he seen the kid again—he had the sneakers on. Me and my cousin just asked him 'what's the deal?' He went to reach [for a gun], and we shot him.

INT: He went to get his gun?

THEO: Yeah, and we shot him.

INT: You don't know nothing about the guy you was fighting?

THEO: Yeah. He lived in my cousin's projects.

INT: Oh, you knew the dude, and he knew you when he robbed you?

THEO: Yeah. He just played hisself, that's what he did right there. That's what the whole point was. He disrespected me.

In the next example, Alonzo participated in a gun event related to the drug business. The initial shooting was an attempted takeover of a drug spot. The respondent reported the day's events to his boss, who then got into his car and went looking for the opponents. Alonzo described the situation:

> INT: Alright so what happen, did something happen after that?
> ALONZO: It was a little beef had started. So, one day we
> went back. It was, like, all of us, so the boss gave us a gun so
> we can hold up the spot then. So, we went to hold it down.
> We was just walking, and one of our people came over there.
> They was working too. Everybody—he gave everybody a
> little position, so, we was like 'all right.' So, one day the guys
> came back. So, we saw the guys and one of my friends started
> shooting at the guys. The guys started shooting back. So, we
> all running, running frantic, everybody running and shooting.
> So, then, nobody got hit.
> INT: Was you shooting?
> ALONZO: Nah, I wasn't shooting, but, I was there. Then I
> got out, we all ran back to the—back to our complex, and we
> lounged there. Bought some beer, told the boss what happen.
> So, we told him what happen, so we came driving around,
> blah, blah, blah. He—he saw one of the kids and one of the
> kids that he was with they was walking in the store. So, and
> then he killed both of them.
> INT: Who, the boss?
> ALONZO: Yeah. He came around he's like 'yo I'm gonna
> take care some business.' Then he drove off, and then when he
> came back he asked us to go around there and check, see what
> was going on. 'Just go around the corner and check and see
> what's going on.' We went around there and seen two niggas
> laid out on the floor.
> INT: So, how that made you feel?
> ALONZO: Ahh, in a way I was, like, 'yo, man.' That's my
> first time I ever seeing somebody killed. And it was like, it
> was like, yo, my conscious—it didn't bother me 'cause I was
> like, yo, the way I seen it was the timing was for a good,
> 'cause they probably would have came back for us and did the
> same. There's no saying who would've been in the spot at the
> time, boy. They just had to go down that way, you know? It's
> like 'oh, whatever, whatever.' I could see I had that I-don't-
> care attitude. Now I'm developing that attitude, because of
> that attitude I don't care. Because I see that in order to be
> around these people you gotta be real, and in order to be real

it's like being true to yourself, who you be with, and whatever goes on stays. Whatever goes on, what happens, it stays in, in, it stays where it's at. And you gotta keep it real with you people, . Anything happens with you, you know, if you get knocked you gonna have to keep it to yourself. You can't snitch 'cause you be breaking the—you just be breaking the code.

INT: What's the code?

ALONZO: Like I'm saying, being real.

INT: Being real? What's being real like?

ALONZO: Like I was saying, you gotta be real. It's, like, a dedication. It's, like, you gotta dedicate yourself.

INT: To your clique?

ALONZO: Yeah, to your clique. You know, all the peoples you with, anything go down they gonna be there for you, which—anything I have been through they been there for me. And everything they went through, I was there with them. And that's how it was. We ain't never looked at ourselves as a clique or a posse, we looked at ourselves as a family, but we did dirt, fell. We did a little dirt and shit.

INT: All right, so what happen after that?

ALONZO: After that, they—they got killed.

## GOSSIP, RUMORS, OR "HE SAID, SHE SAID" SITUATIONS

Rumors or what respondents called "he said, she said" situations, usually involving the discovery that an individual was talking negatively about another behind the other person's back, cause some violent events. In other cases, false information spread through gossip caused actors to engage in violence. Eighteen conflicts developed as a result of rumors or gossip. One respondent described a rumor-based event in the following way:

GLEN: Just had a fight. I got beat up one time.

INT: Why y'all was fighting?

GLEN: Oh, he thought I said something. I ain't said nothing.

INT: Somebody told him you said something?

GLEN: Yeah.

INT: And he came back and asked you did you say it?

GLEN: Yeah, and I said just [said] 'get out my face, man what you talking about?'

INT: Why didn't you just say 'no, I ain't said it.' You told him to get out your face?
GLEN: Yeah.
INT: Then when you said that, what did he do?
GLEN: He said 'come on, I want to talk to you over here.' Kid live on the other side, though.

Often these situations related to females and relationships. Gossip or talk about who's seeing whom, who's talking to whom, and who's having sex with whom often creates problems for adolescents, leading to violence. Sometimes these situations were resolved with very little violence; in other cases the outcome was injury or death. One situation in which violence was avoided is described below:

INT: Have you ever been in a situation where nobody ended up getting hurt? Like you confronted somebody, or..?
JEFF: Oh yeah. Yeah. When I was in high school I had it happen. Where, like, you know, there was, like, a lot of 'he said, she said' thing going around, you know. And, like, some guy had felt that he was disrespected 'cause his girl or whatever—he thought, like, his girl wanted to talk to me or something like that, you know. And he thought that I was disrespecting him. So I just, like, spoke with him about it, and... I was, like, there's plenty of women out there. There's plenty of women in the school. I don't need to stress you. Yours ain't really all that. You can keep her, I ain't already talking to your girl. We came to the point that we spoke about it and we said—we just left it at that.

Another respondent found himself in a near-violent situation resulting from false information spread by his opponent's girlfriend, who happened to be a friend of Tyrone's girlfriend. The situation was heated, but ended peacefully as Tyrone walked away from his opponent:

INT: What happened? Tell me about that.
TYRONE: It was over a girl, telling my girl something about me. When it wasn't true. Her man got into it. So me and him are arguing. I'm telling him to mind his business. He telling me to shut up.
INT: Word?
TYRONE: 'My girl ain't say none of that.' I'm like, 'your girl did so, my girl told me.' So he arguing with me and then it

almost lead—to a real—it was going to lead to something real big, man, but I just walked away.

INT: You knew the kid?

TYRONE: Nah, I ain't know him, I just knew his girl, and his girl was going with—his girl used to be [friends] with my girl.

INT: Did they hang out?

TYRONE: Yeah, they hang out together, but she told my girl something about me that wasn't even true.

INT: Yeah. So 'he say, she say' shit?

TYRONE: He say, she say. [laughs]

INT: So what happened after that? Everything dead?

TYRONE: Everything. I ain't never seen him no more.

INT: Oh, so how about—how about your girl and her homegirl? They still hang out?

TYRONE: They still hang out, still telling those stuff.

## TERRITORY OR NEIGHBORHOOD HONOR

Events were classified as erupting out of non-drug-related territory or neighborhood honor issues when either the respondent or the opponent reported being in the "wrong neighborhood" as the reason for an attack. Violence could occur if an outsider was walking through an area that, according to the "insiders" of that neighborhood, he should not have been in. Sixteen events were coded as having erupted out of non-drug-related territory or neighborhood honor issues. In the example presented below, Terry described a inter-project conflict that has continued across generations. He explained:

> TERRY: One time and shit, we had a little prob, problems with these guys and shit from their projects and shit. So, we used to constantly [get into] it, really. It started from the older dudes in our projects. They always had beef with the dudes in this next project. From us, whatever. It started from them. And it, like, it was passed down to our little generation or whatever. You know, we end up getting into beef with these heads...
>
> INT: What kind of beef was it though, like drug- or gang-related or projects?
>
> TERRY: Yeah, it was like a project thing. It was more—it was basically a project thing. We didn't get along with them. They didn't get along with us. We always consider them as

pretty boys or whatever the case may be. They always thought of us as hard nigga dogs or whatever. But we always bumped heads and shit. I recall one time. It was like an ongoing thing. Every night we was getting it on with 'em. One night they had called us on our pay phone. They—we beefing with 'em on the pay phone and they're like 'yo, meet us at so-and-so and we going to settle this.' Like we was going to end it that night or whatever. Whatever the beef was, whatever the case may be. So we goes up there and shit. They like, 'no guns,' whatever, shit like that. So we goes up there with bats and shit. But we got 'em stashed or whatever the case may be. Some dudes got bottles and little, you know, razors or whatever. So we waited for them and shit. They took a little minute to show up and shit. So when they did show up, you know, we get up, start walking towards the street. And it's only like three of them. So we know it's like 'yo, where is the fuck those bastard niggas at?' So we, like, looking at the corner or whatever. So we walking over there or whatever. So while we walking over there the niggas just unzipper, man, like one of them gym bags and shit. So we looking, we walking or whatever. Some nigga just drawed and shit, man, slow. It's like he taking his time with a gun and shit. So we looking at the like hell this nigga got.... By the time anybody could really realize what it was. Man, the nigga just started hitting off and shit. He had a HK. ...Nigga was hitting them shits was hitting garbage cans everything man. We took the fire whatever the case may be and shit.

## DEBTS OR MONEY

Some incidents were sparked by unpaid debts of money, including loansharking and drug business debts. In most of these situations, violence was used to force payment. Money or unpaid debt was given as the reason for 16 violent events. One example of a gun event resulting from an unpaid debt is described below:

INT: So how 'bout when you shot that guy?
DERRICK: My only mistake with doing that was that it was over a hundred dollars. I say he got the drop. I guess it was my time to float. But if he freeze and I could get away...
INT: But at the time, what was you thinking?

DERRICK: At that time I was thinking about he owed me money and he tried to play me. And he tried to play me bad. It's just that he tried to take something that that was mines and it was mines.
INT: It was bothering you?
DERRICK: It was bothering me. I felt that he tried to really play me. I was worrying 'bout me getting money.

## CHEATING OR UNFAIR PLAY

Respondents occasionally were involved in events in which "unfair play" resulted in conflict. The majority of these situations occurred while the respondents were playing sports, shooting pool, or gambling. Cheating, unfair fouling, and rule violations typically resulted in fights. In most cases, the "cheater" denied the claim of cheating and reacted by counter-challenging the accuser until the situation escalated to a physical battle. In some "unfair play" situations, an actor left the scene, got a gun, and returned to express his grievance. Fifteen conflicts resulted from unfair play in either a gambling or sports situation. Fights erupting out of sports or gambling situations usually consisted of non-weapon situations, like the example presented below:

INT: Would you tell me a little about that? What happened?
DANIEL: Well, one time we were playing football and the kid, you know, played rough with me so I was and we were gonna fight. So then we kept playing. So, he made me fall so I got up and I just swung at him. We were fighting and fighting.
INT: So you all went a fair one?
DANIEL: Yeah, we went for a fair one. Nobody stopped us. We just kept fighting and fighting. It was like a year ago.
INT: What happened? Who started what?
DANIEL: He was the one that started it 'cause he was pushing me. I told him to stop pushing me. I did. I just hit him. I had enough of him. I hit him and we just started fighting and fell on the floor and...
INT: What were you trying to accomplish when you was fighting with him?
DANIEL: We was struggling and I hit him.
INT: How did this situation end? What happened? How did it end?
DANIEL: We left. I left.

INT: But how you all broke up?

DANIEL: Donnie, he's the bull, he broke it up. The dude was like, 'Yo, break it up, break it up.' The kid wanted to get me...

INT: After the fight, did you all keep on playing? I mean what happened after that?

DANIEL: Nah. We stop playing and we left. I left.

INT: Everybody left?

DANIEL: Smoke blunts. Smoke blunts with my boys.

This chapter described heterogeneity of violent events focusing specifically on type of weapon, type of weapon use, and the sparks or motivations for the violent events described by respondents. Much of the research on decision-making in violent situations has focused exclusively on adult behavior. This research suggests that the public nature of violence among adolescents, especially coupled with the ready availability of firearms among this population, make social conflicts more significant and potentially deadly. Adolescent males presume that their counterparts are armed, and if not, could easily become armed. They also assume that other adolescents are willing to use guns, often at a low threshold of provocation. The next chapter explores the relationship to the opponent(s), the role of co-offenders in violent situations, the role of third parties, the linkages of violent events to subsequent events, arousal states, the role of alcohol and drug use, the role of formal agents of social control, event outcomes, and aftermaths.

CHAPTER 8

# The Processes and Contingencies of Violent Events

Research suggests that violent situations occur under specific relational, social, and physical conditions (Anderson, 1990; Anderson, 1994; Anderson, 1999; Fagan & Chin, 1990; Miethe & Meier, 1994; Oliver, 1994). These situational contexts offer some type of facilitating features where violence is likely to be tolerated, if not expected. Most theories of criminality hold that a facilitating environment with a motivated offender, a suitable target, and the absence of agents of social control are necessary conditions for violent behavior (Cohen & Felson, 1979; Hindelang, Gottfredson, & Garofalo, 1978). However, these theories fail to account for the interactional dynamics between actors and observers in these settings.

Several important factors of violent situations must be examined in order to explain why some actors choose to be violent in some situations and not in others. An event-level analysis must identify which factors are needed for an encounter between two parties to result in a violent outcome. For example, the victim-offender relationship significantly affects the type and sequential process of violent situations. Each actor's perception of a situation, both in terms of threats and risks, also were important. Perceiving a personal threat or identity challenge, as discussed in Chapter 8, sets up a number of contingencies that actors typically address through the use of violence. For adolescents, peer group involvement and support for violent events further accounts for individual-level participation in those events. Peers often act as co-producers (or at least cheerleaders) in many violent situations.

Violent events among young males in the inner city by and large are public performances with multiple participants and observers. According to a symbolic interactionist framework, the focus of event analysis should be on the interactions between and across actors in specific socio-cultural contexts. Indeed, the findings presented in TABLE 8-1 through TABLE 8-8 illustrate how frequently violent events involve collective definitions of the situation by multiple actors. Heise (1979) states:

A definition of the situation identifies the setting and relevant persons and objects that are present, so it presents the actors and objects that can be combined into recognition of events in that situation. The definition of the situation also entails inferences about social institutional context, knowledge on the part of the observer of ritual or scripted behavior, and negotiation with other observers present at the scene (Heise, 1979: 9).

One aspect of defining the situation is for respondents to make sense of what happened by attributing blame and responsibility to some "defining moment" of the interaction. Respondents used a variety of information sources to develop definitions of the situation. Events were coded across different domains with the aim of understanding the basic "facts" of each event including who was present, who did what, and how each party's involvement affected the respondent and his actions.[11] Other researchers have emphasized the contributions that third parties or bystanders make during violent encounters (Decker, 1995; Oliver, 1994; Tedeschi and Felson, 1994). Slaby (1997) explained:

> As a conflict escalates toward violence, the participants often seem to take turns auditioning for the roles of aggressor, victim, and bystander, as though they were involved in a game of "musical roles." When a gun fires, the music stops. Then, and perhaps forever after, the individual holding the gun has been cast in the role of an aggressor, the one on the ground is a victim, and the one who has been encouraging the violent encounter is a bystander who has contributed to violence (Slaby, 1997: 175-176).

## LOCATION OR SETTING OF VIOLENT EVENTS
Some settings or locations have been shown to be "hot spots" for violence. More than 90% of the violent events described occurred in

---

[11] It should be noted that descriptions of violent events presented in this book reflect accounts offered by respondents during research interviews. It is unclear to what degree their reconstructions of these events fully captured the arousal states during these situations. The best use of these data is to document the level of arousal in vague terms after the fact. The data provide some insights into cognitive processes; however, additional analysis and data are needed on cognition during heightened arousal states such as the life-threatening situations presented herein.

five types of locations: drug spots (locations for drug selling and/or use), the corner or block, house parties or clubs, schools, and jail. As shown in TABLE 8-1, nearly 50% of events occurred on the block or street corner. Respondents described 19 events that transpired inside jails, 31in drug spots, 36 in clubs or parties, and 36 in school or on school grounds. The remaining events occurred at stores, inside houses/apartments, public transportation areas (stations, trains, or platforms), parks, or outdoor pools.

Location played some role in determining the choice of weapon in violent events—locations with less strict social controls were more likely to facilitate gun events. As shown in TABLE 8-1, 55% of gun events, 49% of other-weapon events, and 45% of non-weapon events occurred in the street or on the corner. Drug spots were the setting for 19% of gun events, none of other-weapon events, and 3.7% of non-weapon events. Events at clubs or parties accounted for 14% of gun events, 12% of other-weapon events, and 10% of non- weapon situations. Respondents reported no gun events in jail, 16% other-weapon events, and 11% no weapon events in that context. Events that occurred at school accounted for 4% of gun incidents, 12% of other-weapon incidents, and 22% of non-weapon events.

Place or location is significant in violent and potentially violent situations because place facilitated social interaction among participants and played some role in defining situations. The affect of place in understanding violent behavior includes its attractiveness to potentially violent people, the level of social control available, and the activities that routinely occur in the context. The two inner-city neighborhoods studied clearly were danger zones in which high levels of risk for victimization, frequent exposure to violent experiences, and a normative framework supportive of violent behavior were documented.

One example of the significance of location is presented, however readers can glean information about event locations from many of the other event narratives presented later in the chapter. Respondents often indicated that drinking places themselves were especially prone to violent confrontations, often independent from the drinking patterns of the people present. Young men prepared for these potential dangers by carrying guns to parties or clubs in anticipation of violent events.

**TABLE 8-1. Intersection of Type of Weapon by Location of Event (N=306)***

|  | Total<br>n (%) | Gun<br>n (%) | Other<br>Weapon<br>n (%) | No<br>Weapon<br>n (%) |
|---|---|---|---|---|
| **Location or Place of Event:** |  |  |  |  |
| Jail | 19 ( 6.4) | 0 ( 0.0) | 8 (15.7) | 12 (11.2) |
| Drug Spot | 31 (10.4) | 27 (18.6) | 0 ( 0.0) | 4 ( 3.7) |
| Party/Club | 36 (12.0) | 20 (13.8) | 6 (11.8) | 11 (10.3) |
| Street/Corner | 149 (49.8) | 79 (54.5) | 25 (49.0) | 48 (44.9) |
| School | 36 (12.0) | 6 ( 4.1) | 6 (11.8) | 24 (22.4) |
| Sports | 9 ( 3.0) | 0 ( 0.0) | 1 ( 2.0) | 7 ( 6.5) |
| Gambling | 5 ( 1.7) | 2 ( 1.4) | 0 ( 0.0) | 3 ( 2.8) |
| Store | 13 ( 4.3) | 11 ( 7.6) | 2 ( 3.9) | 1 ( 0.9) |
| House or Apt. | 13 ( 4.3) | 8 ( 5.5) | 2 ( 3.9) | 3 ( 2.8) |
| Train/Station | 10 ( 3.3) | 3 ( 2.1) | 2 ( 3.9) | 5 ( 4.7) |
| Park | 9 ( 3.0) | 4 ( 2.8) | 1 ( 2.0) | 4 ( 3.7) |
| Pool | 3 ( 1.0) | 3 ( 2.1) | 0 ( 0.0) | 0 ( 0.0) |
| Missing | 7 | 3 | 0 | 4 |
| Total Valid | 299 | 145 | 51 | 107 |

*Data were missing on different domains. Percentages are for valid cases only.

Many youth associated the danger in those settings with a certain amount of excitement as long as he was prepared to adequately defend himself. In other cases, the risk of injury at parties deterred future attendance and participation. One person described an event in which he was nearly injured:

> INT: You ever been shot?
> STEVE: Nope. I been grazed.
> INT: You been grazed, where?
> STEVE: My back.
> INT: What happened? Tell me about that.
> STEVE: It was a whole bunch of things. It wasn't meant towards me, it was meant for somebody else, and I was just

sitting on the corner drinking beer and it just happen. I was in the wrong place at the wrong time. But I thank God that it didn't hit me, you know what I mean?

## SORTING OUT THE ROLES OF PARTICIPANTS AND OBSERVERS

Youth described a wide range of violent situations, including events in which the respondent was the initiator; the opponent was the initiator, and those in which no party dominated the opening stages of the confrontation. The variability in types of involvement by actors further complicated the task of assigning roles in violent incidents. Each event was coded according to the respondent's description of his own actions and role in the events. This information was drawn primarily from the descriptions of how an event started and the interpersonal exchanges that transpired. Each role was analyzed to get a clearer understanding of how the respondent made sense of his own actions in the event. Each type of action was coded by the actor that completed the action, for example, individuals could initiate, get attacked, support, seek revenge, come to mutual consent, or witness an event. The variable "role" was not an important predictor of any of the observed patterns. Events in which the respondent was the initiator looked very similar to events in which the opponent started the conflict.

In addition, each category was analyzed for intersections with theoretically relevant categories among other dimensions. Often it was difficult to differentiate between the roles of aggressor and victim in a violent event. No significant differences were seen across the situational domains between events in which the respondent described being the clear aggressor and those in which he was attacked. This finding supports Slaby's (1997) notion of "musical roles" in violent events. The only exception was for injuries: in situations in which the respondent was attacked, he was more likely to also be injured, while in situations in which the respondent attacked his opponent, the opponent was more likely to suffer an injury. The involvement of peers in the assault of others also was important in this role-injury relationship.

### Relationship to the Opponent

Violent crimes typically are classified according to the relationship between the participants. Respondents' relationships with combatants were frequently a key element in defining a situation and shaping the way events unfolded. Respondents described violent conflicts with friends, co-workers, neighborhood acquaintances, rivals, and strangers. As shown in TABLE 8-2, opponents were strangers in nearly half (46%) of situations, were acquaintances in 30% of conflicts, were rivals in 19% of altercations, were friends in 12% of situations, and were co-workers 7% of the time. Relationship to the opponent was an important factor in choice of weapon, type of weapon use, and subsequent reconciliation between adversaries.

Events have different trajectories and characteristics according these relationships. When respondents had no prior relationship or knowledge about an opponent (e.g., "never seen him before," "didn't know him from a hole in the wall," or "just some head"), they were classified as strangers. Respondents reported having little or no knowledge about opponents who were "strangers" and often suspected that these young men harbored not only hostile, but lethal intent. Violent events with strangers more often resulted in weapon use, serious injury, and a lack of closure compared to the other relationship types (see Table 8-7).

Violent events with acquaintances from the neighborhood were those situations in which the respondent knew that the opponent lived or hung out in the neighborhood. In most cases, respondents reported recognizing the opponent by face, previously attending the same school, previously meeting through others, growing up together but not being friendly, or seeing the opponent hanging out regularly in the neighborhood.

Conflicts with opponents classified as "rivals" included situations of ongoing dispute between parties. Rivals typically resided in adjacent neighborhoods and competed with the respondent for drug business, females, or status/identity. Although a rival may also have been an acquaintance from the neighborhood, individuals who were considered rivals were classified as such and not as acquaintances or strangers. Many of the conflicts classified as ongoing were between rivals.

Violent events that erupted between the respondent and a close friend rarely involved serious violence. For example, potentially violent conflicts between friends often were likely to get "squashed" before violence occurred; less frequently involved weapon use, and resulted in minor fights with few serious injuries. The majority of these situations were fair fights, even when one or both parties were armed. Respondents seemed to rely upon the relationship to assess the potential risk in conflict situations. Violent events among friends most often included closure and reconciliation, although in some cases friendships ended after a violent interaction. Violent events between co-workers were related to the drug business and typically involved some type of dispute related to cheating, stealing, or encroaching on someone else's territory. Situations between co-workers rarely moved beyond threats (with and without guns); co-workers frequently backed down or complied with the demands of a more powerful opponent. Gun use among drug workers was considered detrimental to the drug business because of the increased likelihood of police attention. Conflicts among drug workers were more likely to have lethal consequences if allowed to escalate, however, gun use was also important for ending business associations and avenging betrayal.

**TABLE 8-2. Intersection of Type of Weapon by Relationship with Opponent (N=306)**

|  | Total n (%) | Gun n (%) | Other Weapon n (%) | No Weapon n (%) |
|---|---|---|---|---|
| **Relationship with Opponent:** | | | | |
| Friend | 34 (12.0) | 11 ( 8.0) | 9 (17.6) | 14 (12.6) |
| Acquaintance | 86 (30.4) | 33 (24.1) | 10 (19.6) | 42 (37.8) |
| Rival | 53 (18.7) | 35 (25.5) | 9 (17.6) | 11 ( 9.9) |
| Stranger | 130 (45.9) | 67 (48.9) | 17 (33.3) | 44 (39.6) |
| Co-worker | 21 ( 7.4) | 16 (11.7) | 1 ( 2.0) | 4 ( 3.6) |
| Missing | 23 | 11 | 6 | 6 |
| Total Valid | 283 | 137 | 51 | 111 |

*Data were missing on different domains. Percentages are for valid cases only.

## THE CO-PRODUCTION OF VIOLENT EVENTS

Third parties may be viewed both as part of the socio-cultural context and as participants in the co-production of violent events. These "third parties," for lack of a better term, may be neutral, aligned with the respondent or opponent, or aligned with both. They may play an actively violent role in the situation or may make up the supporting audience for the violent performance. The role of peers or members of an actor's social network in co-producing violent events also is discussed.

The involvement of friends or associates in the co-production of violent events complicates the analysis of roles. The respondent's friends were present in 79% of the violent events described while the opponent's friends were present in 75% of the events. The respondent's friends were more likely to be present if the situation involved a gun (86%) compared to other-weapon (68%), or non-weapon (75%) events. The presence of the opponent's friends showed a similar pattern with the opponent's associates were present at 79% of gun events, 71% of other-weapon events, and 70% of non-weapon events. One interruption of this finding was that when conflict situations were serious, individuals will be more likely to garner assistance from others in order to enhance self-protection. Alternatively, the presence of others may promote the use of guns because with more people present the more potential source of the gun or onlookers may push the conflict to a more violent resolution. Another possible explanation is that much of the conflict is group conflict to begin with. Studying violent events by interviewing individuals about their individual involvement in violent incidents could potentially miss the group processes. Friends/associates also were more likely to participate in violence if guns were involved. Specifically, respondents' friends used violence in 69% of gun, 55% of other-weapon, and 39% of non-weapon events, while the opponent's friends used violence in 82% of gun, 71% of other-weapon, and 30% of non-weapon events.

The subsequent example shows the importance of rallying peer support in a violent event. In the incident classified as an accusatory identity challenge, Dean described the involvement of his friends as a source of backup and protection. The respondent's friend "shared" the burden of the initial attack. He explained:

> INT: Was there any third parties around?
> DEAN: Yeah, his friends was there, my friends was there. I only had one friend with me 'cause we had went to this school out of the 'hood and he lived over by the school. He knew a whole lot of people over there and I didn't hardly know nobody over there.
> INT: Did anyone else get directly involved?
> DEAN: Yeah, my man who was with me, 'cause we was going out for each other. If he was going to get in a fight I was going to jump in, if I'm in a fight he jumping in. That's how it was.
> INT: Did having your people there affect the fight?

DEAN: Yeah. If he wasn't there, they could have all just focused in on me. But when—I mean, they still had the advantage, you know, but when we was fighting he could just come in and snuff somebody, boom, and get somebody up off me. And I could do the same for him.
INT: After the event, did you do anything extra to protect yourself?
DEAN: Yeah. The next day I came up there with my peoples and jump them.
INT: What sort of relationship did you have with the guy after the fight?
DEAN: You know, it was like—we still had hard feelings for each other, but they was going to kick us out the school if anything was happening with us. So niggas just cool shit down, it was squashed. We didn't ever talk like friends or nothing, though.

Peers frequently got involved in situations where their friends were being disrespected or victimized by others. Respondents described violent situations in which they come to the aid of others and also those in which others come to their aid. One respondent described a scene in which a teenager was being 'rude' to his friend and answered Alonzo's request for respect with a second challenging remark. When the 'rude' man refused to back down, Alonzo shot him in the head and later attempted to rationalize his actions by denying the opponent's worth or social status:

INT: Did you ever shoot anyone?
ALONZO: Yeah. I shot somebody. We had this conflict, this kid, I don't know him but we was just sitting next {to him}, and he exchanged words with my friend, so he told..., he came to the kid, the kid came to my friend and my friend told him to move... so my man was like 'move, what you mean move, man, the word is excuse me,' he was like 'no, move' ... some rude boy. So he was like, I heard them, so I turned around and said 'yo, what the fuck is going on, yo,' the kid talking about 'what you gonna do,' so I said 'what you mean what I'm gonna do,' so I shot him...

A second example shows an older and tougher friend attempting to 'get justice' for the respondent. Brandon had a history of problems with an opponent, and his friend attempted to force the return of Brandon's stolen property. When the opponent ordered the friend to mind his own business, the friend decided to shoot him. Clearly, the opponent did not properly acknowledge the status of the shooter according to Brandon's account:

> INT: Can you remember of a situation where the beef went down, where a beef went down and somebody got hurt involving you?
> BRANDON: Yeah. ...I had problems with this Puerto Rican kid. ...So he was just talking a lot of shit to me, 'cause he beat me for a remote control car. He kept my shit.
> INT: When was this?
> BRANDON: This was like, I was 15, I was like between 15 and 14... So he beat me, he kept my shit. So my man came, so he came home and shit. ...I had a ghat (gun) on me that night, because I wasn't going to take it to that level. So I seen the Puerto Rican kid, I stepped to him. I'm like, 'yo, when am I going to get my shit?' He's like 'yo I don't got it.' So my man, my man I was with was like 'yo, when you going to get his shit?' So the Puerto Rican kid telling my man 'yo, mind your business, you don't have nothing to do with this.' So we broke (left). I told the nigga, 'yo that's my man.' So he talking shit, 'fuck y'all niggas, man, I'll flip on both of y'all.' So I snuffed him. So me and him 'bout to... then my man snuffed him. So he heard that my man told him 'I'm going to kill you, watch, I'm going to kill you, don't let me catch you,' so I had the ghat on the side of my hand. But I ain't know what my man was going to do, so I'm off guard that minute, looking at them argue 'bout. My man just grabbed the ghat from my hand, popped him twice in the leg, boom, boom, in front of the building, in front of, like, five people. So we standing there, and I'm like 'yo, oh shit, what did you do that for, son?' So boom. The Puerto Rican kid went through the back—through the back of the building.
> INT: He was shot.
> BRANDON: Yeah, he was shot twice in the leg. So I'm about to leave—so I'm about to go back in the building, my man went through the back of the building followed him, so I'm going to get him so we can jet. {I} get to the back of the

building, my man finished him off, boom, boom, boom, boom, boom, boom, boom, boom, loaded nine shots at him. Shot him twice, had seven left, let off the rest at him. Next thing you know we both scheming, I don't know what happen then, we both left.

INT: You don't know if the guy got killed?

BRANDON: Nah, he didn't die though, he didn't die. He came home, but walks down to me. I didn't have nothing to do with it. He didn't have to say nothin' to me, next thing you know my man got locked up for that, 'cause he snitched. The Puerto Rican guy snitched, so my man got locked up. Yo, I don't know what that nigga was thinking in his head, bro, I can't tell you that.

In order to capture the group nature of violent events, the interviews were coded to capture the active participation of all relevant actors described by the respondent. As shown above, many violent events were group conflicts with multiple actors on both sides. In fact, 76 of 280 events (27%) were situations characterized as group-conflict or "crew-on-crew" battles. Another 23% pitted a respondent and at least one friend against a single opponent; respondents alone faced multiple opponents in 8% of violent events. Despite the high frequency with which third parties were present at these scenes, 42% of events were classified as one-on-one conflicts, i.e., one respondent versus one opponent with no one else getting physically involved in the situation. Pooling the three categories of co-offending yields a total of 163 violent events; co-offenders actively were involved in 58% of the violent events in the sample.

Again, there were stark differences across the three weapon types in violent situations. For example, 67% of gun events involved multiple offenders (42% were crew-on-crew situations) while only 23% were one-on-one incidents. In contrast, situations without weapons more often were of the one-on-one variety (59%). This finding may in part reflect the seriousness introduced by guns in conflict situations. In situations without weapons, an actor's friend(s) may actually play a controlling role by preventing the escalation of one-on-one fights without weapons. The role of third parties as amplifiers and co-participants is illustrated by the event described below. In this

**TABLE 8-3. Intersection of Type of Weapon by Co-offending Status**

|  | Total n (%) | Gun n (%) | Other Weapon n (%) | No Weapon n (%) |
| --- | --- | --- | --- | --- |
| **Single or Multiple Offenders:** | | | | |
| One on One | 118 (42.1) | 33 (23.4) | 24 (50.0) | 60 (58.8) |
| Two + on One | 63 (22.5) | 41 (29.1) | 12 (25.0) | 12 (11.8) |
| One on Two + | 23 ( 8.2) | 10 ( 7.1) | 6 (12.5) | 7 ( 6.9) |
| Crew on Crew | 76 (27.1) | 59 (41.8) | 6 (12.5) | 14 (13.7) |
| Missing | 26 | 7 | 3 | 9 |
| Total Valid | 280 | 141 | 48 | 102 |

*Data were missing on different domains. Percentages are for valid cases only.

example, both the respondent's friends and the opponent's friends played roles in the violence process. Individuals on both sides of the conflict promoted the use of violence; the respondent described the crowd as "rowdy" and giving specific instructions for him to inflict harm on his opponent, comments that registered with the respondent. JP described how others were involved:

> INT: So umm, did any of your...did any of his people get involved with it as soon as he and you walked outside?
> JP: Yeah. All his...you know I'm saying he was with all his boys. I'm saying, I was with a couple a niggas. That's why he was acting rowdy. 'Cause he was with his peoples.
> INT: So your peoples from your crew...
> JP: Yeah, my boys was telling me 'shoot the nigga. Slice him, stab him.' Shit was running through my mind.
> INT: So how 'bout his peoples?
> JP: Yeah, you know, they were shouting shit out. 'Just shoot that cat.'
> INT: How you was feeling when your peoples was instigating?
> JP: I was gonna do it. Cops pulled up too quick.

Housing authority police officers disrupted the initial event; the combatants fled the scene to avoid arrest. The conflict later continued and intensified into a shootout between the opposing sides. In the subsequent incident, previously uninvolved third parties become actively engaged as co-offenders in the "retaliatory" gun event.

INT: So what happened when they left? They broke out?
JP: Yeah, they broke out. We just...we broke out too. But we caught the niggas the next day.
INT: Hmm. Y'all caught them the next day. What you mean?
JP: Yeah, we caught ' em like I said. We went back over there the next day. With a bigger crew. We just—we did what we had to do.
INT: So when y'all went back, what y'all—what y'all...you say? You went back with a stronger crew?
JP: Yeah, we saw them out there. We rolled up on them. We just flipped on them. So everybody bugged the fuck out.
INT: So everybody got violent?
JP: Yeah. We pulled out on them. They pulled out too.
INT: Oh, so y'all had a shootout?
JP: Yeah.
INT: The next day?
JP: Yeah.
INT: So umm, this shootout—anybody got hurt?
JP: Yeah. Yeah, the kid that I was fighting with, I'm saying he got shot in the chest.

Robberies, for example, often involved groups of young men as co-offenders. One respondent described a robbery of a drug spot that did not unfold the way the group had planned—it became a robbery-turned-shootout. First, Travis described "the robbery plan," then he described the actual encounter. Note the very detailed account of his thought processes during the event:

INT: What happened?
TRAVIS: Well, somebody got shot and shit, the man and shit. We went up in there and shit and.... do you want to hear exactly what happened?
INT: Yeah. Yeah.
TRAVIS: Alright. I had the 'Bama. The shit was in Queens. We went over there, we parked there. This kid was setting up the plan and shit, me and my man. My man had .45 and I had

a .32 and shit. So the kid, he just told us the plan. 'You go in there, tell 'em Dan sent you, and tell 'em this and that' and shit. So me, as being Spanish, should have an advantage, for I could talk my Spanish and shit, boom boom bam. And since them being Spanish too and shit, know I could blend in and they give me a little more...

According to Travis, this was the first time he took a leading role in setting up an exchange with a victim. He described being nervous and worrying about how his performance, if inadequate, would affect his standing back in the neighborhood. The respondent was reluctant to carry out his mission and described his behavior as procrastination. His actions were determined in part by cues he received during the event from his partner:

TRAVIS: So I went up. We went up in there and shit. It was a record shop, a regular shop. Fat Colombia man in the front and shit, bitch in the back. So when we went up in there we like, 'yo what's up?' and shit, and I'm waiting for the people to leave and shit. So he like, 'what's up?' and shit, you know. That's when I stepped in and started kicking my Spanish, *yo quiero un viento cinco*, it's a one twenty-five, a hundred and twenty-five grand and shit. So he was like, 'umm, all right, who sent you?' and shit, so I said 'Dan' and shit. So he started getting suspicious. So he was like 'all right put it right here.' So he went to the back, I guess he made a phone call. So he came back. And [my partner] was like, 'umm, man, damn, set it off. Set it off.' My man wanted me to set it off and shit but I was procrastinating, so he waited ...
INT: You was nervous?
TRAVIS:... yeah I ain't gonna front. I was kinda nervous and shit. So we waited for a little second 'cause I wanted him to set if off, if he wouldn't have set it off no matter what, which I had to. That was the... it was the destiny I had to do it. I wasn't going back to the projects, 'ahh, he fronted!' so I had to do it. So I was just waiting for them and shit.

The respondent described waiting for the right moment, but then being forced into action when someone else entered the room and his partner ordered him to act. At that point Travis took a more aggressive position:

TRAVIS: So we waited... waited. All a sudden another man came. When the other man came my man was like, 'fuck, you gotta do it now and shit!' So another man came, my man pulled out click. When he pulls out I pulls out. Put the shit to the fat Columbian nigga head, so I searched him. Boom pulled out, he had a nine... nine-shot Taurus. [I] pulled it out put it in my, umm, pouch. I had a, umm, Columbia windbreaker type shit. So we backed him down and shit run him to the back. So when we brought him to the back my man was deep inside shit. So you know I'm like—look I could see the front door and shit from the back of the, umm, store. So my man backing him down. My man just start, 'fuck that, where the fucking money at?' shit like that. So, all of a sudden I just heard some motion-type shit. 'Oh shut up, 'this and that and shit.' So I hear shot, Bow, so I said 'ahh fuck it. I got to shoot somebody or shit.' So I shot the nigga. I had him down on the wall so I shot him, but I shot him in the leg though, bow, bow, twice and shit, and I ran. When I ran and shit I left, you know, I—mistakenly I left my man and shit. I should not did that, so I—when I was leaving the door and shit, I turn around, you know. My man call me, he's like 'yo son.' I turn around see my man get on the floor. This fat motherfucker shot him in the leg and shit. So I run back and shit. When I run back I shoot the nigga two times in the back ba bow. My man get up and shit, you know. A clip fell out the gun and shit, like, damn, so we running out the store and shit. We get in the car and jet. After that we was doing more shit though, man. We was running up in bodegas, sticking guns in...

The respondent described this event as the beginning of a series of stick-ups of corner stores. This situation clearly was a learning experience for him. One of his primary concerns was how others, both at the scene and back in the neighborhood, would view him after this incident.

## OTHER ROLES OF THIRD PARTIES

The presence of other bystanders or observers at violent event could be determined in only 137 of the 306 events; of those third parties or observers were present in 101 (74%) violent events and absent in 36 (26%) events. From the respondents' perspective, bystanders sided with the respondent in 40% of violent events and with the opponent in 9% of situations. Bystanders verbally pressed or "amped up" the actors in 37% of violent events, broke up 10% of conflicts, and did nothing in 23% of the events. Several examples of bystander affects were presented below.

In the next example, Jose described third parties as "instigating" on the side of the opponent. Although the crowd was involved by verbally "amping" the situation, no one else got physically involved in the conflict:

INT: There was people around when you and him—when the beef was going down?
JOSE: Yeah, they was people...
INT: What they were doing?
JOSE: Yo, instigate, Bee. Instigate. 'Oh shit, oh, oh shit,' that's that type of shit. They want to make a nigga take out a gun or some shit. Be all about 'blast this nigga. I want to be the fucking man. Everybody saw that shit. Nobody gonna fuck with me.' I don't think like that. You gotta think about yourself.
INT: True true. Did anybody get in?
JOSE: Nah, nobody got in. We just a fair one, one on one.
INT: Was they people talking shit?
JOSE: Yes. Never heard so much shit, have to be that night, man. People 'oh, hit him, hit him, take out your shit, stab him, shoot him.' Yo man, ain't no need for none of that shit. Nigga had to pull shit out on me, fuck, I'ma pull out some shit. I consider that shit being pussy. Word up, kid. I eat the shit. I don't be a pussy. Word up.

Clearly, Jose was concerned about how he handled the situation and how the audience would view him after the performance. He recognized the negative pressure of the crowd and felt compelled to make his own decisions despite their cheers. In this regard Jose demonstrated a level of maturity not frequently seen among the sample. He felt satisfied with his performance in the fight and with the fact that the two combatants had a fair fight without using firearms.

In several situations, third parties got involved to stop a violent event. Below, Morris explained how one fight at school was broken up by a gym teacher:

INT: How did the situation end? What was the outcome?

MORRIS: Gym teacher broke it up. Grabbed him, I busted his fucking nose. He just went to the doctor to get his shit patched up, get a little ice pack for that eye piece.

INT: After the fight, did anything change about where you hung out at?

MORRIS: Nah. Fucking niggas ain't scaring me.

INT: Did you do anything extra to protect yourself?

MORRIS: Just let my peoples know what time it is. If the niggas want to jump me, jump me.

INT: What sort of relationship did you have with the guy after the fight?

MORRIS: What's up? That's about it. No words, keep it moving.

INT: Was there any talk after the fight?

MORRIS: Yeah, this bitch in class tried to gas shit up. They got into a little argument. She that is why he lumped your shit up. Look at your eye.' She was like, 'nigga fucked you up.' Nigga said, 'he didn't fuck me up. I'll go back there and snuff the shit out that nigga.' So I said, 'what?' I jump up, 'what?' Teachers came and broke the shit up. His bitch jumped up, my bitch jumped up, getting ready to go at it.

INT: How did you feel about what was being said?

MORRIS: Nigga trying to play me, we already see one eye, he want the other one bust the fuck open, what the fuck wrong?

In many cases, third parties merely observed these situations. According to Patrick, witnesses to violent events often were intimidated or ordered not to report what they have seen.

INT: Beside you and them two guys, were there other people present during the altercation?

PATRICK: Yeah, there was. There was a lady out there where I did it.

INT: What was she saying?

PATRICK: That bitch better not say anything or she would have got smoked too.

## ROLE OF ALCOHOL AND DRUG USE

Drinking, drug use, and drug selling were clearly part of the social context of violent events among our sample. As shown in TABLE 8-4, respondents reported being drunk or high in the majority (64%) of violent events, and were certain that their opponent was also high or drunk in 12% of incidents.

**TABLE 8-4. Intersection of Type of Weapon by Alcohol or Drug Use (N=306)\***

|  | Total<br>n (%) | Gun<br>n (%) | Other<br>Weapon<br>n (%) | No<br>Weapon<br>n (%) |
|---|---|---|---|---|
| **Alcohol or Drug Use:** |  |  |  |  |
| Drunk/High | 111 (64.2) | 61(80.3) | 13 (50.0) | 38 (53.5) |
| Not Drunk/High | 62 (35.8) | 16 (21.1) | 13 (50.0) | 33 (46.5) |
| DK/Missing | 133 | 72 | 25 | 30 |
| Total Valid | 173 | 76 | 26 | 71 |

\*Data were missing on different domains. Percentages are for valid cases only.

Respondents frequently were involved with gun events while under the influence. Gun events were 3.8 times more likely to occur when a respondent was under the influence of drugs or alcohol, in fact, respondents report being drunk or high in 80% of the situations; for non-gun events the ratio was 1.2: 1. A range of dynamic processes was identified that showed the interactions of intoxication effects, situational contexts, and individual propensities to contribute to violence or its avoidance. Some involved affective states following intoxication, others involve events that occur in drinking or drug use locations, and still others involve problems in drug businesses that spill over into other areas of social life. Throughout all of these, guns were present as a strategic factor and also as a threshold criterion in decision-making about violence.

Drug and alcohol effects were evident in decision-making, cognition, intensified emotional states, exaggerated affect, and diminished capacity for self-regulation, deviance disavowal, and other cognitive processes. For example, respondents indicated that language when intoxicated was more provocative, and such language often "amped up" otherwise minor disputes into violent encounters. Some said they tended to take bystanders' provocations to fight more seriously. More boastful language and exaggerated verbal displays of toughness and "nerve" were common during drinking events:

INT: Do you know if he was high?
LUKE: Yeah. He was drunk, high or drunk. The nigga was fucked up, man. I think that is why he thought he was Superman for that night.
INT: Everybody drinking think they somebody.
LUKE: That just goes to show that Superman can't stop a bullet. Everybody got skin. This flesh. Under that is bone.

Respondents read cues about whether or not their opponents were drunk or high based on the way the opponent looked, acted, smelled, or spoke:

INT: Do you know if the other guy had been drinking or using drugs before you guys started fighting?
JEFF: He looked pretty much out of it. So I guess yeah.
INT: Do you think the use of alcohol influenced the way he handled the situation between you and him?
JEFF: The way he spoke, yeah.
INT: How?
JEFF: 'Cause he just, you know, he said, like a lot of dumb things that, like, just really, like—heated up the moment more.

In retrospective many respondents felt that they would have handled the situation differently if they had not been under the influence.

INT: Do you feel, think that the situation was related to you using, drinking?
VINCE: Yeah, I think so. Yeah, I know so matter of fact because if I wouldn't have been drinking I would have handled it in a more calm manner.
INT: It was more impulsive because of the drinking?
VINCE: I was very much more aggressive.

One common problem associated with drinking or getting high was the tendency to become more boisterous, verbally provoke others, find amusement in playing mind games with people, and feeling more bold:

INT: Umm, you ever have got into any beef or a fight while you was drunk?

STEVE: Yes, I did.

INT: What you—what that was about?

STEVE: Well, about me having a big mouth.

INT: What happened with that?

STEVE: Well, I was smoking weed one day, all right. My man, I was smoking weed one day, drinking, getting fucked up, we got into a little technical difficulties, you know. We had a fight. I got my ass wiped.

INT: What y'all fought over, some bullshit?

STEVE: Just bullshit, just talking, you know, talking out your ass, arguing back and forth, you know what I mean. So niggas said 'yo pipe that shit down, dead it,' nigga ain't pipe it down, I'm still talking out my mouth.

INT: Who said 'pipe it down, dead it?' Somebody else?

STEVE: Yeah, one of my homeboys, you know what I mean? Nigga said 'I ain't with that shit no more, you know,' and I'm still talking out my mouth. So you know, niggas told me it was a lesson to be learnt, so it happened it happened, you know. It happened to me, like, three times, you know, but you learn from that.

INT: All three times, was anybody trying to calm the situation down?

STEVE: Yeah, but I wasn't trying to hear that. I was in the influence of drinking and everything and like, 'fuck you, get the fuck outta here,' you know, 'let me do my thing, let me handle my business.'

Some individuals used drugs as a way of preparing themselves for a violent encounter:

INT: Did you plan to do this?

PATRICK: Yeah. I told you, I meditated the night before. I said 'I hope it snow all night.' I ain't going to lie, I used to smoke cocaine. I sat up and smoked cocaine blunts mixed with weed. About five of them bitches talking about how I'm going to kill this nigga in the morning.

INT: Were you high at the time?

PATRICK: Yo, back then I was smoking angel dust, kid. So I probably was high from an angel dust blunt the night before. You know how that angel dust is.

INT: Did you know if them two guys was high on drugs?

PATRICK: Hell yeah, them niggas was high. Them niggas was smoking trees.

INT: How about the other party? Do you think they were on drugs at the time?

PATRICK: Yeah. Yeah, he looked like he was high, but I fixed his ass 'cause he wasn't high when I got finished.

INT: Do you think alcohol and drugs influenced the way he handled the situation?

PATRICK: Yeah, I'm sure it did, because if he wasn't high he wouldn't have touched me that day. And if I wasn't high it wouldn't have happen. It was like we both was high or whatever, 'cause I had just came from down south so, you know, I went and got me a bag of weed. And if he wouldn't have touched me—I knew he was high, I seen the high. It is like regardless of whether he was high or not, me being God, I ain't got to let no man touch me.

Some people reported having made bad decisions while high, leading to fights that might have been avoided in other circumstances:

INT: Did you have any kind of strategy you were going to use to win this confrontation?

MALIK: Not at the moment, no. I was tipsy. I was off focus.

These mind-altering behaviors often increased the stakes in everyday interactions, transforming them from non-challenging verbal interactions into the types of "character contests" which often involved violence. Alcohol exaggerates the sense of outrage over perceived transgressions of personal codes (respect, space, verbal challenges), often resulting in violence as a means of exerting social control or getting retribution.

A wide range of drug effects was reported. Some "chilled" when smoking marijuana, others sought out victims to dominant or exploit, and a few reported becoming paranoid and avoiding any type of human interaction. But for some, paranoia created an air of danger and threat, leading to defensive or pre-emptive violence:

INT: I noticed you were drunk when all of this happened.

JAKE: I wasn't really drunk. I was just, like, "nice."

INT: But the drug—did the liquor had anything to do with your actions?

JAKE: Nah, you crazy? It's worse—I feel I'm worse when

I'm not drinking, not that. Like, when I smoke weed I turn soft. Like, when I smoke weed, I get nice and shit—shit be having me nervous and shit. Yeah.
INT: And you don't really wanna get into it?
JAKE: Nah, when I smoke weed, nah. Sometimes I get paranoid. I don't like smoking weed.

Several respondents described an intensified need to prove their machoness, and also a skewed ability to handle joking, teasing, and other verbal games when drinking alcohol:

INT: Thinking back, why do you think you did what you did?
VINCE: In that instant, 'cause I was drinking and my state of thinking was altered to a more, how would you say, "machismo." When I had to prove that, I guess at that moment feeling the way I was feeling, buzzed up like that.
INT: You felt dissed...?
VINCE: I felt disrespected, and you got to prove yourself.

Others note the human guidedness[12] of drinking behaviors, where drinking often was an intended behavior that creates the emotional and affective conditions in which violence was likely. Consider the two opposite descriptions of marijuana effects:

INT: Had you been drinking or doing drugs before that fight? Were you high?
NATHAN: Smoke some weed.
INT: So you was high?
NATHAN: Yeah, I was kind of fucked up.
INT: Do you think alcohol or drugs influenced you, the way you handle the situation?
NATHAN: Nah. Marijuana keeps you fucking... it keeps you down. It keeps you more or less in a mellow state. Alcohol will take you to that level you wanna fucking hurt someone. I wanted to chill and watch a basketball game. I didn't want to go out there and fight on no hot fucking summer day.

---

[12] Human guidedness refers to the internalization of justifications or expectancies for one's behavior after consuming alcohol or getting high. Aggressive behavior is blamed on the substance use as a "guiding force" leading to such behavior. It is a complex socialpsychological process (see Pernanen 1991).

TOMAS: Sometimes I think it depends on the smoke too, like some smoke. You be finding out you go to that store. Smoking the trees over there. I don't fuck around with weed personally, I used to fuck around. Like you said sometimes you do shit for fun, I do shit for fun, I smoke weed and go fuck somebody up for fun. That is why don't even fuck around with that shit, that is why I leave that shit alone, I drink my litter beer here and there, little 40 here and there but I don't get so drunk I hate throwing up, son.

Several respondents reported that intoxication compromised their decision-making during violent events. Some respondents felt invincible and instigated fights that they would end up losing. Some engaged in aggressive responses that, in retrospect, seemed unnecessary and stupid. Still others said they were "too fuzzy" when high to make good decisions about whether or how to fight.

While cognitive impairment was evident for some, others noted that their decisions while drinking reflected complex strategic judgments about the "chess game" that often precedes the decision to fight or withdraw. The decision to "squash" or to "dead" a fight involves reading a series of cues and perceptions as well as using verbal skills. One respondent told how he and his friends withdrew from a potential fight at a party after deciding that they could not win, that their opponents outnumbered them, and that even if a temporary peace could be negotiated, it would be fragile and short-lived. But their withdrawal required that they offer accounts that permitted both sides to maintain a share of the "props" while not appearing to be weak. This required both mental and verbal agility, skills that had to be summoned despite a long night of drinking.

Intoxication also appears to indirectly influence violence, and may even be an outcome of violence. Some respondents described violent events while intoxicated where drinking or drug use was unrelated to violence, while others disavowed responsibility for their violence, blaming it entirely on being high. Others got high after violent events as a form of self-medication or celebration:

INT: You was high that day? Drunk, high, weed?
EDUARDO: No, I wasn't high. I wasn't drunk.
INT: What about after that? After the fight?
EDUARDO: After the fight, when I got back around my way, I told my friends about it and we planned to go back.

INT: Y'all got high and started laughing after that?
EDUARDO: No, we didn't. We got high, but we wasn't laughing.
INT: What kinda drug did y'all use to get high?
EDUARDO: Marijuana.
INT: And that's it?
EDUARDO: That's it.

Finally, one respondent told of how the complications of drug addiction and the drug business spilled over into other social interactions. In the street context, the social standing of frequent drug users was quite low. Drug users were used, played, and manipulated into a variety of chores and actions by more powerful characters on the street. As the example below illustrates, people who were close to friends or family members addicted to drugs were pitied as "fallen victims." Consider the following story that integrates these themes:

CLARENCE: And then, like, my cousin, right—I had a cousin. He was black too, and he was skinny. You know, he was a good kid and he was young. Then he started smoking, he got caught up in the game. He started smoking. And you know, the rest of his friends was looking down on him. They was like, 'yo what's wrong with you, supposed to be chilling with us. Look at us, we chilling, we phat. What you over here smoked out (from crack)? Why go there?' They used to diss him and all that. They use to look out for him and all that, pay him, 'yo, here, go to the store for me, yo. Here, here.' Look out for him. They always took care of him and all that. But he never degraded himself where he was robbing people, snatching anybody's chain, robbing people's moms of something like that. He never went low like that. But he just liked to smoke. He liked to get high. And umm, he was chilling with this other crackhead that was the bad—he was the opposite of him. He would always be sticking nigga's moms up, stickin',—he stick anybody up. Catch a little nigga for his work, take him, take his money, take whatever. And he used to always rob this one guy constantly. And them two—since they stood together, you know, a lot. And they liked to get together because the nigga, he would rob mad people and he would have mad work and he would come and be 'yo, what's up, man, come get high with me.' 'All right,

fuck it, yo.' So they kind of stood together and the other person saw that. He was like 'yo, damn, I want that nigga but I guess I'm gonna have to use him to get to him.' So they kind of made a setup one day. He tried to set him up in the building. And my cousin he didn't know what time it was. He was like, 'yo, what's up, come get high with me.' All right. He was supposed to bring the other nigga, that's were they went wrong. 'Cause he told my cousin, he was like, 'yo, come get high. Go tell Billy come' and the other guy Billy, he was like, 'Nah. Nah. I'm not trying to hear that, yo.' So he tried to stay away from that. He was like 'Nah.' He felt funny. He was like, 'Nah. I'm going with that. I'm always sticking you up and you trying to light me up (get me high) now. Nah. I ain't fucking with you.' So he got one. He got my cousin into the building and for one reason or another there was somebody waiting in the staircase with a "shotty" (shotgun) but it was supposed to be for the other guy and it was a case of mistaken identity, and they shot my cousin in the face boom.
INT: He killed him?
CLARENCE: Killed him.
INT: Pssst.
CLARENCE: And that kind of—it didn't happen to me—it happen—it was my birthday that day. The last time I saw him was right there on the corner before I went upstairs. I had a little joint, I was puffing it and boom. And he, you know, whenever I had blunts I always smoked with him too, 'get high off of this.' Leave that other shit alone. That stuff ain't good for you.
INT: Yeah.
CLARENCE: So I was smoking my joint with him and before I went upstairs I gave it to him. I was like 'yo, I'm out. See you tomorrow' and he was like 'ah-ight.' Usually sometimes and—I was kind of close to him. In the mornings he used to come to my house, I used to cook a phat breakfast for both of us. He used to always eat with me and we used to just kick it, chill, bugging, watching TV and everything. Then it happen, like, three in the morning that night and I had went upstairs about twelve. That was the last time I ever saw him.

In this story, Clarence's cousin who had a drug addiction was lead to his death by the promise of his next high. Although the cousin was not the intended victim in this case, his addiction was the primary reason for his death.

Many respondents reported avoiding serious drug use before planned violent events such as robberies. These individuals explained that drug use would impair their ability to successfully carry out the crime. When asked about being high during the robbery described earlier, Nick explained:

> INT: Was you high when you robbed that dude?
> NICK: Nah. When I do my shit I like to be sober. 'Cause I'm better on that point. There's some people that smoke weed and they be all like commando. But I got to be sober, 'cause I got to have my thoughts correct. I can't be slipping out here.

## THE ROLE OF LAW ENFORCEMENT

In a small percentage of cases, police officers were involved in controlling, mediating, and sanctioning participants in violent events. The classification of police presence for this domain includes any mention of the actual or anticipated presence of police including sighting a car or officer, hearing sirens, directly interacting with a police officer, and any subsequent investigations.

Using this conservative definition of police presence, respondents report that police were present in 47% of the 172 valid cases. In the majority of these situations, police arrived well after the actors had fled the scene of the violent incident. As shown in TABLE 8-5, police were more likely to be present (typically after the fact) if a weapon was used. Police were considered present in 61% (49/81 valid cases) of gun events, 63% of other-weapon events, and 29% of non-weapon events.

Respondents rarely described using law enforcement or the justice system following criminal attacks or victimization experiences. These adolescent males generally were heavily involved in the illegal economy, where legal means of resolving conflicts generally were unavailable. Not only were they involved with criminal activity, but also the prevailing normative system punished or sanctioned the use of police or other authority figures to resolve disputes. Respondents described their experiences with the police as hostile, abusive, and oppressive. Cooperation with the police was viewed as disloyalty to members of the community and may be punished.

**TABLE 8-5. Intersection of Type of Weapon by Role of Police (N=306)***

|  | Total n (%) | Gun n (%) | Other Weapon n (%) | No Weapon n (%) |
|---|---|---|---|---|
| **Police Involvement:** | | | | |
| Police Present | 81 (47.1) | 49 (60.5) | 15 (62.5) | 20 (28.6) |
| Not Present | 91 (52.9) | 32 (39.5) | 9 (37.5) | 50 (71.4) |
| Missing/DK | 134 | 67 | 27 | 41 |
| Total Valid | 172 | 81 | 24 | 70 |

*Data were missing on different domains. Percentages are for valid cases only.

Respondents generally described police as absent when needed and not at all helpful when present. Respondents complained that police officers were more concerned with gathering evidence and making arrests then trying to save the life of a gunshot victim. Despite frequent and heated expressions of dissatisfaction with the police, respondents described at least 20 violent events in which police officers played a significant role in stopping and/or preventing a situation that would have otherwise escalated. Events in which police intervened and either made an arrest or broke up a fight often reached closure more readily and the opportunity for retaliation was reduced at least temporarily. In addition, hearing police sirens during an event often resulted in the premature ending of a fight or shootout so that the combatants could successfully flee the scene before police arrived. The story of one respondent's drug-related gun event illustrated the most common scenario of police involvement:

> INT: Did the police come to the incident when you shot the guy?
> PATRICK: Yeah, they came, but I was gone already when... They was looking for me because they told them who I was. Police just coming through looking for me. Going in my grandmother crib. My pops, they walking up to my pops giving him cards, like 'tell your son to come see me.' I thought I was going to hit 'America's Most Wanted' for a minute.

In this case, Patrick fled New York until he felt he could return without risk.

## DEFINING CLOSURE OR OUTCOMES OF VIOLENT EVENTS

Previous research generally has neglected the importance of defining closure in violent events (See Oliver, 1994 for an exception). Data on the outcomes of violent events beyond the immediate incident generally are unavailable in traditional data sources. The issue of event closure is especially problematic for adolescents. This section examines the "outcomes" of these violent events with a primary focus on defining closure. Different aspects of "squashed," completed, and ongoing conflicts were compared to identify situational contingencies. At least seven different types of outcomes are described; descriptive results are presented below in TABLE 8-6.

One goal of this study was to define respondents' involvement in potentially violent situations and compare those situations to completed events. Accordingly, respondents were asked to describe "squashed" or "deaded" events. They described at least three types of situations in which conflicts were "squashed:" before violence occurs, after violence occurs, and temporarily until the next opportunity arose.

### Squashed Before Violence

In the sample, 9% (27/298) of situations resulted in a non-violent outcome, i.e., the conflict was settled before violence ensued. In these situations, mutual agreement to end the dispute without violence was achieved. In some cases, third parties served as mediators to prevent situations from escalating. In these situations, both parties usually enjoyed the approval of others in the setting for squashing the conflict before violence. Nonviolent resolutions most often occurred in situations without weapons, especially, for squashing the conflict before violence. Specifically, 20 of the 27 squashed events involved no weapon, 5 involved guns, and 2 involved other weapons. This represents 18% of no weapon events, 4% of gun events, and 4% of other-weapon events.

One common feature of events that were ended before violence was the respondents' relationships to their opponents: the closer the relationship, the more likely the situation would be resolved without violence. The more closely tied the two combatants were the more likely they were to defuse heated situations.

**TABLE 8-6. Intersection of Type of Weapon by Outcome (N=306)\***

|  | Total n (%) | Gun n (%) | Other Weapon n (%) | No Weapon n (%) |
|---|---|---|---|---|
| **Event Outcome or Closure:** |  |  |  |  |
| Squashed Before Violence | 27 ( 9.1) | 5 (3.5) | 2 ( 4.0) | 20 (18.0) |
| Disrupted | 21 ( 7.0) | 7 (5.0) | 4 ( 8.0) | 9 ( 8.1) |
| Ongoing | 83 (27.9) | 57 (40.4) | 12 (24.0) | 16 (14.4) |
| Retaliation Anticipated | 29 ( 9.7) | 20 (14.2) | 3 ( 6.0) | 7 ( 6.3) |
| Squashed After Violence | 57 (19.1) | 17 (12.1) | 6 (12.0) | 33 (29.7) |
| Just Ended | 88 (29.5) | 33 (23.4) | 25 (50.0) | 33 (29.7) |
| Compliance | 24 ( 8.1) | 21 (14.9) | 2 ( 4.0) | 2 (1.8) |
| Don't Know/Missing | 8 | 7 | 1 | 0 |
| Total Valid | 298 | 141 | 50 | 111 |

\*Data were missing on different domains. Percentages are for valid cases only.

In the example presented below, Wesley described being angry at the opponent, but stated that the relationship bond took priority:

> INT: What happened?
> WESLEY: What I did? This nigga was bitchin' at me in my hallway and he pulled out a gun on me. So I took it from him. I disarmed him and pointed it at him, threatened to shoot him. Get the fuck out of my hallway.' Told him to get out.
> INT: What you all riffin' about?
> WESLEY: Nigga was like, 'yo, you a bitch-ass nigga,' you know, acting all big 'cause he got the gun there. You know. One thing led to another. Well, I had took this gun from my man, caused. What kinda gun?
> WESLEY: Little nine.
> INT: Did you think it was gonna be a shootout when things started to heat up?
> WESLEY: Nah. I mean, the nigga was my man, so I didn't really think he was gonna shoot me, you know... I knew neither me or him was gonna shoot each other. It was just the fact that we was mad at each other that time.
> INT: Alright. What did he do or say after that?

WESLEY: He's sorry.

INT: What did you do or say after that?

WESLEY: I gave him the shit back, threw it out the window to him.

INT: He saw it?

WESLEY: Mm-hm. Took it back home.

INT: How did the situation end? What was the outcome?

WESLEY: After, he went home and came back to my crib later on that night and apologized.

INT: You accepted it?

WESLEY: Yeah. Yeah, it's my man.

Providing apologies and backing down from threats were sometimes sufficient reason for actors to drop a conflict before it escalates into physical violence. In the example below, the opponent verbally insulted Antoine's friend. By reinforcing the norm of no fighting inside his aunt's house, Antoine may have helped to defuse the situation; however, it is the opponent's apology that allowed the actors to back down while still saving face. Antoine described the situation in the following way:

ANTOINE: This kid started arguing with my man. And so when we was—when (we) was ready to do our thing, he came back. He just got punk-ass with my man.

INT: What caused the beef?

ANTOINE: I don't know. I ain't know what was going on. I just know my man was arguing with him.

INT: And you got your man back? And I seen him arguing.

ANTOINE: I told my man to go downstairs and handle his business. 'Cause I didn't want—I didn't want no fights in my aunt's house.

INT: Um, who made the first move towards violence?

ANTOINE: My man had bottle in his hand. Ready to pop his head open. There wasn't a second move. After that he [the opponent] apologized. That's it. It was over.

### Compliance Before Violence

Another 24 events ended without violence due to total compliance offered by the victim in the situation. Violence was not used in these situations because the actor(s) achieved their goal without it and it was unconsidered necessary. The majority of these situations (n=21) were armed robberies in which the victim complied and the actor engaged in no violence.

In the situation described below, Jessie and a friend were paid by a woman to stick up a man. The victim complied fully; however Jessie said he and his co-offender would have injured the victim anyway had it not been for the police presence in the area:

> INT: So what he was saying when this was going down? What—what, did he try to fight back or he thought—he thought it was a real gun?
> (Jessie): Yeah, he was cooperating.
> INT: Did you all hurt him?
> (Jessie): Mm? No, I was going to. Like, my friend was going to hit him on the head before we left. And then we heard sirens and shit, so we just left.

In the armed robbery of the jewelry store described below, the owners of the store complied with the demands of the robbers without much resistance. The respondent explained how the group got away, split the proceeds, and spent the money.

> INT: Y'all didn't hurt nobody or nothing?
> NOAH: Nah, we didn't hurt nobody.
> INT: So you said that people saw you. When y'all got away, was there people like chasing y'all?
> NOAH: Nah, nobody was chasing us. Everybody just shocked. We had masks on our face.
> INT: Y'all had masks?
> NOAH: Yeah. Black masks.
> INT: So how did this situation end? How did it end?
> NOAH: It just end like that. Hey, we had a—we got it, got it. Come through with the money. That's all we needed.
> INT: And what you did with the money? I mean, what you bought, you know?
> NOAH: Just bought school clothes. I just bought a lot of stuff, man. Equipment, system. All that.

## Squashed After Violence

Respondents were able to achieve closure after engaging in violence with an opponent in 19% of violent events. Events defined as "squashed after" violence included some type of resolution or abandonment of the conflict. In many cases, incidents of violence may have occurred between combatants, but eventually they agreed that the beef was over. Mutual agreement or mutual disinterest in continuing the battle was necessary for a beef to be "squashed after" violence. In these cases, respondents reported that no additional violence was needed or expected.

The majority of events "squashed after" violence involved situations with no weapons. Of the 57 events in this category, 12% of gun events, 12% of other-weapon events, and 30% of non-weapon events were "squashed after." Clearly, weapon events were more likely to continue or to result in multiple incidents.

An example of a gun event that was "squashed after" violence is presented below. In this conflict, classified as resulting from neighborhood or territory issues, the combatants reconciled after several back-and-forth incidents:

> INT: Alright, how did the situation end? You still got beef with the nigga now?
>
> TERRY: Nah, we all became close. We, like, started—we started affiliating with started hanging out. Started became close. So it was just basically a young thing, I figured out. It was just a young thing. 'Cause we all started getting cool after that.
>
> INT: What you say, your friend got hit with the garbage can? Nobody else got shot, right?
>
> TERRY: Nah, nobody else got shot.
>
> INT: Was it a minor wound, or?
>
> TERRY: Yeah, it was a little scratch. It was kind of deep, though. He needed stitches, 'cause the garbage can or whatever. I think you know, shit is metal, so the shit, it cut into him. But it didn't go in and stick or nothing. But he was alright. each other. Hanging out, whatever. I was telling you about this little team all of us.

In the respondent's eyes the conflict resulted from the immaturity of the parties, and the two groups ended up becoming friendly after several shootouts and fights. Although the potential for serious injury existed no one was seriously wounded. The outcome of these conflicts may well have been less amicable if the gunplay had resulted in death or serious harm. The narrative in which one inmate had taken the respondent's belongings and set him up to fight for them described in

Chapter 7 is an example of an incident that was "squashed after" the fight. Terry explained that by putting up a good fight (despite losing), he won back his property from the opponent. The event defined Terry's status with the opponent, who warned him "not to play {him} close" and told him he would do the same.

**Temporary Closure: Events that Just Ended**
According to respondents, 30% of violent events reported "just ended." In these situations, closure occurred without agreement or resolution, and thus, appeared to be temporary rather than permanent. Respondents noted that they were not actively planning to seek out the opponent to keep the conflict going, but rather that the possibility of future conflict remained. If the opportunity arose, violence may erupt again between the parties. Events "just ended" either as a consequence of what Oliver (1994) called "internal closure" (i.e., the "incident was over immediately after the respondent had dominated his antagonist" Oliver 1994: p 121) or for some other reason. Serious injury often resulted in events that "just ended." The actors in these events frequently (in 53% of event that just ended) were strangers. One interpretation of this finding could be that routine interaction or opportunity plays a part in the continuation of violent events. Social distance may limit the opportunities for future conflict or may offer legitimate reasons to walk away from conflict without losing face.

Actors used a variety of tactics to get away from armed opponents. Often an incident is the last time the two parties ever see each other. In one situation, sparked by a stranger's bump a respondent described how he got away:

> INT: How did the situation end? What was the outcome?
> ANTOINE: I went to... well, when he was shooting at me I tried to run to the train station but then I got up the train. I mean, I got up to the train station and started walking through the police precinct. When we came back over there we didn't find them.

After the incident Antoine returned to that neighborhood to get revenge on the opponent for the gun attack. Although Antoine was motivated to seek revenge, he could not locate his opponent.

In an incident described previously as a personal and material attack in front of a tattoo parlor, Clarence explained how the situation ended:

CLARENCE: ...but the man who own the tattoo place had came downstairs and he was like 'yo, you know what's going on?' And we was like—we was like 'yo, some kids tried to play us.' He was like 'yo, they always doing that, yo, watch yourself. Don't be outside too much.' So we went upstairs and we stood up. But that was kind of an incident—I don't know, I kind of felt happy that I had a joint 'cause I— I wasn't letting nobody take advantage of us like that so I felt I could defend mines. It gave me more confidence. And I intimidated them and it kind of worked out and they broke out.
INT: So that was the end of that, that was the—y'all got y'all tattoos and y'all broke out?
CLARENCE: Yeah. We got our tattoos and stepped.
INT: True... Um. Your aunt never said nothing to you about that afterwards?
CLARENCE: Nah. She was like 'yo, see? Fuck with the bulls, you get the horns.' She made a little joke out of it.

Clarence concluded that the event was a positive experience for him because he successfully defended his rights, friends, and property. As Clarence explained, it was a confidence-builder for him. The owner of the tattoo parlor reinforced the "successful" performance by warning the kids about the dangers of being outside in the neighborhood. His comments like: "they always doing that," "watch yourself," and "don't be outside too much" were supportive of Clarence's definition of his own actions as appropriate.

Compared to other outcomes, there were an equally large number of events that were classified as "just ended" across each of the three weapon types. For instance, 23% of all gun events had this outcome, 50% of all knife and other-weapon events, and 30% of no-weapon events "just ended."

**Forced Endings: Disrupted Violence**
Events ended prematurely in 7% of situations. In most cases, endings were forced by police officers, school officials, security guards, or others. Typically, the immediate threat of punishment or social control prompted actors either to attempt one last punch or shot or to flee the scene. The disruption often was sufficient to allow the conflict to dissipate. In fact, respondents rarely described a desire to ignite additional violence in disrupted situations. There was very little

difference across the three weapon types for this outcome (5% of gun events, 8% of other-weapon events, and 8% of no-weapon events).

Many of the gun situations involved threats and even weapon use but further action or harm was interrupted by some external factors. In the example below, the security guards prevented Eric from shooting his opponent:

> INT: What about after that?
> ERIC: We go to this club. My girlfriend didn't go with us that night. I was talking to a girl, dancing. I had heat on me. I had a .45. Dancing, dancing. This guy push me. I look and said, 'Don't touch me!' [he said] 'What you gonna do? You dancing with my chick.' ' I dancing with your chick. Her, I didn't know she was your chick.' 'Nah, you disrespect me, I gotta do something.' He swung and punched me. I moved back and laughed at him. I pulled out in the club. I tried to blast him. The security guards all charged me. That's it, they busted me. Two months. I stayed there for December to February. Still got in a couple of fights, beefing, but no more jail.

### No Endings: Ongoing Conflicts

Nearly 28% (83/298) of the violent events were classified as ongoing. Ongoing violent events were serious conflicts, and situations continued beyond the first violent interaction for a variety of reasons. Injury to one's health or reputation often evoked the desire to retaliate against an opponent over other, more peaceful alternatives. Harm to others, especially lethal or serious harm, often sparked the continuation, or "torch-taking," by close friends or relatives.

Many event narratives presented in the first half of this chapter were classified as ongoing and likely to result in additional violent events. Some of the events described were the second or third event in a series of incidents.[13]

The violent conflict described below actually consisted of five separate, but connected, incidents between the same combatants. The initial incident resulted from Grover's dislike of the opponent and involved a threat with a gun following a verbal challenge. The second encounter involved a fight without weapons, which Grover lost. The

---

[13] Only portions of those events are described in detail.

third event followed immediately thereafter; Grover attempted to stab
the opponent following the loss. In the fourth event, Grover fired three
shots at the opponent and was grazed on the ankle when the opponent
returned fire. This situation, although an extreme case for the sample,
illustrates how the "end" of one fight could spark the beginning of the
next if the outcome was unsatisfying to the participants:

Event #1 INT: Okay, so what happened describe the situation.
GROVER: Alright. Um, I am coming home one day from school,
right? And I see this black kid right next to me, you know. So I
am smoking a blunt. I puffed the blunt. I flicked all the ashes on
his leather jacket on purpose because he was acting like a monkey.
Listen to that rap music, diddy-bobbin mad hard. So the next thing
you know, we walk down a block. So we beefing and shit. He go,
he went up in his building. I went into my projects, right. So
boom, I went upstairs I go get my toast [gun], boom. So he in the
middle of the project, boom. He just ripping [talking loud].
'Ahhh, you talking mad shit.' Yeah, boom boom, so I show him
my shit and all that. He know that I got my burner on him but he
still want to pop shit. So I aim but didn't bust him in broad
daylight.
Event #2 GROVER: The next morning we going to school. I see
him, so when that next day, whoop, we shoot a quick 5 minutes.
Do do do do da da do da doom. You know. He did his thing. He
had a little weight. He lift me up on my feet, got me down, boom.
But I rocked him 'cause I am good with the hands.
Event #3. GROVER: I went back upstairs. I ran back—I ran up
got a butcher knife. I knew—and he was going to school. So I
chased up after him in the school. I try to stab him up in front of
all his friends. Like six kids. His friends helped him, pushin' him
away from me and everything. He got on the train, then I broke
out.
Event #4 GROVER: Then the next night. I hadn't seen him and
shit. So boom, he was coming with his people and shit. But he
ain't had no gun on him. I had my gun on me. So next thing, I see
this man in the store, right. Soon as I seen him in the store, I just
open the door like 'yo, what up, nigga, hold your head man, it's
coming for you.' So boom, as soon as the door closed. I walk up
into my projects. So he walk through. I started licking on him.
Beka beka beka, I let off three shots at him. He started ducking.

He started running under the benches. Started throwing the garbage can on the floor. I am starting to run too. I smell cops all over. So the next thing you know, his man come down. His man, already he had his. He was ready downstairs with a burner. He had like some fucking—he had a TEC (automatic handgun), yeah, some shit. Yeah, 'cause this shit was licking. So next thing you know I am running up in my building. One of them shit hit me in my fucking ankle. I ran upstairs to the ambulance. You understand? I didn't snitch on him or nothin'. I said to myself 'Yo, you know what? This nigga shot me. I got caught by a unknown bullet and I am going to see this nigga. Wait til he try to blaze me.'

Event #5 GROVER: ...So I seen him the next weeks, right. I got my hoodie on. He ain't even see me. I got a couple of peoples with me. I got like three fellows with me. So the next thing, we at a party and shit. We drinking 40s and everything like that. I didn't drink nothing that night. Everybody started drinking the most. He gets happily drunk and everything. So the next thing you know—I got a hoodie. He couldn't see me. ...I put on my hat, my gloves, and everything. Ran up from behind with my three boys. My two boys grabbed his arms. I just ran up through him and just cut him. Slashed him in the neck. I don't know if he lived or died. He was drunk. He thought everything was all forgotten. Little do he know in his sleep is the kiss of the death. But I never see this guy after that day.

INT: Did you know the guy?

GROVER: Nah. Some cornball, some cheesecake-ass nigga. He live around my way, put it like that.

INT: What was it about the situation that made it necessary to handle beef the way you did?

GROVER: 'Cause he do what he had to do. I do what I had to do.

INT: And what was that?

GROVER: Stand up and approach my business.

INT: What made you shoot at him?

GROVER: 'Cause I ain't I trust him. He had gold teeth in his mouth. He had gold teeth on the bottom. He had fronts, the gold fronts. I don't trust guys with gold fronts.

INT: After all of this happen, did you change where you were hanging out?

GROVER: Yes, I had to change where I was hanging and where I lived at. Because that's provoking danger to me and my family.

Gun use events were more likely to lack closure than other-weapon and no-weapon events; 40% of gun events were classified as ongoing beefs, whereas 24% of other-weapon and 14% of non-weapon events were characterized as such. Respondents reported that they anticipated completing an act of retaliation against the opponent(s) in 10% of all reported events and in nearly 35% of situations classified as ongoing, 24% of those were gun events. According to the respondents, these conflicts would fester in their minds. The event would come to life when the respondent felt the time was right, (or, more accurately, when the odds tipped toward a favorable outcome for the respondent). The remaining 65% of ongoing conflicts would just simply continue, according to respondents, implying that resolution would not occur without some significant change of position.

### The Intersection of Spark or Reason and Other Situational Variables by Outcome

As indicated by the narrative descriptions, certain types of violent situations result in different outcomes. As shown in TABLE 8-7, outcomes correlate with situational factors depending on the type of event. The only significant correlation for events that were disrupted was when a respondent was having a conflict with a co-worker in the drug trade. Situations in which compliance was reached, or rather those in which the victim did not resist, typically were armed robberies of strangers committed by multiple offenders in the absence of third parties. Conflicts between friends were defused before violence tended to be unarmed conflicts. Violent events stemming from unfair play or cheating and events over females significantly correlated with the outcome category "squashed after." Situations that were squashed after violence were not likely to involve weapons. A negative correlation was found between events "squashed after" violence and gun use. Situations that "just ended" had no significant correlation with any of the motivational categories. Weapon type was significant, in that knives and other weapon events were positively correlated with situations that "just ended," while gun use was negatively correlated with that outcome. The presence of the respondent's boys was negatively associated with "just ended" situations, whereas respondents' status as drunk or high was positively correlated.

Events classified as "ongoing" correlate with a range of motivational and situational categories. For example, events sparked over drug business transactions, identity challenges, money or debt, revenge, and self-defense were positively correlated with the outcome category ongoing. These situations were less likely to result in closure. Gun use was positively correlated with ongoing events, while no-

**TABLE 8-7. Correlations of Outcome & Other Situational Factors**

| | Disrupted | Comp. Before | Squash Before | Sqush After | Just Ended | On Going |
|---|---|---|---|---|---|---|
| **Spark or Reason:** | | | | | | |
| Identity/ Status | -.08 | -.11 | -.04 | .08 | -.10 | .15* |
| Girl | -.07 | -.11 | .02 | .17** | -.07 | -.03 |
| Self-Defense | -.02 | -.07 | -.14* | -.01 | .03 | .16** |
| Robbery | -.04 | .35** | -.16** | -.14* | .07 | -.10 |
| Drug Business | -.02 | -.03 | -.05 | -.04 | .01 | .16** |
| Revenge | .02 | -.10 | -.08 | -.06 | -.11 | .28** |
| Defense of Others | .07 | -.11 | .03 | -.07 | .05 | .04 |
| Rumors | -.02 | -.08 | .07 | -.02 | .08 | .00 |
| Neighborhood Honor | -.07 | .09 | -.02 | -.04 | .11 | -.05 |
| Money/ Debt | -.01 | -.07 | .08 | -.00 | -.06 | .12* |
| Unfair Play | .01 | -.05 | -.05 | .13* | -.01 | -.03 |
| **Weapon Type:** | | | | | | |
| Gun | -.06 | .23** | -.19** | -.16** | -.14* | .26** |
| Knife | -.02 | -.11 | -.08 | -.05 | .13* | .01 |
| Other Weapon | .06 | .05 | -.02 | -.03 | .13* | -.07 |
| No Weapon | .03 | -.18** | .24** | .19** | .01 | -.23** |
| **Relationship with Opponent:** | | | | | | |
| Friend | .05 | -.06 | .17** | .24** | -.11 | -.13* |
| Acquaintance | -.02 | -.10 | .03 | .13* | -.06 | .03 |
| Co-worker | .12* | -.02 | -.08 | .03 | -.05 | .06 |
| Rival | -.11 | -.06 | -.07 | -.06 | -.04 | .25** |
| Stranger | -.00 | .19** | -.07 | -.22** | .13* | -.14* |
| **Presence of Third Parties:** | | | | | | |
| Respondent's Boys | .03 | .12* | -.07 | .03 | -.12* | .06 |
| Opponent's Boys | .03 | -.13 | -.05 | -.04 | -.08 | .20** |
| Bystanders | .05 | -.39** | .04 | .08 | .07 | .09 |
| Drunk or High | .04 | .00 | -.01 | -.02 | .16* | -.09 |
| Injuries | .07 | -.01 | -.07 | -.06 | .07 | .03 |

*Significant at the .05 level; ** Significant at the .01 level.

weapon events were negatively associated with this outcome. Participants in violent events ongoing tended not be friends or strangers but rather conflict rivals. The presence of the opponent's boys was positively correlated with ongoing events.

## INJURIES

Respondents reported that serious injuries resulted in 65% (124 of 191) of violent events. Logically, injury was more likely if weapons were involved. Of the 99 gun events that included information on injuries, 73% ended with a serious injury, and 92% (33 of 36) of other-weapon events resulted in serious injury, while only 36% of non-weapon events did.

**TABLE 8-8. Intersection of Type of Weapon by Injuries (N=306)\***

|  | Total n (%) | Gun n (%) | Other Weapon n (%) | No Weapon n (%) |
|---|---|---|---|---|
| **Injury:** |  |  |  |  |
| Squashed Before Viol. | 27 ( 9.1) | 5 ( 3.5) | 2 ( 4.0) | 20 (18.0) |
| Someone injured | 124 (64.9) | 72 (72.7) | 33 (91.7) | 21 (35.6) |
| No Injury | 67 (35.1) | 27 (27.3) | 3 ( 8.3) | 38 (64.4) |
| Missing | 115 | 49 | 15 | 52 |
| Total Valid | 191 | 99 | 36 | 59 |
| ---------- |  |  |  |  |
| Respondent Injured | 25 (20.2) | 10 (13.3) | 8 (13.6) | 8 (38.1) |
| Opponent Injured | 70 (56.5) | 38 (50.7) | 20 (33.9) | 13 (61.9) |
| Other Parties Injured | 33 (26.6) | 27 (36.0) | 11 (18.6) | 0 ( 0.0) |
| Total Valid (Inj.) | 124 | 75 | 39 | 21 |

\*Data were missing on different domains. Percentages are for valid cases only.

### Concluding Remarks about Closure

As shown above, defining closure in these situations was problematic and warrants further study. Respondents described the anticipation of retaliation by the opponent (and usually his friends), and the anticipation of retaliation by the respondent (and usually his friends), as well as actual retaliation by either. Thus, the ending of one violent event often sparked the beginning of the next. It seems that for a conflict to end with resolution, a number of conditions must be met, including agreement that the conflict was over, conveyed through verbal and nonverbal gestures between the parties and their associates. Again, relationships were the most powerful predictor of the type of outcome for these events. Weapon choice also was influential in determining the outcomes of violent events; gun events were less likely to reach closure, while fights without weapons were much more likely to achieve closure.

## THE AFTERMATH OF VIOLENT EVENTS

The violent events described by the respondents often had consequences beyond the immediate situation. Following a violent event many respondents felt that additional attacks were imminent, their opponents were more likely to be armed in future confrontations and therefore, they needed to be armed more frequently, they needed the protection of their peer group. Finally, the talk or gossip following many of these violent incidents also may have consequences for future violence, drug business, safety, and social identity.

### Additional Violent Events

Additional violence may occur via direct routes such as retaliatory violence or through more indirect means such as leaving individuals behind without protection. The aftermath of one violent event may have unforeseen consequences for competition over power and control of street life. The defeat of a powerful street character could shift the violence hierarchy of social relations on the street. The story presented below illustrates some of the things that can happen after one violent event. In this example, Patrick described his absence from New York as having contributed to the murder of two of his associates:

> INT: After this altercation happened, was there talk in the neighborhood about it?
> PATRICK: Oh, word. Police was looking for me, son. Niggas was like, 'yo, son smoked that nigga, son. Son shot that nigga in the head five times.'
> INT: So what happen, when the police left you came back to check the scene?
> PATRICK: Yeah. Yeah, I went back and they was like 'yo son, you crazy, kid. You rocked that nigga.'
> INT: Niggas was amping you up and shit?

PATRICK: Yeah, son, you know. I had to go get my little props. I always felt like a original killer but I wasn't happy because I was satisfied. I was like 'yo, I fucked up.' That is when I realized I fucked up. When it was too late. 'Cause now I wasn't being able to get no sleep.

INT: Did anyone encourage you not to [do it], dead that shit, dead that shit like that?

PATRICK: Yeah son, my partner, 'cause he was like 'yo, we making money, we can't afford this shit right now. And the shit took down my whole business. Word. I regret doing it because all my business went down. And then after that, my best friend and my cousin got killed.

INT: Was it related to this?

PATRICK: It wasn't related to it, but I could say it was related because if I wouldn't have did that, then I wouldn't have had to leave New York. 'Cause I had to go on the run for a few years 'cause the cops was looking for me to give me 25 to life. My best friend had to go on the run, and by us both leaving my cousin got killed because he was by his self. And by me and my best friend not being around the same way, he got killed. So I can say it is stimulated from this.

### Need for Increased Protection

Concerns about personal safety following a violent event were very common. Many respondents described the need to enhance personal protection. Respondents described the concept of "sleeping" or being "off-point" as extremely dangerous. Most took a proactive stance toward warding off retaliatory attacks by preparing for the worst. Enhancing one's self-protection capability was a common theme that ran through the individual-level descriptions as well as the event-level data presented in the first part of this chapter.

### Gossip or Rumors After an Event

We have already discussed how gossip or "he said, she said" situations lead to specific violent events, in this section I examine how gossip about the violent event extends the life an event and can lead to additional violence. Some type of conversation about what had occurred and who was involved followed most violent incidents described by the sample. Within peer group, retelling of "war stories" was extremely common. It appears that respondents make sense of their actions, look for social reinforcement, and were entertained by the stories. Telling "war stories" was described as a ritualistic part of the violence process. Many times after an incident, there would be talk on the block about what had happened before the individuals involved even had the opportunity to tell their versions of the story. Often these rumors were inaccurate, partial, and fueled additional violence. Positive gossip about one's performance was potentially status-enhancing; however, it could also lead to additional problems. For example, if the performance of one individual was rumored to have been powerful and dominant when in reality it was not, the person with the "one-down" position may become enraged. Gossip may spark undeserved praise or humiliation, or simply distort the reality of the conflict. Gossip was especially powerful between individuals who were acquaintances from the same neighborhood or school. Gossip was a powerful mechanism in promoting the symbolic audience to violent events. Strangers from outside the neighborhood would be less likely to have knowledge of street gossip. Both males and females participated in gossip about violent events.

## SUMMARY

Guns have symbolic as well as strategic meaning. Gibbs and Merighi (1994) suggest that guns are symbols both of masculinity and identity. Respondents in this study reported that showing a gun (threatening someone) was a sign of disrespect, a violation of one's social and physical space. Guns also changed the calculus of a dispute, raising the stakes both in terms of status and strategy. Once a gun was introduced into a conflict situation, it was perceived as a life-or-death situation. Following this type of disrespect, the opponent was expected to retaliate by getting a gun and shooting the other person. In a gun face-off situation, the main strategic move reported was to take the first shot in anticipation of the opponent using his weapon first if given the opportunity.

Violent events were described as public performances with often-serious implications beyond the immediate interaction. Violent events in which guns were involved included the active participation of "co-offenders" in 67% of cases compared to 33% of non-weapon events. The violent performances given by our respondents reflect concerns about gains or losses in individual and group status as one of many possible outcomes. Respondents were more likely to engage in gun violence with a stranger or rival than with a friend, co-worker, or neighborhood acquaintance. Gun events were more likely to occur on street corners, in unregulated clubs or parties, or other public spaces with limited social controls, and were less common in schools or jails. Respondents frequently became involved with gun events while under the influence of alcohol or drugs. Gun events were 3.8 times more likely to occur when a respondent was under the influence of drugs or alcohol, in fact, respondents report being drunk or high in 80% of the situations; for non-gun events the ratio was 1.2: 1. Naturally, serious injuries were more likely in situations with firearms compared to no weapons. Situations in which knives and other weapons were used also resulted in a high rate of injury. Gun events were less likely to reach resolution, while fights without weapons were much more likely to achieve closure.

The neighborhoods studied here could be best characterized by an absence of effective adult informal and formal social controls. Both the process and outcome of violent events was significantly different when an able party got involved to end a conflict. The majority of the events had no such agent of social control. Although we recognize the need for positive adult influences in the lives of young people and we see the presumed outcome of the lack of adult involvement, we do not fully understand how the lack of capable adult guardianship effects youth from their perspective. Further, if our nation's streets are "controlled" by the tough delinquent and criminal youth it may be difficult for adults or government-funded service providers to redefine the social norms at the community level. The level of effort required to make a significant change in a local community is virtually unknown. Perhaps there is a "tipping point" at which community adults are motivated to become more involved in the daily activities of neighborhood youth. The viewpoints of youth on the roles that adults play in the regulation of daily life in low-income inner-city neighborhoods could generate important hypotheses for further research and policy reform. The next chapter examines the role that violent events play in the process of status or identity development among adolescent males.

# CHAPTER 9

# Violent Events and Social Identity:
## Specifying the Relationship between Respect and Masculinity

"Toughness" has been central to masculine identity in many social contexts of American life. Issues of respect, honor, and pride are repeatedly described as central features of male identity formation beginning in early adolescence. Physical prowess, emotional detachment, and the willingness to engage in violence to resolve interpersonal conflicts are seen as hallmarks of adolescence (Anderson, 1994; Anderson, 1999; Canada, 1995; Messerschmidt, 1993). While these terms have been used to explain high rates of interpersonal violence among nonwhites in central cities, toughness has persistently been highly regarded, a source of considerable status among adolescents in a wide range of subcultures from streetcorner groups to gangs (Canada, 1995; Goffman, 1959; Goffman, 1963; Goffman, 1967; Goffman, 1983; Hagedorn, 1997; Hannerz, 1969; Miller, 1958; Toch, 1969; Whyte, 1943; Wolfgang & Ferracuti, 1982).

The process of self-preservation through displays of toughness, nerve, or violent behavior is considered a necessary part of day-to-day life for inner-city adolescents, especially young males (Anderson, 1994; Anderson, 1999; Canada, 1995; Wilkinson & Fagan, 1996). Violence often is used to perpetuate and refine the pursuit of toughness, and to claim the identity of being among the toughest. Acquiring fighting skills (and perhaps more importantly shooting experience): is considered important as a means of survival in the inner city (Sullivan, 1989:113). Perceived insults or transgressions typically have been grounds for fighting (Anderson, 1978; Cloward & Ohlin, 1960; Strodtbeck & Short, 1968; Suttles, 1968; Thrasher, 1927; Whyte, 1943; Wolfgang, 1958). "Fair fights" have consistently represented the most elementary form of interpersonal violence among inner city youths.

Impression management seems to be an important aspect of negotiating the street world. The status and reputations earned through violent means provide inner city adolescent males with positive feelings of self worth and "large" identities especially when other opportunities for identity development are not available (Hagedorn,

1997; Messerschmidt, 1993). The concept of respect or honor refers to granting deferential treatment to what Goffman called one's "personal space." One who grants another respect would acknowledge and esteem the other's individuality and personal space (or least not attack it). The adolescent male is looking to others to reflect back ("looking glass self" phenomenon): aspects of his own self-image which is constantly shaped and reshaped within the context of social interaction with others.

Until the 1960s, fatalities were rare, whether by firearm or any other weapon. And the circumstances that called for fighting generally were confined to territorial disputes, ritual displays of toughness, or family and ethnic solidarity (Fagan & Wilkinson, 1998a). Rising homicide rates among inner city adolescents in recent years suggest sharp changes in this social and behavioral landscape. The ready availability of guns increases the stakes of toughness among socially isolated inner city adolescent males (Fagan & Wilkinson, 1998a; Fagan & Wilkinson, 1998b). The use of guns has instrumental value that is communicated through displays of dominance and urban "myths," but also through the incorporation of gun violence into the social discourse of everyday life among pre-adolescents and adolescents. I have argued in earlier chapters that guns play a significant role in shaping the lives of many inner city adolescent males. There appears to be a growing number of situations and contexts where conflicts arise that may escalate to lethal violence. The use of violence may reflect both an apparent lowering of the thresholds for using weapons to resolve conflicts and a socialization process into a world where gun use is valued and necessary. The presence of firearms influences decisions both in social interactions with the potential for becoming disputes, and therefore affects the public identity making process.

Social identity and respect are the most important features of the street code. As one respondent puts it: "To you it's all about respect. You gotta get your respect out here, man. Gotta get your respect." Within this context, there are clear-cut rules for using violence to gain respect. The public nature of a person's image or status identity often requires open displays of "nerve," including attacks on others, getting revenge for previous situations with an opponent, protecting members of one's social group, and having the right to "props." There is only a limited amount of respect available and the process of acquiring respect is highly competitive. Projecting the right image is all-important in this context and backing up the projection with violent behavior is expected.

Anderson (1999): suggests that the alienation, social isolation and despair about the future experienced by many inner city residents, may have created an alternative system of developing positive identities and building self-esteem that is reflected in what he calls the "code of the streets." According to Anderson, the street code provides rules for how individuals are to communicate with one another, how respect is to be earned, how and when respect is granted to another, and what should happen when someone disrespects you. Violence is used as a tool in promoting one's self-image. Developmentally, as children begin to approach adolescence there is a stronger need for social approval and status. Ecological theories would predict that these needs would be even stronger in an inner city context where fewer opportunities for receiving positive status (according to middle-class values): are available to young adolescents. Though Anderson's work provides a cohesive framework for understanding aspects of inner city life and violence, this framework is limited in that it was primarily derived from a single research tool (ethnographic study), derived from a restricted setting (Philadelphia neighborhoods): and, most importantly, focused on an adult-oriented perspective.

Symbolic interactionist studies of social identity emphasize the group or public nature of interaction that enables individuals to form and maintain personal and social identities (Cairns & Cairns, 1994; Eder, with Evans, & Parker, 1995; Kinney, 1993; Schwendinger & Schwendinger, 1985). According to Goffman (1963), group formation crystalizes one's personal and social identity. Social identity has a stronger influence because "individuals have little control over situations and especially going outside of the expected role for their particular social identity" (Goffman, 1963: 128). Many of the vital functions of adolescent social life operate through these groupings whether they are loosely or tightly connected (e.g. social learning and mentoring, play, nurturing, social support, and economic opportunity). Goffman argues that the "norms regarding social identity pertain to kinds of role repertoires or profiles we feel it permissible for any given individual to sustain" (Goffman, 1963:63).

The process of categorizing others (from one's own frame of reference): shapes human experience. Researchers have described the dynamic nature of social identity during different periods of adolescent development. Kinney (1993): for example, found that "identity recovery" was possible through increased opportunity and diversity of peer groups (Kinney, 1993). These school-based studies show that the school setting offers a myriad of opportunities and constraints to identity development. The street, as a social context, offers a similar opportunity for adolescent identity formation, trials, and maintenance.

The complexity of developing positive social and personal identities among inner-city minority males is both structurally and situationally determined (Anderson, 1990; Anderson, 1994; Anderson, 1999; Billson, 1981; Majors & Billson, 1992). The physical and social isolation that young people experience in the inner city undoubtedly shapes the range of behavioral and cognitive repertoires. Advanced segregation and social isolation of inner-city communities create social boundaries that effectively seal off adolescent networks from potentially moderating influences of other social contexts (Massey & Denton, 1993; Sampson & Wilson, 1995).

The social position of the inner city affords limited avenues for adolescents to obtain the types of social status and roles available to children in other ecological contexts. Street-oriented peer groups dominate social roles, with limited opportunity for broader participation in community life such as after-school groups, volunteer organizations, or supervised athletics (Short, 1998). In the absence of opportunities to participate in prosocial activities at the local community level, inner city adolescent often are unable to demonstrate the types of refined skills that bring status in later years.

Alternatives to conventional status attainment then, may be limited in the inner city to manifestations of physical power or domination, athletic performance, verbal agility, or displays of material wealth. Social status inordinately depends on one's position within social hierarchies, and for males those hierarchies often are established through manifestations of physical power or fighting (Anderson, 1999; Guerra, Nucci, & Huesmann, 1994; Hagedorn, 1997; Messerschmidt, 1993). The continual demand for personal respect coupled with limited avenues by which to attain it, sets up conflicts often resolved through fighting, an available pathway to high status. In these circumstances, cultural diffusion transmits such views and behavioral norms quite efficiently. See, for example, (Tienda, 1991).

The process of placing or defining oneself and others among adolescents has been studied primarily within the context of elementary and secondary schools (Brown, 1990; Brown, 1994; Eder & Enke, 1991; Eder et al., 1995; Kinney, 1993; Schwendinger & Schwendinger, 1985) and primarily with white samples –see (Billson, 1981; Cairns & Cairns, 1994; Majors & Billson, 1992), for an exception. Studies of adolescent identity in school settings consistently show that a status hierarchy exists within the setting and those individuals who are the most popular and visible get the most status (Cairns & Cairns, 1994; Eder et al., 1995; Kinney, 1993; Schwendinger & Schwendinger, 1985). Peer groups are very significant in the formation of personal and social identities in childhood and adolescence. The vast array of social interactions or "events" adolescent males participate in within this context is also important for identity development.

The current study shows that in the mid 1990s violence was still a viable tool for identity formation and maintenance among inner-city young men. The majority of our sample felt that violence was essential from their daily survival in their neighborhoods. The chapter describes a typology of situational identities that respondents report, how those identities are won and lost, and how young men compete for desirable identities. These complex processes unfold over time and have specific developmental stages. This chapter explores what appears to be a hierarchy of social identities among late adolescent males with regard to violent behavior. Young inner-city residents must learn to negotiate the street world by building a social identity, projecting a reputation, and developing a protective peer group in the neighborhood. The process of finding a niche and forming a "safe" identity typically includes engaging in violent behavior. Violent events occurring in the public context of social interaction serve as "defining moments" for identity formation and maintenance.

The importance of a dominance hierarchy of toughness appears to be most salient during the adolescent and early adulthood years for males. The data presented here illustrate several possibilities of how this process unfolds, and suggest that guns play a significant role in forming and sustaining "positive" social identities within the neighborhoods. As noted above, taking on one or more of these social identities varies by interactional context, stage of development, and social network. There is a competition for respect in the inner city, and the quantity of respect seems to establish one's place on a dominance hierarchy as well as one's social status (the two are intimately intermingled). I argue that information and impression management are the most critical tools young men use to negotiate the street. Knowledge of the "players" in the neighborhood is needed to determine what type of action is appropriate in a face-to-face encounter and how respect is to be apportioned. Individuals who have higher levels of status on the street expect to receive displays of respect. However, attacks on that status are also to be expected. The quest for respect in this setting may include both symbolic and overt expressions of violence.

## SOCIALIZATION AND IDENTITY

The social construction of male identity in the context of the street world follows specific age-graded tracks. It appears that violence plays a central role in defining social identities during different age periods in the inner-city street context. Development, age-specific expectations, and ritualized "rites of passage" add legitimacy to gaining and withholding respect through violent means. The examples and quotes illustrate respondents' experiences with victimization and the perpetuation of violence during these periods. Children growing up in this context learn to negotiate the neighborhood through both the use and avoidance of violence. Whether judged as right or wrong morally, boys find that violence is one of a small number of available resources that enable them to gain status. Violence is a resource for passage from one status or identity to another. Crafting a powerful social identity is a critical tool for survival in the inner-city context.

Social standing can be achieved via several routes with the common thread of the threat or use of violent force. The socialization process into this dynamic is quite clear, according to our respondents. At an early age, males frequently experience violent attacks and must learn "how it is in the street." One respondent reported: "All right, say you're small, probably let people pick on you and stuff like that, just let them do what they want, but as you get older you start fighting back. You stop letting people take advantage of you." Developing a desirable social identity on the street appears to become important for males between the ages of 7 and 11. Defining one's status in comparison to others involves a number of staged plateaus or schedules. According to one respondent: "Everybody's a herb[14] when they're—in the beginning,

---

[14] A herb is a person who shows weakness and does not adequately protect himself from a physical assault or robbery. A herb is easily

...everybody I know who's keeping it real (being honest): has gotten fucked up so bad that they just don't wanna get fucked up no more. So that's why they act the way they act."

Two themes emerge in this analysis: young males have low status initially, and establishing status requires public acts of violence. The process, described by our sample as a kind of "who's who" of the street serves as a way of identifying potential threats and resources within neighborhood associations. Participation in violent social interaction provides young men with information about the abilities and potential of others with whom they share social space and time. The violent analysis described herein illustrates how performances in potentially violent situations work to make or break social identity.

This public performance allows others to classify and categorize males in terms of threat, power, "heart," and status:

DONNELL: Back in high school, I was new in school, and, you know, I was a freshman and the niggas thought shit was sweet, I used to go to school uptown. And of course the fact that I was from Brooklyn, I had to represent Brooklyn, so there was other freshmen that was getting hurt and beat up and, you know, stuff like that as part of initiation into the school. And I could not see that happening to me. So I retaliated with my violence, and I beat up the biggest nigga out {of} the crew in the school, you know, just to let niggas know what I was capable of doing. So that was the only time I really used violence (to get reputation), you know...

As with other social contexts, peer groups play a significant role in defining social identities. Belonging to a clique or streetcorner group may fulfill a variety of needs for young men, including protection, income generation, adventure, companionship, love, identity affirmation, partying, and drug/alcohol consumption in a social atmosphere. The social network, among other contexts, enables masculine views to take shape. Groups also take on social identity, and group affiliation brings with it privileges and obligations. According to our data, criminals and those who exhibit tough qualities and behavior were the "populars" and got the most attention from others. One

---

manipulated by others to run errands, do dirty work that others did not want to do, or easily cheated out of money or property.

respondent described the attention that "bad guys" got in his neighborhood as very appealing to him as a young adolescent:

> TRAVIS: It got a lot... to do with people I was hanging with, and I seen that all the attention was going to the bad guys at that time. All the attention used to go to the criminals... everybody used to hang out in front of the school was known, and all the regulars known was the criminals. So I used to see that. So I used to get that 'damn, I want some attention, I want to be like them' and shit, you know. That's like damn I want to be like them and shit I want to be known. That's, that's what it is, I wanted to be known.
> INT: True.
> TRAVIS: And... my moms too, she wasn't giving me the money I needed and shit so, as you know, robbery was the best thing at that time. But this go—this is back in a—before I put that 10 month {incarceration} you know, I was into that bullshit. Then I moved up levels and shit, you know.

The pressure among peers to "be part of the scene" or to "prove that you are capable of using violence to fit in" to the street life is intense. Group influence seemed especially important in establishing one's identity. Tyrone described the pressure he felt at an early age:

> INT: Alright. Can you remember a time when you felt like a punk[15] or a herb?
> TYRONE: Yeah, when I was little.
> INT: When was it?
> TYRONE: I was in a public school.
> INT: What happened?
> TYRONE: {laughs} There was these guys that I used to hang with. But they was doing a lot, they was starting fights and everything and, but I wasn't with that, but I still wanted to be with these dudes. So they calling me a herb and punk.
> INT: 'Cause, 'cause you ain't wanted to get with?
> TYRONE: 'Cause I ain't want to get with them, I wanted to be with them, but I couldn't do what they was doing.
> INT: True. How old was you?

---

[15] Punks and herbs also are called "soft," "sucker," "wimp," "pussy," "bitch," "ass," and "chump."

TYRONE:  I was, like, nine.

Another respondent described how peers made assumptions about him based upon the type of house he lived in.  His belief that others felt that "shit was sweet in a private house" made him feel like an outsider.  Boys from the projects intensified this distinction by teasing and threatening Donnell.  To prove he was "status worthy," Donnell became the first kid on the block to have a gun.  The gun was used strategically to demonstrate his capacity for violence:

INT: Have you ever felt you needed to do something violent to amp up your own reputation?

DONNELL:  When I was young, yeah.  Being that I lived in a private house and the projects was right across the street.  You know, project kids automatically assume that shit was sweet in a private house...

INT: So what did you do?

DONNELL:  Kids from project(s): just came over with no problem because they figured all right, ain't that many niggas on the block and obviously if we living in the private houses, we must be pussy. {When I was} young, I always had a little burner {gun} or my pops always had a burner in the crib. But being that I had a burner, you know, as soon as they came with the drama, they came with bats and sticks, I already had a gun so I squeezed it off at them. Actually, I didn't really squeeze it off at them. I just pulled it out to let them know that I wasn't afraid. I pull(ed): it out to let them know that ain't nothing sweet over here.  And I wanted to squeeze after but, you know, back there and I still had some of my little teachings in me, so I didn't really do it. ...But they got the message by just seeing me pull out. They had sticks and bats and I had a gun.

INT: So did that help?

DONNELL:  Yeah, that helped.  No one really saw me as no punk or herb after that situation. They'd bring the drama to everybody else except me and my brother, my other man that was on the block...

Identity challenges occur when the status of others is not known or when the situation calls for definition and classification.  Shows of disrespect, or "dissing," often were defined by young males as an intentional attack or attempt to downgrade someone else's identity.  In order to preserve one's social standing, these challenges must be addressed aggressively. All parties in this type of interaction will define the situation from their reference point, which may include the collective meanings attached to the action. This identity negotiation or testing process clearly was central to the making, remaking, and breaking of identities. Respondents described the testing process as a necessary part of social development stabilized and strengthened their identities. One respondent described how "testing" occurs:

> INT: So what usually happens when nigga gets like this with you in your face or something?
>
> MALIK: Oh, man, that's like, testing your manhood. That's like, anything you ever been taught since you was younger, what's gonna come out now. Should you wait now, do it now, or handle it? Do you try to talk? Usually that don't even work, 'cause nobody's talking to you, they either—the more and more you try to talk, the more and more they gonna disrespect you. That's how I feel.
>
> INT: So, what happens if somebody, I mean, disrespect somebody, what—what happens?
>
> MALIK: They fight. I mean, they fight or they—or they threaten. They make threats to your mom, all types of threats, and you, like—you can't let this dude come after your moms.
>
> INT: Yeah.
>
> MALIK: ...{people} don't even be fightin' each other, they be teamed up, you know, they be tryin' hype it up. There may be one just two, three people and they—just buck wild over there. It didn't even {used to} be like that. And the more and more they hype it up, the more and more people read, damn, it's like? So, now they feels -- that's how they see somebody doin' that shit -- he ain't fuckin' with me. And it just keeps growin,' keeps growin,' almost nonsense—
>
> INT: Yeah.
>
> MALIK:—hate and that. Somebody don't know you or know who you are, what you about, they all gonna test you, all are gonna try to see what you about. It goes both ways, too. Maybe somebody think you cool and wanna know who you are. They wanna know if you blood or a bad guy, want to know if you good.

Robbery situations frequently provide young males with opportunities to impress their peers and upgrade status. Several of the examples described herein were ordered or set up by peers to define status:

> INT: Have you ever felt like you needed to do something to, like, fit in with your peoples?
> DAMONE: Maybe like smoke or something like that, or rob a nigga. Make sure you ain't no herb or nothing like that. Yeah, I did shit like that.
> INT: Yeah, what you needed to do?
> DAMONE: I had to steal a chain from a fucking lady.
> INT: Why for your little crew?
> DAMONE: Yeah, they told me to steal a chain so I stole it, to see if I had heart. So I went and I grabbed the chain and I whacked it. Went up to her and grabbed it, asked her a question and grabbed it.
> INT: What you asked her?
> DAMONE: I asked her where 42nd Street is at, and I was standing right on it. I just snatched the chain.

The projected identity or reputation an individual achieves has multiple dimensions. Violent performances can be seen as representations of self, group, and neighborhood territory and word of mouth can increase the social benefit of violent acts:

> INT: What is reputation about? Why is that, like, so important to young brothers?
> JABARI: It is like fame. Every time you do something to boost your rep that makes on a street level, it brings your fame higher and higher in your own little community. Boom, I live {in the projects}. It is divided into five sections. Every time a section come in and beef {with} my section, I get down for mine. Not only my section and that section will know. The other three section will know too. So my street level right there will go higher. Then it will hit the Cherry Valley Mall area and it'll just keep getting higher. So I'll be going to {a guy} from section three, 'Oh, I heard about you this, that,'...Yeah. 'Cause I mean it is bad. In a way, life is fucked up 'cause all the shit you did, you get in trouble for doing, is what you got to do. There is no way to avoid it. 'Cause it is

coming at you at every angle. I mean at first I thought All
right stay in school if you can stay smart and stay in school,
I'll be all right but...

## A HIERARCHY OF SOCIAL IDENTITIES

Teenagers may situationally engage in violent behavior to form and/or
maintain certain social identities within the broader social context of
the neighborhood. Projecting the right image may have consequences
for personal safety, social acceptance, and self esteem among
individuals. Within an isolated social world where respect and valued
social standing is limited, the threat of gun violence introduces new
complexities to the development of social identity. Respondents
described social identities such as: being "crazy," "wild,"or a "killer"
(one who performs extraordinary acts of violence), "holding your
own" (a functional fighter/shooter), and being a "punk" or "herb" (a
frequent victim struggling for survival).[16] Social identities become
more salient through repeated performance; the social implications of
each performance determines when and how an actor will be known to
others in the neighborhood, and, in turn, affect subsequent interactions.

Strauss (1997): explained that "face-to-face interaction is a fluid,
moving, running process; during its course the participants take
successive stances vis-a-vis each other. ...The initial reading of the
other's identity merely sets the stage for action, gives each some cues
for his lines" (Strauss, 1997:57). In addition, Strauss points out that
individuals classify their own identity in the situation, and "may also be
acting toward an invisible third, much as if the latter were actually
present" (Strauss, 1997: 58). These classifications are bounded by the
limits of personal experience and social structure:

> The person who knows his world well, who is familiar with all
> its pathways, is strongly committed. Committed to what? To a
> conception of himself as a certain kind -or kinds - of person,
> who is expected to, and himself expects to, act in certain ways

---

[16]The three types of social identity described here were the most common!
described by our sample. Most of the interactions were defined in terms c
avoiding being classified as a punk or herb. Respondents also did describe othe
violence-related social identities including "the avoider," "the nice guy," "th
beef handler," "too cool for violence," and others.

in certain situations. If the situations that arise are not entirely familiar, they are nevertheless somewhat like the old ones and demand similar lines of action (Strauss, 1997: 41).

Social identity may be built, earned, applied, or assigned (Strauss, 1997: 145). During the course of social interaction, individuals "may force each other into such statuses" (Strauss, 1997: 79). Strauss explained the process of "status forcing" with the following statement:

...Status positions exist not merely to be filled at appropriate times by appropriate persons -as in rituals; but they get assigned according to the witting judgments and often unwitting impulses evoked during interactional encounters. (Strauss, 1997: 85)

Status forcing has different consequences for the identity of actors depending upon the duration and permanence of that status. Strauss argued "it makes a difference whether the placement is temporary (banishment), permanent (exile), or of uncertain duration (idolization)" (Strauss, 1997:83). He explained that some forced statuses were "reversible" and therefore would have less long-term impact on identities. According to Strauss, social identity is extremely dynamic because it is in motion (e.g., identities on the way up and the way down, as well as those holding on).

An elevated social identity can both prevent violence from coming (he won't get picked on): and promote additional violence (other young men will attempt to knock him off his elevated status). The individual who performs poorly becomes known as a punk or herb. One who performs admirably gains status and becomes known for "holding his own." One who gives an extraordinary performance is labeled as "wild" or "crazy." These social identities may be temporary or permanent. The following section briefly describes the characteristics of these three ideal identity types.

The majority of respondents classified themselves as being someone who holds his own; a small number described themselves as fitting into the "crazy," "wild," or "killer" identity at the time of the interview. Few, if any, of the respondents classified themselves as a punk or herb; however, most respondents, 78% of those queried (71 of 96 respondents with available data), described one or more situations during childhood or adolescence of feeling like a punk or herb as a direct result of violence perpetrated against them by older, more powerful males. Every respondent described the importance of using violence to gain social status and personal security.

### Being Known as "Crazy," "Wild," or "Killer"

At the top of the identity hierarchy of the street is the "crazy," "wild," or "killer" social identity. Individuals who perform extraordinary acts of violence were feared and were granted a level of respect that is not easily attained. Approximately 14% of the sample described themselves or others as being "wild," "crazy," or a "killer." Some took on this identity temporarily or situationally while others described the identity as permanent. The performances that lead to these identities often were considered shocking or judged to be beyond what was necessary to handle a given situation. Once an individual gave an extraordinary performance, he may have noticed changes in the way others related to him. He may also have begun to view himself differently. This status brought with it a level of power and personal fulfillment that may be reinforced by projecting this identity and future violent performances would enable him to maintain the image of the most violent or toughest on the street. Bo, Austin, Alonzo, and Jose explained:

> BO: I seen him, one kid everybody used to look up to, and he thought he was impossible, he thought nobody couldn't –he thought he was a serious gangster. Couldn't be killed. ...He was the big man, he used to walk up to spots and rob people.
> INT: What made him a big man?
> BO: I guess the way he presented hisself. The way he went after people's spots, take their drugs, he didn't care. Like he was God or something. He got shot maybe a couple of times and thought he couldn't die. So I guess that's what made him the big man or made him feel like he was the big man.

> AUSTIN: Well they get respect like that, they want respect. Now-a-days niggas bust their gun, they ain't got to be trying to shoot you, they just bust their gun at you, make themself look big, that's the only thing, that's how it go, then they get respect, everybody going to be thinking he's a killer, he know he ain't no killer, but everybody think he a killer, unless he shine a gun.

INT: So when you shot the guy you shot... or when you found out he was dead or something, how did that make you feel?

ALONZO: It ain't hype me. It didn't make me feel like going out there and doing it again; it just made me feel like... I just got a stripe, that's how that made me feel. I got a stripe.

INT: Did you get a reputation after that?

ALONZO: Well, I kept a reputation but... 'cause I was into a lot of stuff, ...and thing(s): I did. Came to where I was like one of the people, I was like one of the most {violent} people they would come and get when it was time for conflict, than anybody. ...that I really be around when there {is} beef, when it's beef time they know who to come get. And out of those people, I was one of the top ones they would come and get... 'cause they always known me, ...for being trigger happy and...

INT: So what you was saying when the beef was going down?

JOSE: Yo, when the beef, at that time kid, yo, you mind blanks out. You just go crazy, man. Especially me, I went crazy. I didn't give a fuck what was going to happen to me, B. I just want to get the shit done. To you it's all about respect. You gotta get your respect out here, man. Gotta get your respect.

A person who has an identity as someone who is crazy, wild, or a killer gives off the impression that he has extreme "heart," is untouchable, and is unconcerned with the repercussions of violent acts. He has the capability to use extreme violence and gets respect for dominating others. Others may want to associate with him to benefit from his high status on the street. The identity itself carries privileges, expectations, and obligations that may catalyze additional violent encounters. The powerful identity may be downgraded by someone else's extraordinary performance.

**Being Known as "Holding Your Own"**
Many respondents characterized the process of "holding your own" in violent situations and described how personal identities formed around displays of "doing what you got to do" were generally positive on the street. The majority of the respondents would be categorized as "holding their own." Individuals who 'hold their own" were respected on the street, largely due to the numerous challenges that must be

overcome to attain and retain such an identity. A person who has an identity as someone who "holds his own," gives off the impression that he has the capability to use extreme violence but does so only when necessary. This person will face a challenge directly and is respected for that position. This identity allows an individual to be considered an "insider" with the street world; however, this status can be unstable and may require acts of violence when faced with public challenges. Most respondents described themselves as having this identity. Consider the descriptions provided by Rashard, Norm, Patrick, Donnell, and Malik:

> RASHARD: {Someone} who can just handle their own, who's not no troublemaker, but who finishes trouble when it comes.

> NORM: ...It's a lot of popularity, you know. Your image that you hold is your reputation. You need that on the streets 'cause without that then anybody... and everybody can do what they want to you. If...if you let them. But the rep that you have shall keep... you know, if it's a good rep, it will keep these people away from you, keep 'em on your good side. I mean, most people who know of you and know how you get down for yours, they know you don't play, that they won't mess with you, because they don't wanna get hurt, because of the reputation that you had. Maybe they don't wanna start because they know you cool, whatever.

> PATRICK: Yeah, you will go through people trying to get to know you. This, of course, is a problem because it starts when you younger by getting that reputation, you know, you not trying to be a killer or a thug, but you just want people to know, yo, who you is 'don't fuck with me I won't fuck with you.' So you got to break up a few heads you got to do whatever to get that reputation.

> DONNELL: I was always one holding my own. I always had peoples behind me. I was always a fighter.

> MALIK: Somebody who doesn't fight over B.S. Somebody who think, you know, who wants to shoot a fair one, it will be just a fight and he could hold his ground, hold his own. But it gotta be over somethin' important. It gotta be either somethin' personal between that nigga—you know, everybody ain't

gonna get along, but if you have a fight you might as well fight and get it over with. One lost, one lost, you know. They don't always go down like that. That's why I hate that, too.

As illustrated by the above examples, an individual who 'holds his own' has used violence as a resource for obtaining that status. These young men face the same type of testing process as the punk or herb; however, it is expected that this class of men will handle their conflicts with violence and it will be effective. If violence is not effective, someone who is known to 'hold his own" will be granted respect for putting up a good fight or taking a bullet "like a man." If someone gives a poor performance with a low status opponent, his social standing or identity could face a downward slide.

**Being Known as a "Punk" or a "Herb"**
At the bottom of the status hierarchy of the street is the "punk" or "herb." Like, the school-based "nerd" or "dweeb," the punk or herb identity is assigned to those who have failed to attain a high status or tough identity. In the inner city, those who cannot fight or prove their toughness may instead be stigmatized either temporarily or permanently, and other guys in the neighborhood will act upon that stigma. The process of "punking" or "herbing" someone, as respondents called it, closely resembled the process of 'fool-making' described by Klapp cited in (Strauss, 1997). Strauss states:

> Orrin Klapp has suggested the different conditions that determine how a person can become a fool and remain one: 'Because fool-making is a collective imputation it is not necessary, however, that a person actually have the traits or perform the role of the fool. A person is a fool when he is socially defined. ...What makes a fool role stick? Among the factors responsible for permanent characterization as a fool we may particularly note (1): repeated performances or obvious personal traits which continually suggest the role of a fool; (2): a striking, conclusive, or colorful single exhibition which convinces the public that the person is irremediably a fool; (3): a story or epithet so 'good' that it is continually repeated and remembered, making up an imperishable legend; and (4): failure to contradict a fool role by roles or stories of a different

category.' (Klapp, 1949, 159-160, cited in Strauss, 1997: 80-81)

If someone had the punk or herb identity, he was considered "fair game" for attacks and robberies. The attacks were motivated both by the need to restate the dominance hierarchy and as a punishment for not living up to group norms. If a young man did not have a tough identity or at least have close associates or relatives who could protect him, either by association or literally, he was a punk. Others in the setting degraded, dominated, and victimized individuals who have punk or herb characteristics, typically via direct or implicit emasculation of the "weaker" males. Punks and herbs also were called "soft," "sucker," "wimp," "pussy," "bitch," "ass," and "chump." Given the intensified acceptance of hegemonic masculinity in the inner-city context, these messages would have a strong negative impact on a punk or herb's self-image (Hagedorn, 1997; Majors & Billson, 1992; Messerschmidt, 1993). Most young men assumed that "outsiders" in the neighborhood (and relevant social network): were punks or herbs until the outsider proved otherwise. Several respondents offered definitions of the punk or herb identity:

> JOEL: The definition for a punk or a herb, well, around my 'hood {it} is like somebody that don't want to fight and shit. Like somebody would go up to them and push them or whatever and they won't fight back. So, you know, everybody call him a punk. And the definition for a herb is like, say, somebody who is being nice, or somebody who is scared of somebody, and they tell him 'yo, go do that, or go, do this.' And, you know, he is just, he listens to whatever they say. {The guy} is just sunning him, he's herbing him.

> GREG: Psst. That's easy yo. A punk or a herb is somebody who, it's somebody ...who let ...some next person ...make him do shit, make him feel like a sucker. Like if somebody walk up on you... and start talking and start mushing you in your face or putting his fingers in your face ...and you ain't constantly doing nothing about it or he's constantly motherfucking disrespecting you on the real, that's a herb. When you let that nigga get away with it you {are} a herb.

DAN: A person who can't defend himself or {is} scared to defend himself.

SCOT: Punk or a herb, getting played and not doing nothing about it, you know.

RASHARD: A herb is a bad ass nigga, someone who's bad and who snitches. You know, {he} gets into a altercation and they lose or something and {then} snitch...

## STATUS FORCING AND SITUATIONAL IDENTITIES

Negotiating the street necessitates tests of character, knowledge of the rules of respect, familiarity with the players on the street, and open displays of violence. Since the social identities of actors in the setting are ever changing, the testing process appears to be continuous until at least 20 years of age. The "mixed contacts" between young males of differing social standing provides the clearest context for observing all facets of status forcing—identity on the way up, on the way down, and holding steady. As Goffman states, "the very anticipation of such contacts can of course lead normals and the stigmatized to arrange life so as to avoid them. Presumably this will have larger consequences for the stigmatized, since more arranging will usually be necessary on their part" (Goffman, 1963:12).

For example, those who were attempting to transcend a punk or herb identity must interact with those who hold their own or those identified as killers in order to avail an opportunity for "identity recovery" (Kinney, 1993). Punks and herbs absorb all manner of abuse in inner-city neighborhoods. More powerful street guys use lower status males to test their nerve. A young male who "holds his own" may face threats from punks who were attempting to ascend into a higher social identity. An identity shift also can be publicly constructed through reinforcement and praise by observers and/or those hearing about the performance. Observers and others in the neighborhood offer rewards for these performances in the currency of respect. Violent behavior motivated by other issues may also have side benefits for social identity, especially among members of the peer group.

The street environment serves as the "classroom" for violent "schooling" and learning about manhood. One theme that emerges from this analysis is evidence of an age grading of identity building via violent performances. The data suggest that mixed age interactions play an important role in this process.  It appears that older children and adolescents exert downward pressure on others their own age and younger through identity challenges which, in part, shapes the social identities of both parties.  At younger ages, boys were pushing upward for status by challenging boys a few years older.  The social meaning of violent events reaches a broader audience than those immediately present in a situation.  Each violent event or potentially violent interaction provides a lesson for its participants, first-hand observers, vicarious observers, and others influenced by stories about the situation.  Children learn from personal experience and by observing others use violence to "make" their social identity (or at least one important vector of a young male's identity): or "break" someone else's identity on the street.  Three types of performances (poor, successful, and extraordinary): may occur in a violent event.  A poor performance is status depriving, a successful performance is status maintaining, and an extraordinary performance is status enhancing. The main focus here is to emphasize the role that violence plays in shaping situational identities.

Gun use may involve "crossing a line" or giving an extraordinary performance that shifts one's view of oneself from a punk or even holding your own to crazy or wild. Guns were used as a resource for improving violent performances.  The abundance of guns in these neighborhoods apparently has increased the severity of violent performances.  Guns have changed the meaning of toughness.  For the majority of our sample, guns became relevant for conflict resolution at around 14 years of age.

### Transcending the Punk or Herb Identity

Punks or herbs need to develop 'nerve' or a willingness to commit violence in order to deter future attacks and improve their standing in the neighborhood. As Goffman explains:

> The stigmatized individual can also attempt to correct his condition indirectly by devoting much private effort to the mastery of areas of activity ordinarily felt to be closed on incidental and physical grounds to one with his shortcomings (Goffman, 1963:10).

Countermeasures would include building fighting skills, aligning with tougher peers, acquiring and using firearms, and staging winnable violent events. Our respondents explained this process repeatedly when they reflected back on past experiences.

Face-to-face interactions that involve identity tests or challenges in the form of insults, looks, bumps, and other confrontations also represent status-forcing situations. In interactions on the street, social status is defined both individually and collectively. A lack of acknowledgment or denial of status by others may result in violence that under these circumstances may be justified as maintaining the dominance hierarchy.

The first example presented below illustrates the stigma a young man experiences when he was labeled a punk or herb. In this event, the respondent was jumped by a group of teenagers from another neighborhood after two of them demanded a hit off his blunt. Arlo refused to share and was offended by the request because the opponents were strangers to him. His friends were present but did not get involved in the fight. He described the situation as a learning experience that resulted in him arming himself, not relying on his friends for backup, and being better prepared for future violence:

INT: Alright. Can you remember any time when you were growing up that you felt like a punk or a herb?
ARLO: Yes. I felt like a punk and a herb when I fucking, when I was in the streets, and ...I used to get jumped. And niggas, you think you have boys, but niggas really don't look out for you... So you got to look out for yourself. So, yeah, I felt like a punk and a herb at one time.
INT: Did it bother you?
ARLO: Of course it bothered me. Everybody in the neighborhood, you know, saying, calling you a herb. Even the bitches make fun of you...
INT: So, can you tell me a little bit about an experience you went through when you was a punk?
ARLO: Yes. There was fucking one time I was chilling in front of the building ...just rolling the fucking blunt, trying to get my shit. And fucking two niggas came up to me and I didn't know them niggas. They fucking from another neighborhood. I was chilling and they were like, 'yo, let me get something,' ...like coming out all ruggedness. And I said, 'what the fuck?, ...I don't know your ass. I don't know what the fuck you have to pass my shit to you. Get the fuck out of

here.' And niggas came out. They broke out. Five minutes
later niggas came back with like six other niggas and fucking
just started beating on my ass. I took the one nigga and I was
knocking him, but I got my ass kicked.... My boys was
watching and they didn't do shit. So, I felt like a punk and a
herb.

INT: Why they didn't get in? They your boys, right?

ARLO: To tell you the truth, yo, in my neighborhood there
ain't no such thing as boys. ...Nobody looks out for nobody.
You got to be on your own. They your boys and everything,
but if they see a nigga that's bigger than him, or ...got more
props, {then} they punks.

INT: So, what happened with that? How did that situation
end?

ARLO: ...I had to go to the hospital for two or three days ...but
you know, I came back up. It's not like I fucking died or
nothing like that. I didn't get no broken bones or shit like that.
But they fucked me up, yes. I got to learn a lesson. I
experienced something.

INT: After that, you felt like you needed to do something to
amp up your reputation?

ARLO: Yes, like get a fucking ride, fuck up somebody, have a
piece. To be strapped and...

INT: What made you do that? I mean, you know, tell me a
little bit about that?

ARLO: Well, it's like I was fucking—I would go around and,
you know, if anybody looked at me hard, I would just fucking
snuff the shit out of them and if they wanted to fucking keep
going, I would just buck them right there, or fucking go with
my ride and just blast niggas. Fuck that. I don't give a fuck
about po-po (police).

For some respondents, a gun was the best solution to the punk or
herb stigma. In the next example, Jamal contrasted his current status as
a "hit man" to how he felt when bigger males in the neighborhood used
to pick on him. At age 19, he solved his conflicts with guns:

JAMAL: Yeah, man, I felt like a punk. When I didn't have no
motherfucking money I felt like a punk, man, 'cause
everybody have fun. I also feel like a punk when big

motherfuckers are bothering me. Big niggas like—big niggas when I was small used to always kick me in my ass. Ain't no motherfuckers kicking me in my ass in '96, 'cause I'ma put a fucking bullet in they ass, they want to kick me in my ass.

INT: Do you ever feel like a punk or a herb now?

JAMAL: Man, I don't feel like a punk now. I feel like, I feel like a motherfucking hit man right now, I feel like a hit man.

INT: You feel like a hit?

JAMAL: Yeah. Why I consider myself a hit man? 'cause my motherfucking man tell me that somebody did something to him, you ain't got to tell me too long 'cause I'm going to get him, that's why I consider myself a hit man. You give me the gun, the utensil; I'm going to use it.

## Avoiding the Punk or Herb Identity by Pushing Upward

The next example illustrates how one respondent, at 11 years old, fought with an older opponent to avoid being treated like a punk. As he explained the opponent was known as a bully and often picked on younger kids. The respondent described the importance of standing up for himself against his opponent:

INT: Umm, who was the guy you was fighting with?

LATRELL: Some nigga named Mike.

INT: What was your relationship with the guy?

LATRELL: We ain't have none. I knew was a bully, so I tried to keep away from him.

INT: How was he in size? Bigger, taller, smaller, shorter?

LATRELL: He was taller than me at the time, and wild.

INT: Around the same age?

LATRELL: Nah, he was 20. I was 11.

INT: Psst, you fighting 11, you fighting a 20 nigga? ...Go ahead, tell me what happened with the fight?

LATRELL: We playing football together out in the streets, this nigga hitting me, boom. I got away, I had two pieces of stick and started booking at this nigga, swinging at him, constantly.

INT: Y'all was playing football, and he just hit you in the back of the head with no kind of reason?

LATRELL:  See, we playing three second hold, right? Shit's dead, that's how I look at it. The play was dead. So {I said} 'why you swinging on me for?' I felt he swung at me.

INT:  You feel when he swung at you, or you know he swung at you?

INT:  For nothing?

LATRELL:  I thought it was for nothing. I said 'what the fuck you doing?' What the fuck he thinking, I'm the little man, since I was a little man, at the time, and he tried to push me away and shit, you know. I was like 'what the fuck this nigga trying to do.' So I got the stick—I got my little bat and went to work on his ass. I wanted to kill this nigga.

INT:  Was there any kind of argument before you went and got the weapon?

LATRELL:  Yeah. He hit me over my head, that's it. This nigga's right there, he like a bully, the bully of the block. He took advantage of the little niggas. I didn't go for that shit.

INT:  What happened next after that, what you did?

LATRELL:  I couldn't hit him in his head, so I hit him in his arms and shit... It was like three, four times, then he grabbed the bat.

INT:  And what he did?

LATRELL:  He was like 'shorty, don't be playing me like that.' That's when everybody came outside and broke it up.

## Getting Even for Punk or Herb Experience

The detailed gun event described below illustrates the significance of overcoming a punk or herb identity for a young inner-city male. This "revenge of the nerds" tale is an interesting story of how a 19-year-old African-American male got revenge for a punk/herb experience that occurred in junior high school. The incident started when Ben ran into someone who took his hat a few years earlier. Although Ben remembered his opponent readily, the opponent did not remember him. He was instantly heated upon seeing his enemy and remembering the previous negative encounter. Ben described the event as a very important experience of regaining something that was lost by humiliating and terrorizing his opponent. The respondent pulled out 9mm semi-automatic handgun and put it to his enemy's neck. He attempted to restore his opponent's memory by reminding him of the previous encounter when Ben's hat was taken and the opponent publicly humiliated him. Ben wanted to kill his adversary but instead robbed and pistol-whipped him. Clearly, Ben enjoyed the event, the event was especially rewarding because of his previous status as a victim. He explained:

> BEN: Yeah, a lot of niggas used to be scared of this punk-ass nigga. I mean...I ain't gonna front, you know I was a new head in school, niggas was like 'yo, he's a big man.' I was like, 'word,' I was a little punk-ass too, I was scared of him—I wasn't scared, I was just like, yo, I didn't want to get jumped. Back then I didn't really know how to fight.

The opponent showed fear, cried, and apparently believed that his life in jeopardy. The respondent and his friends were able to totally dominate the victim. The attack was a group activity that included six of Ben's friends against one unarmed victim. The respondent described the situation as if he were controlling all of the actions of his opponent as well as the behavior of his friends. He explained:

> BEN: I'm not really a killer, you know. I hit {him} with my pistol, I pistol-whipped his ass, he just fell to his knees. I just let my mans do what they wanted to do, they—they took off his pants and ...we let him run home in his underwear.

As Ben explained the gun played a central role in this event:

> BEN: Yeah, 'cause all he... {said was} 'just don't kill me,' he was saying that shit, niggas laughing at him. He was looking like a little sorry ass. Nigga really act pussy if they don't got a gun.

During the event, Ben was under the influence of alcohol and marijuana, a combination that he believes is explosive:

> BEN: Yeah, because I feel like when you drink you be, like, you become more looser. When you smoke you become more meaner. Both of them combined, it's just like total destruction.

When asked why violence was necessary in this situation, Ben expressed concerns about justice and revenge. He declared: "Because yo, whoever took something from me always pay the price. If not that

day, {then} someday. And they always did." He explained that this
situation compensated for negative experiences he had in his youth.

> INT: Thinking back, why do you think you did what you did?
> BEN: Because, see, I always {was} like a fighter, you know,
> but when I feel like I'm outnumber{ed}, {like} back in the
> days, I would just let it be. But as I got older I couldn't let it
> happen no more so you know I just had to do what I had to
> do."

The respondent was arrested but not convicted for this incident. He
said he felt good about the situation afterward because he performed
well. Ben was asked what was gained or lost from the situation:

> BEN: I didn't have nothing to lose and I gained everything.
> INT: You gained everything, like what?
> BEN: Respect. Yeah, man he took my hat. I ain't never seen
> nigga since. ...I heard he moved out of state.

## Status Forcing Among the Tough

Young males who hold their own or have thug status may face identity
challenges from peers outside their social network or geographic
territory. Many young males capitalize on situational opportunities to
force others' status downward, as described below:

> INT: Could you tell me how it occurred?
> LUKE: All right. I had a little problem with this kid for a
> while, ever since I has in high school, all right. He was a thug.
> He used to come around my projects, 'cause—my projects that
> I moved to. I'm originally from a certain project that is known
> for having a reputation of having all thugs in there. I had
> moved to these projects where it wasn't too many thug niggas.
> I was probably one of only thug niggas in there. So he would
> come around my way, fuck around with niggas, the herbs
> around my way, and he must've thought he knew where I was
> coming from, {like} once I moved to those projects I turned
> herb or some shit. My name ain't Herb. One day {his boys}
> had jumped me. I let that slide. I don't think he was there, it
> was he boys that did that. ...Then one day my peoples come
> over there to see me from my old projects. He there with his
> men. My man like 'what is the verdict, son, what's the
> verdict." Niggas try to take it out in the street. He acting like

he got a guard jewel {gun} on, he acting like he got something on him so. My man come to me like 'yo, let me get the heat,' {gun}. Yeah, all right I go in alive, I grab it, make sure it is loaded. ...When he get around the kid he gives it back to me, and said 'no, I'm fight him straight on. He fights the fair one with the kid. They fight for a while, break it up, start fighting again. Now they fought for ten minutes, they both tired. This dude still wants to fight. This dude starts a fight with my other man that came to visit, too. My man's like, 'yo, you don't know me, get out of my face. First he tried to give my man five, like 'what's up,' like 'good one.' My man don't know him, he was like 'what you mean give you five, 'he was poking my man in the eye and shit, some pussy shit. So he was like 'what you mean give you five? I don't know you, you don't know me, 'he was like 'what you want to fight with me, man...Then so he come over to me and tried to give me five... He said 'you're a pussy' or some shit, I said, 'what? you talking to me?' I had the gun that my friend had gave me. I had {the} gun off safety, loaded, in my pocket and this dude is trying to fight with me. I had one of two choices. I could fight with him now. The police was already on their way. It was just a 15-minute fight, everybody {was} outside the building, you know, somebody had to call the cops. I had a choice. I could fight with this dude. He could of had a gun on him, which he was acting like he had a gun on him, and his man was there. Or I could take care of my business, hit with it, shoot him, whatever I got to do, and break out. The cops is on their way. I could fight with him, it could go off while we fighting, wrestling, bong. I'm getting shot as a motherfucker. Or I could just hit him with it. I choose to hit him with it. I pull it out boom. I hit {him} over the head with it then he started coming at me I hit again in the head with it then he tried to wrestle me for {it} and I shot him in the shoulder. That is what happened. The shit jammed, son or he would have been done off. It jammed because I had hit him with it. It was only a .25, brand new, we just got it that day, chrome .25. I hit him here and here, gave him stitches, boom. After I hit him he started running. I'm like this, 'aw, shit,' then I started breaking out. I went to the back of the building.

INT: Did you know the guy before you shot him?

LUKE: Yeah I knew him, I had a few incidents with him.

INT: You all didn't get along, right?

LUKE: Nah he tried to play too much of a thug I didn't never have a problem with him but, you know what I mean, he wanted a problem with me.

In sum, there were many ways in which young males "force status" on each other. Violence was instrumental in this process. There are status consequences for all parties involved in a violent event. The respondents described a number of status-forcing situations including upward movement, downward movement, and status maintenance. Identity challenges were very common; there is a developmental component to identity-based violent events and these examples show the perpetuation of toughness norms of masculinity.

Based on the data presented in this chapter, several conclusions can be made about the relationship between social context, violent situations, and social identity among adolescent males in these inner city neighborhoods. The street context offers a variety of mechanisms for the development of social identity. The two inner-city neighborhoods studied here clearly were danger zones in which an "ecology of danger" including high levels of risk for victimization, frequent exposure to violent experiences, and a normative framework support violent behavior. The public or interactional nature of violence among adolescents allows the airing of identity contests to take on a more significant and potentially deadly meaning, especially coupled with the ready availability of firearms among this population. The social space becomes even more closed when the experiences of active violent offenders is examined. In other contexts, such as middle-class schools, we see adolescents forming desirable identities via athletic ability, attractiveness, charm, and wealth (Cairns & Cairns, 1994; Kinney, 1993). The current data, and previous research, suggests that for inner-city males prestige is granted to those who are tough, who have gained respect by proving their toughness, and who reenact their appropriate role in public. As Messerschmidt (1993): points out, toughness or displaying a willingness to fight when necessary exists in these contexts; however, the current data show that violence is the single most critical resource for gaining status among those inner-city males who frequently participate in street life.

The dynamics of violent events reflect several interesting processes: (1): achievement of a highly valued social identity occurs through extreme displays of violence, (2): achievement of a "safe" social identity may also require the use of extreme forms of violence, (3): the ready availability of guns clearly increases the stakes of how one achieves status, (4): much behavior is motivated by avoiding being a punk or herb, (5): identities can change from being a punk or herb into a more positive status such as holding your own, (6): guns equalize the odds for some smaller young men through the process of "showing nerve," (7): one can feel like a punk for a specific situation but not take on a punk identity, (8): one can feel like a crazy killer in a specific situation but not take on a crazy, wild, or killer identity. (9): If "compulsive masculinity" or Anderson's (1990): "street orientation" is as dominant in public spaces and personal safety as our data suggest, then those who do not conform will be victimized.

The reproduction of social identities constructed through violent behavior, and the eclipsing or devaluation of other identities spreads in increasingly socially isolated networks. These identities reinforce the dominance hierarchy built on toughness and violence, and its salience devalues other identities. Those unwilling to adopt at least some dimensions of these norms either overtly or symbolically are vulnerable to physical attack. Accordingly, these identities are strategic necessities to navigate through everyday dangers of inner city life.

The maintenance and reinforcement of identities supportive of violence is made possible by an effective socio-cultural dynamic that sets forth an age grading pathway to manhood that includes both behaviors and the means of resolving violations of respect. The incorporation of violent attitudes and behaviors as a "rite of passage" has been documented in this study. The illustrations above show the strong influence of a street code, similar to the codes identified by Anderson (1999), or the code of honor described by (Toch, 1969), over the behaviors of young children, adolescents, and young adults. The absence of alternative means of attaining valued masculine identities further compound the problem. The transmission of these social processes occurs on both the micro and macro level. Children growing up in this environment learn these codes, or behavioral-affective systems, by navigating their way through interpersonal situations that oftentimes involve violence encounters. Negotiating safety within this context is extremely difficult especially when much of the social activity available to young men who have left school and are "hanging out" on the inner-city street corner involves expressing dominance over others. The effects are a hardening of street codes, and an eclipsing of other avenues for social status and respect. Attempts to reverse this cycle must address its manifestations at the individual, group, and societal levels.

# CHAPTER 10

# Discussion

I started this project with the goal of gaining the trust and confidence of young violent males in order to give voice to their complex social worlds. In particular I wanted to examine the decisions they made in moments of time when they were armed and angry. I wanted to know about the ways that they coped with the daily stress and strain of inner-city life. Once inside this world I felt profoundly grateful that I could go home to a safe neighborhood and that I do not have to struggle against racism and classism on a daily basis. Throughout this experience, I have never stopped wanting to make a difference with this population but grew to recognize just how difficult and complex that process is. It will be a lifetime effort for certain.

The young men in this study realized that their chances to obtain wealth and power were so miniscule via legitimate pathways that many opted for the fleeting glory of the street over a life of unremarkable toil. Most of the young men in this study choose to live "short and large" rather than long and boring lives. At a fundamental level these young men demonstrated a level of denial of personal responsibility for their actions and an unwillingness to acknowledge cause and effect. Their choices to adhere to a normative code that calls for frequent violent competition for limited rewards enables the worst sort of cycle to perpetuate. Individuals actively engage in violent power plays with others in their environment because the environment is dangerous. By using violence to resolve these conflicts the environment becomes even more dangerous ensuring that those after them will face the same limited set of behavioral choices.

## UNDERSTANDING THE EPIDEMIC OF ADOLESCENT GUN VIOLENCE

While youth violence has traditionally been a problem in American society, the modern version of it seems distinctly different: it is more lethal, in large part due to the rise of gun violence by urban adolescents. This research provides a new perspective and unique data on the role of guns in shaping the recent epidemic of youth violence. At the descriptive level, the answer is clear: urban adolescents in cities are possessing and carrying guns on a large scale, guns often are at the scene of youth violence, and guns often are being used. This is historically unique in the United States, with significant impacts on an entire generation of adolescents. The impacts are most seriously felt among African American and Latino American male youth in America's inner cities.

For a generation of adolescents, gun violence has had instrumental value that was integrated into the social discourse of everyday life among urban youth. Guns were, and remain salient symbols of power and status and strategic means of gaining status, domination, or material goods. This research demonstrated how adolescents use violence to achieve social status or identities in economic contexts with attenuated routes to adult roles. The current cohort of young men, who were born from 1973-1982, grew up during a time of alarmingly high rates of violence in their neighborhoods. Many young men presume that firearm possession will increase personal safety and equip the individual with a perceived necessary tool for self-protection. The event level data clearly show that weapon carrying increased the seriousness and likelihood of conflict situations turning violent. It does not appear that the nature of disputes (e.g., motivations) changed in any meaningful way during the study period—what had changed was the relative frequency with which a dispute would involve the use of a gun by an adolescent. The event narratives suggest that there has been a breakdown in the age grading of behaviors related to violence. Previously researchers have documented a segmentation of younger adolescents from older ones, and distinctive behavioral transitions from one developmental stage to the next. The experiences described here show that the presence and use of firearms, the involvement of younger adolescents in street-level drug sales, and intensity of a violent normative has effectively short-circuited some of the traditional age barriers. The data presented in the chapter on neighborhood context suggests that adults attempt to enforce of norms regarding fighting behavior among children (8-12 year olds) but not fighting among adolescents (those older than 13). The lack of adult involvement in social control processes leaves control of the street to older adolescents who are more likely to be supportive of violence.

Violence has become an important part of the discourse of everyday social interactions, with functional (status and identity), material and symbolic meaning (power and control), as well as strategic importance. The development of violence "scripts" and violent identities reflects processes of anticipatory socialization based on the perceived likelihood of violent victimization and the perceived necessity to deter violent attacks by projecting an aura of toughness and danger. The result is a developmental "ecology of danger," in which beliefs about violence and the dangers of everyday life are internalized in early childhood and shape the cognitive frameworks for interpreting events and actions during adolescence. In turn, this context of danger creates, shapes, and places value on behavioral repertoires skewed toward violence and underscores the central, instrumental role of violence in achieving the goals of aggressive actions or defensive violence in specific social contexts.

## GUNS AS SOCIAL TOXIN

The complex interactions among gun availability, gun ownership, gun carrying, and gun use among those youth most likely to be at risk for involvement in gun violence or to be victims of gun violence have been documented in this book. The spread of discourse, fear, and identity occurs through a process of social interactions not unlike social contagion (Burt, 1987; Fagan, Wilkinson, & Davies, 2000). In the contagious dynamics of violence, the social meaning of violence is constructed through the interrelationship of its action and its context. Weapons serve as an environmental cue that in turn may increase aggressiveness (Slaby & Roedell, 1982). Adolescents presume that their counterparts are armed, and if not, could easily become armed. They also assume that other adolescents are willing to use guns, often at a low threshold of provocation. Many of the respondents in this study described their neighborhoods as "war zones," where violence, especially gun violence, was very likely to erupt. The social meaning involves actions (violence) that have both returns (identity, status, avoidance of attack) and expectations that, within tightly packed networks, are unquestioned or normative. Conduct impregnated with social meaning has influence on the behaviors of others in immediate proximity. The social meaning of violence influences the adaptation of behavioral norms, expected responses (scripts), and even beliefs about systems of behavior. Social norms are the product of repeated events that demonstrate the meaning and utility of specific forms of conduct.

Social influence thus has a dynamic and reciprocal effect on social norms. In poor neighborhoods, social interactions are dominated by street codes, or local systems of justice, that reward displays of physical domination and offer social approval for antisocial behavior. The setting or context of contagion reflects the susceptibility of populations to the transmission of a socially meaningful behavior, and its exposure to the behavior that has acquired meaning. This can be as true for fashion and art as for problematic social behaviors such as drug use, teenage pregnancy, and gun violence.

## DECISION MAKING IN VIOLENT EVENTS

This research began with the hypothesis that violent events reflect the convergence of motivation, social and situational context, and symbolic interactions between opposing parties. To specify a theory for adolescents, perspectives from developmental psychology that influence both motivation and decision-making were explored. Does the integration of these perspectives result in a specialized theory of violent events? And, is a special theory of violence necessary? Based on the current research, the answer to both questions would be no. None of the processes in the situational or symbolic interactionist conceptual frameworks are unique to violence. The data suggest that violent events are a specific case within a generalized pattern of social interactions.

The motivations for violent events among adolescents can be located within a general framework of functionality and goal-orientation of adolescent deviance: competition for status, development of social identity, accrual of material goods, establishment of autonomy, and affirmation of gender roles. The social control components of violence also require no special explanation; crime as self-help or social control includes several types of action, from physical violence to aggression-motivated property crimes to relational violence through shaming and social disclosure. Adherence to a behavioral code —whether social, antisocial, or simply current fashion— is normative for adolescents.

Yet the escalation of disputes into violence requires a specific explanation within this generalized framework of situated transactions. It is theoretical specificity, not theoretical specialization that is needed to explain the escalation of social interactions into violence. There are two features of this puzzle that provide relevant focus for the explanation of violent events among adolescents. First, the social cognition and social judgmental capacities of adolescents are limited (Steinberg & Avenevoli, 2000; Steinberg & Caufmann, 1996). Accordingly, responses to provocation, threat and arousal are less likely to be modulated among adolescents, whose behavioral repertoires and scripts are more limited compared to mature adults. Second, clearly the evidence suggests that violent status hierarchies influence adolescents' decisions to engage in or avoid violence.

In specific social contexts, scripts develop, decision-making processes are shaped, meaning is made of potential conflicts, and violence serves particular functions. These contexts shape normative definitions, imperatives or expected behaviors, and the costs and rewards of violence. The event level analyses highlight that much of the violence experienced by youth during adolescence relates directly to normal issues that are important to most youth—independence, identity formation, peer acceptance, task mastery, sexual exploration, etc. Avoiding being stigmatized as a "punk" or "herb" was central to the experiences of many young men in the study. Victimization experiences were common during childhood and early adolescence, however they were especially damaging during mid adolescence. Some of the violent incidents described in this book reflected the need for adolescent males to perform well in combat situations to impress an audience. The circumstances of a particular violent event determine the parameters of a quality performance. The youth violence problem is cognitive, behavioral, and normative.

The analysis of violent events in specific socio-cultural contexts underscores the importance of understanding the heterogeneity of violent conflict handling among actors in settings. While there were many similarities across different types of events the differences were important. This study provided a closer look at violent actors decision-making in "heated" or emotionally charged situations. These situations are scripted, that is, they reflect the internalization of action sequences that are elicited when situational cues deem appropriate. Guns may have altered violence scripts toward more lethal outcomes. For adolescent males gun and non-gun events have different processual dynamics. The choice structuring properties are limited in gun events by threat of lethal action, thus actors make fewer decisions in gun events. Identity challenges and physical threats are significantly correlated with negative outcomes in conflict situations, especially among strangers. Consistent with previous research victim precipitation, or aggressive actions by the victim, result in more aggressive actions by the "offender."

The social identity or gendered component of these violent behaviors is especially relevant for developing prevention strategies. The use of violence or coercive action as a resource in obtaining a desired status can be found throughout American culture. In the inner-city context, violence is one of a small number of resources available to be competitive and gain status. The negative ramifications of violence are seen most severely in that context. Clearly, on a neighborhood or block level, violence begets violence and victimization begets violence. The narrowing of outlets for learning more positive masculinity roles needs to be addressed through early childhood intervention, parenting, and community-based programs.

The prevalence in inner city neighborhoods of social toxins such as guns, and the recurring episodes of lethal violence throughout childhood and adolescence negatively affect healthy socialization. Gun violence has altered scripts for conflict resolution from toughness and fighting to lethal violence. In conjunction with spatial and social isolation, there have been basic shifts in the perceptions of threat, for escalating disputes into violence, and for the use of severe forms of violence.

Violence scripts have to do with how the key actors (victim(s) and perpetrator(s)) define what happened in the situation and the nature of the relationship between the actors. Both of these factors are important for defining event closure. Events experienced by violent youth in our sample a number of general conclusions can be made about the salience of situational factors for predicting future behavior and identifying potential points of intervention. An event perspective can be a useful framework for the work of public health, criminal justice, and educational professionals because these adults frequently interact with youth in response to such incidents. Having a clearer understanding of how youths make sense of and cope with these experiences provides clues to their resolution and reduction. Criminal justice officials are interested in understanding how to anticipate when and under what circumstances a given offender is likely to engage in subsequent violent events. Professionals who work with similar populations should consider the following comments relevant to understanding the thought

processes of young males in violent events: [the comments in brackets
are the types of questions youths might ask themselves].

> the individual's past experience with violent situations
> [what have I done in this type of situation in the past?]
> normative beliefs about violent behavior in terms of what
> is expected in this type of situation including issues of
> injustice, [what do I think is the right thing to do in this
> situation? Did the opponent handle him or herself in the
> "appropriate way" ?]
> the individual's perception of the normative beliefs of the
> other party (ies) in terms of what is expected in this type
> of situation, [what would other people I respect do if they
> found themselves in this situation?]
> the individual's perception of the reaction from the
> generalized other [what are others expecting me to do?]
> his knowledge of the desires and intentions of the other
> party(ies) involved in the event, [what is the likely
> response/action from the other party?]
> his assessment of the level of harm or damage resulting
> from the event, [How serious is the damage and how can I
> get compensated or make "things" right? Will there be
> further damage (potential injury or reputation loss) if I do
> nothing?]
> his assessment of the level of reward or benefit from the
> event, [Will I gain something from continuing the
> conflict?]
> the expectation of negative gossip or talk in the
> neighborhood [Will this injury harm my reputation?]

Agreement between parties is critical for a violent event to have
closure. Public health professional who work with injured youth
operate under the assumption that an injury incident represents a
"teachable moment" in the youths' life in which the youth are more
reflective and malleable directly after a traumatic event (Rosenberg &
Fenley, 1991). It will be important to try to get some sense from the
victim about the status of the conflict between the parties after the
injury. It makes sense to think that a violent injury serious enough to
require hospital care would cause an individual to pause and search for
meaning. It also seems reasonable to think that shooting another

person or causing a serious injury would invoke as similar process of meaning making.

Although the assumption seems logical it is untested and unproven. In order to establish how experiencing or causing violent injury has affected an individual it is important to understand the weight of that particular event in context with the individual's other life experiences. Typically after a violent event (especially events that occurred in public settings) there is some gossip, teasing, threats, peer pressure, avoidance, withdrawal from the street, anger, emotional stress, and etc. Adults including parents, teachers, police officers, social workers, physicians, counselors, and therapists need to focus their efforts on assisting young people in making sense of the violence that they encounter. Once a young person has experienced a violent event, that event shapes future experiences. Young people need help in identifying positive ways of coping with such experiences so that the behavioral and affective repertoires include non-violent responses and alternatives. Building on the "teachable moment" concept I have developed a conceptual framework that highlights the processes of violent events. In high violence neighborhoods youth are exposed to and experience multiple violent events over the life course. When adults or other authority figures get involved or become awareness of a violent event, their actions (or non-actions) become part of the definition of that event for a young person. For example, if adults break up fights between young children in the neighborhood young people internalize those experiences. If adults do not intervene young people process another message. Several hospital-based intervention programs in Philadelphia are currently implementing strategies that are consistent with this model. I am currently engaged in a study to test the framework with victims of youth violence.

The choice to be violent in specific situations may not be a morally good decision, but it is a rational decision based on a calculus of the consequences of other behavioral choices. For adolescents in dangerous, potentially lethal contexts, threat trumps morality in a context in which there is a reasonable expectation of lethal attack. The developmental context of (violent) inner cities shapes a decision-making heuristic among adolescents based on their best and immediate interests, rather than an abstract code of norms that exist only outside the immediate context. These youth see themselves as products of an environment in which the need for self-preservation leaves them with the perception of having no choice but to act in accordance with the street code. Adolescents face two developmental issues simultaneously –concerns for social status among peers and concerns for personal safety. These two developmental needs often go unmet in these contexts of danger –to many youth legal compliance has doubtful value and low payoff for adolescents.

## IMPLICATIONS AND POLICY RECOMMENDATIONS
This research highlights the complexities of youth violence among inner city minority males as a social problem. Multiple levels of influence have been identified and described including: structural, institutional, familial, situational, and individual level factors. Unfortunately, there is no simple or singular solution to the problem. At the most fundamental level, the personal safety of children in these distressed urban neighborhoods must be a critical starting point and focus. Healthy development will continue to be compromised as children grow up with truncated life expectancies and over exposure to environmental hazards. This research has accentuated the absence of adult caretakers and agents of control over the behaviors of young people on the streets. For all intents-and-purposes, it appears that violent youth regulate the day-to-day activities of the study neighborhoods. Obviously, a variety of factors (e.g. economic inequality, poor housing conditions, departure of stable middle class families, overcrowding, high rates of violent crime, fear of victimization, early parenthood, limited parenting skills, and drug addiction) have contributed to the decline of adult involvement in the lives of children in these neighborhoods. Violence prevention efforts must include a comprehensive approach targeting multiple sources of influence on youth. Comprehensive programs that involve diverse strategies and multiple resources are more likely to impact the problem than narrowly defined programs. However, such programs are more difficult to implement and evaluate. Community development and grassroots efforts that springboard from the rich data presented herein need to be developed and evaluated.

Formal social control processes also need to be enhanced in these neighborhoods. It appears that law enforcement efforts do make a difference in terms of reducing the likelihood of retaliatory action and helping youth to find closure. It is unclear exactly how those processes are operating from the available data; however, one could speculate several possible scenarios. For example, once a violent incident comes to the attention of the police the likelihood of getting caught for retaliating increases. In addition, if police officers regularly work in the neighborhoods officers' actions can help youth define the situation and perhaps find alternative strategies. Over the course of the larger study, youth reported increases in police presence in the neighborhoods. They responded to the increased police presence by altering their gun carrying behavior. Law enforcement officials and other community service providers should make a great effort to get know young people in the neighborhoods—both delinquent and non-delinquent youth.

A youth development or life-course perspective is most useful in thinking about what can be done to reduce the negative outcomes and failures described by the respondents. Interventions programs need to be geared toward the inter-related problems and deficits that youth like those in this study experience. A holistic perspective is needed.

Making the transition to adulthood and productive adult role is difficult for most people in America. Common sense tells us that young people need support in making these difficult transitions. Young people do not magically become self-sufficient at the age of majority. Most young adults rely on support—both emotional and financial—of families and friends. If support is not available within those relationships human beings find other ways of coping and surviving. Over half of the respondents did not have adequate social support, guidance, and positive modeling. Forty-five percent of respondents were involved in voluntary help-seeking behaviors following their release from Riker's Island.[17] The young men in this study would benefit from comprehensive youth development interventions that include: life skills training, employment readiness, educational remediation, parenting and family planning, housing assistance, counseling for violence, alcohol and drug abuse, and relationship issues, family support, and cognitive therapy. Interventions that incorporate the issues and concerns facing inner city adolescent males

---

[17] We did not specifically ask about their involvement with the Friends program because the study was not designed as an evaluation of that program. The program was early in its development and did not have the resources to provide comprehensive services to youth. In addition, the program was located in Manhattan. Individuals are recruited and introduced to the program only after being incarcerated.

should attempt to alter the way social cues are interpreted to equal hostile intention, expand the repertoire of options in high arousal situations, reduce the frequency with which young people are armed with dangerous weapons, and teach individuals to understand the full reality and impact of their actions. It is important that strategies that target these youth are youth empowering. By youth empowering, I mean strategies that identifying and building on the individual's strengths rather than focusing exclusively on the negative behavior that may have brought the individual into the program. Peer leaders frequently had the most success in recruit young people into the Friends of Island Academy program compared to "professional" types.

Economic development and life sustaining job creation is needed in these neighborhoods. The lack of employment opportunities affects both the respondents' outlook on the future (lack of successful role models) and their choices to pursue illegal avenues (lack of available jobs). The experiences described by the sample herein suggest that young males make choices as early as 11 years old that will circumvent future employment and educational opportunities. In many cases, the criminal pathway to income generation is viewed as the only viable avenue. Summer youth programs offered many respondents their first experience with the formal economy and neighborhood institutions. Localized initiatives may be more effective in providing viable alternatives to criminal and other anti-social behavior for youth. Programs such as YouthBuild and JobCorps may offer promise (Schochet, Burghardt, & Glazerman, 2000). Efforts should be made to provide apprenticeship programs and affordable vocational training for this population. Youth will need ongoing support to make successful transitions from illicit market to the licit job market. Their criminal histories will create additional obstacles for permanent employment. Job readiness and placement programs are needed to prepare youth to get jobs, develop proper employment habits, socialize the youth on workplace norms, and manage the complexities of his other demands. Most middle-class teenagers get practice in the workplace through part-time employment and volunteer work. Without early work experience youth are at a competitive disadvantage in the workforce. Funding for these types of programs should be expanded and the programs should be systematically evaluated.

Since drug and alcohol use is involved in 66% of the violent events described and 84% of the young violent offenders report being involved in drug selling behaviors, it is clear that these issues are an important part of the violence problem. After more than thirty years of a lost national war on drugs I am critical of policies to increase enforcement and stiffen penalties for drug offenses. The young men in this study described widespread devastation to families of addictions and abusers. Additional government resources should be put into reducing the demand side of the drug problem by increasing the number of treatment beds available in the local community, drug treatment programs for inmates returning to the community, and self-help through twelve-step and other voluntary programs. It appears that drug selling has become institutionalized in these neighborhoods. Although some adults do not like the activity many others seemed to either be involved or at least tolerant of it. Changing the norm or adaptive stand toward drug selling will only come when viable employment opportunities are readily available to citizens in these neighborhoods. Even then, illegal markets will remain as long as there is money to be made.

The book has uncovered multiple needs among respondents for support and social services. For example, respondents reported substance abuse problems, depression, domestic violence, victimization, persistent fear, hopeless attitudes, and criminal thinking patterns. Most of the respondents in this study attempted to detach themselves from their emotions, denied responsibility for their decisions, and/or externalized being aloof from their feelings about particular events while internally the events would bother them. Culturally sensitive therapy and counseling services are seriously needed among this population. Community level forums or workshops may reduce the level of denial that currently exists and afford the opportunity to reverse the stigma attached to help seeking behaviors.

For many respondents, the research interview provided the first opportunity in their lives to speak openly about their experiences without negative affect or consequences. Many of the respondents had never verbalized their feelings about their lives. The peer interviewers proved to be effective agents at getting most of the young men to open up and talk about troubling experiences. It appears that a "peer mentoring" approach has, on a basic level, broke through the barriers and stigma attached to discussing and expressing feelings among these males. Some respondents ended up joining the youth membership group at Friends of Island Academy that afforded them opportunities to get additional support via group discussions.

The idea of young men who have had similar experiences reaching out to other young men holds promise but remains unstudied. One component of the Friends program included formal presentations of an anti-violence, anti-crime message presented to middle school and high school students by young ex-offenders. The dialogue around community violence was seen as a positive effort to change attitudes and norms although we have no evaluation of its effectiveness. The problems must be addressed at the community level including within- and across-age group problem solving.

School-based curriculum on conflict resolution, anger management, peer mediation, and peer discussion groups about masculinity and toughness need to be refined to include context specific examples and evaluated. School-based interventions will have limited success without broader community level changes (Gottfredson, 2001). Unfortunately, the current knowledge base about what works in violence prevention with this older adolescent population is rather limited. Efforts to collect "best practices" information about programs are important and should be expanded. Collaborations between practitioners and researchers should facilitate lessons grounded in program experience and tested with scientific methods.

## RECOMMENDATIONS FOR FUTURE RESEARCH
Any examination of the trajectory of individuals' identity pathways must closely examine the specific social contexts in which their development is situated. The data presented herein highlight the importance of social networks and peer groups in the social construction of violent events. A number of important hypotheses have been generated from this study. Future research should focus on breaking down event narratives into sequences of social transactions so that researchers can evaluate more closely the micro-decisions actors make during the course of disputes that lead to using guns or avoiding violence. The current and previous research has established that violent interactions follow systematic patterns of action. Interactions involving adolescent actors have similar patterns to those identified for adults in terms of the naming, blaming, and claiming processes (Luckenbill, 1977); however, violent events among adolescents is skewed toward

events that reflect adolescent-specific concerns like establishing tough identities.

The life history data gathered from our sample allowed us to generate hypotheses about social identities, status forcing processes, and developmental pathways to status. While the data is suggestive, it is far from complete or definitive especially on issues related to social identity. Future research should move toward longitudinal qualitative studies to capture more closely the age specific developmental processes hypothesized from these data. The important role of age-grading also suggests longitudinal designs with both younger and older cohorts. If identity is a central focus of these dynamics, research with younger children is necessary to assess how behavioral progressions are tied to identity development and situational techniques of avoiding violence. The interactions of adolescents across age cohorts also are important points of diffusion of behavioral norms and identity development.

Studies of networks of violent and non-violent adolescent and young adults are needed to fill important knowledge gaps about the influence of group processes on violent events. Future inquiries must consider by the structural features of group and institutional settings as well as the processes that operate within those contexts. Observational studies of potentially violent settings examining youth "in action" such as Sullivan's recent study in three New York schools should provide additional insights that were not captured in this study (Sullivan, 1998).

The findings of this study need to be replicated with other samples and in other locations. Similar data needs to be collected from individuals from Caucasian, Native American, and Asian American backgrounds as well as for females. For example, comparable analyses of 16-24 year old females from East New York and the South Bronx should be conducted to further explicit the gendered aspects of violent events. In addition, studies in rural, poor, white communities may provide additional insight on decision-making and scripts among adolescents in potentially violent situations.

# The Columbia Youth Gun Study Final Interview Protocol

I would like to start by having you tell me a little about yourself and your neighborhood.

**\*\*PERSONAL CHARACTERISTICS**
Tell me about a little bit about yourself.
PC1. Age. How old are you? When is your birthday?
PC2. Ethnicity. What is your ethnic or racial background?
PC3. Neighborhood (Raised in). What 'Hood do you live in? (Specific name, more than just "the Bronx")
PC4. What have you been doing during the past six months? (PROBE: Locked up? In school? Working - legit? Hustling? Chillin?)

**\*\*FAMILY**
Tell me about your family.
FAMSIZE1. Do you have a BIG /large family?
FAMSIZE2. Are your parents married? If yes, are they still together? If no, when did they split up? Did you have any step parents or mother's boyfriends/ pop's girlfriends around?
FAMMOMS1. Tell me a little something about your mother. Was your moms around much when you was growing up?
FAMPOPS1. Tell me a little bit about your father? Was your pops around much when you was growing up? FAMBRO1. How many brothers do you have? Older/ Younger? How well do you get along? (FOR EACH ONE)
FAMBRO2. What does he do? What is his occupation (or in school)? ($$$$) Is he a GOOD OR BAD INFLUENCE ON YOU? HOW?
FAMSIS1. How many sisters do you have? Older/Younger? How well do you get along? (FOR EACH ONE)
FAMSIS2. What does she do? What is her occupation (or in school)? ($$$$) Is she a GOOD OR BAD INFLUENCE ON YOU? HOW?
FAMSIZE3. What about your extended family, [Grandparents, aunties, uncles, cousins] are you close to them? Do you see them a lot? Who?
FAMSIZE4. When you were growing up, how many people lived in your household besides your parents, brothers, and sisters?
FAMCARE1. Who was primarily responsible for taking care of you when you were younger?

FAMCARE2. Who do you live with now? Does anyone in your family support you financially?

FAMCARE3. Who are you closest to in YOUR FAMILY? Why?

Okay, Let's talk a little more about your parents..

FAMMOMS2. Did your mother work when you were growing up? If yes, What was your mother's occupation when you were growing up? If no, What did she mainly do for money?

FAMMOMS3. Do you think she was a good influence on you when you coming up? Why or why not?

FAMMOMS4. Do you have a good relationship with her now? Why or why not?

FAMPOPS2. Did your father work when you were growing up? If yes, What was your father's occupation when you were growing up? If no, What did he mainly do for money?

FAMPOPS3. Do you think he was a good influence on you when you coming up? Why or why not?

FAMPOPS4. Do you have a good relationship with him now? Why or why not?

FAMGUIDE1. Do you usually talk to your parents [mom / pop] about your personal problems? How often? Why or why not?

FAMGUIDE2. Do you usually talk to your parents [mom / pop] about your GOALS OR PLANS FOR THE FUTURE? How often? Why or why not?

FAMGUIDE3. Are your opinions about most things similar to the opinions of your parents [mom / pop], or are they different? How are they similar? How are they different? Give examples.

FAMGUIDE4. Some parents [mothers/fathers] have rules for their teenagers and young adults, while others don't. Did or Do your parents have definite rules for you about: -time for being in at night (curfew) -amount of time spent outside with friends -school attendance & homework -against hanging with certain guys -against hanging with certain girls -about dating -eating dinner with the family -helping around the house -dress and hair rules -against smoking, drinking, or using drugs -against selling drugs or hustling -for using violence to protect yourself -against using violence -against having guns -other.

FAMGUIDE5. Of all the rules your parents had for you when you were younger, which ones did you follow and which ones would you regularly break? And why?

FAMGUIDE6. Was there a certain age were you stopped following your parents rules about your activity? What age, what did you start doing, and how did you get away with it?

FAMGUIDE7. Do you think your parents [ mom / pop] approve of most of the things that you do now as a young adult? Why or why not? What don't they like? What do they like?

FAMGUIDE8. How often did your parents [mom / pops] beat or whup you? [Probe: Never, just a few times, regularly, more than once a month]

FAMGUIDE9. How often did you physically fight back? [Probe: Never, just a few times, regularly, more than once a month, all of the times.]

FAMVIOL1. Did your Parents ever fight with each other when you was younger? [IF NO, What about arguing, yelling, screaming out each other] IF YES, Was physical or just arguing?

FAMVIOL2. IF YES, How often did you see your pops hit your mom (or step-mother) when you was growing up? [Probe: Never, just a few times, regularly, more than once a month]

FAMVIOL3. IF YES, How often did you see your mom hit your pops (or step-pops) when you was growing up? [Probe: Never, just a few times, regularly, more than once a month]

FAMNEG1. Does anyone in your family or household have or own a gun? Who? Where is it usually stored?

FAMNEG2. Did your ANYBODY IN YOUR FAMILY ever teach you how to handle or care for a gun of any type? [PROBE: YOUR POPS, MOTHER, UNCLES, COUSINS]

FAMNEG3. When you were growing up, how many relatives did you know who were hustling? Who was that? [PROBE -FATHER, MOTHER, OTHER RELATIVES]

FAMPOPS4. Did your father ever hustle? [IF YES, GO TO FAMPOPS5 / IF NO, SKIP TO FAMMOMS5]

FAMPOPS5. Did your family know about it (father's hustling) at the time?

FAMPOPS6. Did your family approve of your father's hustle? What did they think about it?

FAMMOMS5. Did your mother ever hustle? [IF YES, GO TO FAMMOMS6. IF NO, SKIP TO FAMNEG2. ]

FAMMOMS6. Did your family know about it (mother's hustling) at the time?

FAMMOMS7. Did your family approve of your mother's hustle? What did they think about it?

FAMNEG4. Has anyone in your family been incarcerated that you know of? Who? What was he/she locked up for? When did this happen? You ever go visit?

FAMNEG5. Was anyone in your home a heavy drug user or a heavy drinker when you were growing up? Who? What toll did their problem have on the family?

## **PEERS
Good, tell me a little something about your friends. Think about the people you are closest to when you answer these questions.

PEER1. Do you have someone that you would consider your best friend? IF YES, What makes that person important or a good friend to you? PROBE: qualities, values, similarities, time together, etc.

PEER2. Do you have more than one close friend? How Many?

PEER3. Is it like a group of you all that hang together? How many in your little crew or clique?

PEER4. Are you pretty tight with your friends? Why? (PROBE: Talk about problems, help each other out, just have fun together, etc.)

PEER5. Do most of your Friends (associates) live in your 'Hood? on your block?

PEER6. Are most of these guys your same age or close to your age? IF NO, ask how much older or younger they are.

PEER7. How long have you been friends with these guys? Any new friends in last few years?

PEER8. How often do you and friends get together? What kinds of things do you all do together? (give examples)

PEER9. Who do you think understands you better, your parents or your friends? PROBE: Why would you say that?

PEER10. When you have problems, whose ideas and opinions do you respect more, your parents' or your close friends? PROBE: Why would you say that?

PEER11. Do you think your close friends are a good influence on you? Why or why not?

## **NEIGHBORHOOD
Okay, Let's talk about your 'Hood now.

N1. Where did you grow up? What 'Hood? (Get the name of his block)

N2. How long have you lived in the 'Hood?

N3. Do you live in the Projects or in a house? What projects?

N4. Generally, do you think your neighborhood was a good place to grow up? Why or why not? PROBE: What do you like the most about your 'Hood? What was the worst thing about your 'Hood?

N5. What do most people do day to day in your 'Hood? PROBE: Do most guys in your 'Hood work? What kinds of jobs do they have? (PROBE: legit and illegit?)

N6. When you were growing up, did your immediate neighborhood have any of the following? -Job programs -Parks -Community Recreation Centers -Schools -Health Center-Grassroots community organizations -Homeless shelters -Drug Treatment Programs PROBE: IF YES, Did you use these services?

N7. Generally, do people in your neighborhood help each other out or go their own way? PROBE: Give me examples of situations where a neighbor might help you out. Give me examples of when a neighbor would go their own way.

N8. What do adults do in your neighborhood when they see open drug sales in the street? PROBE: Do they yell at the dealers? Try to stop them? Just ignore them? Call their parents? Call the police? Other?

N9. What do adults do in your neighborhood when they see two young kids (8-12) fighting in the street? PROBE: Do they yell at the dealers? Try to stop them? Just ignore them? Call their parents? Call the police? Other? FOLLOW-UP: Why?

N10. What do adults do in your neighborhood when they see kids destroying property that does not belong to them? PROBE: Do they yell at the dealers? Try to stop them? Just ignore them? Call their parents? Call the police? Other? FOLLOW-UP: Why?

N11. What type of relationship do you think most adults have with teenagers and young men in your neighborhood? PROBE: Do they respect them? Are they scared of them? Avoid them? Do they show them care and love? Explain.

**\*\*STREET CODE**

CODE1. What is the best or easiest way to earn respect in the hood? PROBE: For violent and non-violent ways. Explore --$$, power, guns, girls, being a good provider, etc.

CODE2. Describe the importance of image and reputation on the street.

CODE3. What makes someone tough or "a big man" in your neighborhood? PROBE: What does it mean to have a tough reputation in the hood? How do you get to be tough?

CODE4. What makes someone a punk or herb? PROBE: What does it mean to have a reputation as a punk or herb in the hood?

CODE5. Can your reputation go from being a herb into something better, or is it once a herb, always, a herb? How?

CODE6. Define disrespect or being "dissed" [PROBE: What is it? Why is it important?]

CODE7.  What are some of the different types of disrespect?  PROBE: Ice grills, insults, threats, cheating, stealing, going after a girl, etc.

CODE8.  How do guys generally handle a situation when a guy disrespect him? PROBE: When does it matter most?  --there's people watching, opponent is a stranger, what is it?

CODE9.  How would your friends describe you in terms of toughness? Explain how your friends see you or you see yourself.  PROBE: Are you one of the toughest guys on your block?   Are you tough when you need to be?   Are someone who avoids beef or conflict?  Are someone who gets targeted by other guys for violence?  Other?

CODE10.  How would you describe your friends (YOUR 3 BEST FRIENDS) in terms of toughness? Explain how do you them.  PROBE: Are they some of the toughest guys on your block? Are they only tough when you need to be? Are they people who avoid beef or conflict?  Are they people who get targeted by other guys for violence? Other.

CODE11.  Have you ever felt like you needed to do something violent to amp up your own reputation?  What did you do?  Did it help?

CODE12.  Do you ever feel like you make descisions so that you can fit in with other guys in your neighborhood?  Have you ever used violence so that you can fit in?  Explain.

**\*\*ALCOHOL AND DRUGS**

AD1.  Are drinking and drugs (crack, weed, etc.) heavy in your 'Hood? Explain.  Is it a daily activity?  What about for guys your age?

AD2.  Do you drink or use drugs on a regular basis?  How Often?   Daily? What? and When? How much?

PEERAD1.  What about your friends?  Do your close friends drink and/or smoke weed or use other drugs? (How many friends?  How Often?  Daily? What? and When?

PEERAD2.  Do you think that drinking and/or smoking weed or using other drugs is a big part of what you and your friends do together?  Why or Why not?

AD3.  What affect do YOU think alcohol and drugs have on the people in your 'Hood?

AD4.  Do you think alcohol and drugs have much effect on violence in the 'Hood?  Why or why not?  How does it effect it?

PEERAD3.  What about the drug business?  Are you or your friends involved in that?  Do any of your friends sell drugs? or hustle on the street?  How long have they been doing that?  Are guns part of that scene?  How?  Why?

PEERAD4.  Do any of your friends stay away from alcohol & drugs?  Or hustling?  How many of your friends? Why?

## **GUNS

Now I would like to talk a little about your experiences with weapons. Okay?

GUN1. What about guns, are there a lot of gun in your 'Hood? Is it easy to buy guns in your 'Hood?

PROBE: GUN2. What types of guns could you buy? What's out there?

PROBE: GUN3. What's the going price for say, a 9MM? Cheapest / most expensive?

GUN4. Who is USING or carrying guns in your 'Hood? What ages? Why? For what reasons?

GUN5. Have you ever had a gun?

GUN6. How many guns have you had? What types? Where did you get them?

GUN7. When did you get your first gun? When did you first fool around with a gun? How old were you? What was the situation?

GUN8. What have your experiences with buying or obtaining guns been? Was it easy for you? How did you do it? Explain.

GUN9. What is the main reason you got a gun for yourself? Do you feel it is necessary to have one? Why?

GUN10. Day to day, how often do you OR DID YOU carry your gun on you or make sure you have it close by just in case you need it? (PROBE: everyday, when you got to certain areas or spots, when you hang with certain people?)

GUN11. Why do you carry mostly? (PROBE: to commit crimes, for self-protect, for the drug business?)

GUN12. Have you ever fired a gun? What was the situation? What was the most recent time?

GUN13. When was the first time you fired a gun? How old were you? What was the situation that time?

GUN14. Have you ever used a gun to commit a crime? Oh yeah, how many times? What crime (s)? What was the situation that time?

GUN15. Have you ever been arrested for a weapon-related offense? Oh yeah, what happened? What offense? When was that? IF YES, Explain situation in Violent Event Section.

GUN16. What about other weapons? Do you have or carry a razor, knife, bat, or other types of weapon? Why? Why not?

PGUN1. WHAT about YOUR FRIENDS. Do any of your friends have guns? What is the main reason for them to have guns? Do they usually carry guns when they're on the street? What kind of guns do they have? How often do they carry guns?

PGUN2. Do any of your friends use guns to commit crimes in the Neighborhood? Yeah, what types of things do they do with guns?

PGUN3. Have any of your friends ever shot someone over a dispute that you can remember? What happened?

GUN4. Have any of your friends ever been arrested for a weapon-related offense? What was it? Did he get locked up? How long?

PGUN5. Do you have any friends or associates that don't carry guns? If yes, Why don't they carry or use guns? What do you think of him for not messing with guns?

### **VIOLENCE IN THE 'HOOD

NVIOL1. What do you think is the biggest problem in your 'hood? PROBE: drugs, violence, guns, fear, poverty, no jobs, overcrowding, noise, disorder, teenagers, police.

NVIOL2. How would you describe your 'hood in terms of violence? What about safety? PROBE: Is it safe compared to other areas in New York City? Why would you say that?

NVIOL3. Are there certain places in your neighborhood where violence is very likely to occur? WHERE? (PROBE: certain corners, streets, inside buildings, drug spots, in or near schools, in the park, on the border of a different neighborhood, turfs, at parties?) Can you come up with any reasons why these places attract so much action? For What reasons?

VIOL4. Are there certain times of day in your neighborhood when violence is more likely to occur? When? Why? Any reasons?

NVIOL5. Have you seen a lot of fights (shootouts) in your 'Hood? PROBE: Who's fighting? Guys your age, or younger guys? PROBE: What kinds of beefs are they, usually? Or What causes most beef?

NVIOL6. In your opinion, about what percentage (%) of the guys around your age (15-25) get into fights or have beef in your neighborhood? PROBE: Are there guys in the hood who don't fight or rarely get into beef? IF YES, What are those guys like?

NVIOL7. At what age, do you think guys start fighting or using violence to solve their problems or beef? PROBE: Does it change as you get older? (For example, do 11-12 year olds use fists and 15 + use guns?)

NVIOL8. Do you think it's a good idea that guys your age have and carry guns in your neighborhood? Why or why not?

### **VIOLENT EVENTS

In this section, we are going to talk about particular violent events that you may have experienced in the past two years (in 1994, in 1995, 1996, and 1997). Think back to any drama you have experienced since 1995 (depended on date of interview. (INTERVIEWER USE THE 2 YEAR TIMELINE TO HELP HIM REMEMBER!)

Event TOTAL. During the past two years (SINCE 1995) About **HOW MANY** (ESTIMATE HOW MANY): ARGUMENTS (verbal); BEEFS (physical); FIGHTS (no weapons); KNIFE FIGHTS; GUN SITUATIONS; SHOOTOUTS; OTHER WEAPONS.

Okay, NOW let's go a little deeper into like three or four of those situations. Interviewer: Ask the respondent to pick which events he can remember most clearly. Try to get:

a gun event, (GET AT LEAST 1) a knife event, a fair one, and argument with no violence.

I would like for you to start out by telling me who was there at the scene and who your opponent was.

**\*\*THE OPPONENT**

EVNTO1. Okay, who was the guy you was disputing with that time? Had you heard something about him beforehand?

EVNT02. How did you know YOUR OPPONENT?

EVNTO3. How would you describe your opponent as far as size? Was he bigger, smaller, or about the same size as you? What about strength, was he stronger, weaker, or about the strength as you?

EVNTO4. Was your opponent about the same age as you?

EVNTO5. What was his ethnic or racial background. Was he black, Hispanic, Asian, or white?

EVNTO6. Was your opponent from your neighborhood? Where was he from?

EVNTO7. Were you concerned about whether or not he had a gun or one of his friends would give him a gun in the situation?

EVNTO8. Were you concerned about whether or not he had a knife or one of his friends would give him a knife in the situation?

EVNTO9. Did the opponent have a weapon on him? What kind of weapon was it?

**\*\*WHO WAS THERE: \*\*THIRD PARTIES**

EVNTTP1. Besides you and the other guy, were there any other people present during the altercation? Who else was around?

EVNTTP2. There were NUMBER OF PEOPLE around during the incident.PROBE: EVNTTP2B. NUMBER OF YOUR BOYS EVNTTP2C. NUMBER OF HIS BOYS

EVNTTP2D. NUMBER OF INNOCENT BYSTANDERS OR THIRD PARTIES that were around during the incident.

EVNTTP3. Did their presence effect you /[your opponent] in the conflict situation? In what way? PROBE: Amping, squashing, no effect.

EVNT1. When and where did the incident happened: --MONTH/YEAR -- TIME OF DAY (Morning, lunchtime, evening, late night) --PHYSICAL LOCATION (school, jail, corner, building, train, etc.) --SOCIAL LOCATION (Party, drug spot, etc.)

EVNT2. What started it? WHAT CAUSED THE BEEF. What did it first start over?

EVNT3. WHAT WERE YOU FEELING AT THE TIME?

**\*\*CONTEXT**

EVNT4. What was happening with you that day? Can you remember anything unique about that day or situation? (PROBE: were you WORKING, HANGING OUT, having a good day, etc.?)

EVNT5. What were you doing when you first met your opponent that day? What were you doing when things started to heat up?

EVNT6. Did you plan to have a conflict with him that day? If yes, when did you start planning? If yes, What was your plan?

EVNT7. Did you think it was going to be a SHOOTOUT when it started to heat up? How did you know?

EVNT8. IF WEAPON, Why did you decide to take a weapon with you that day? Was this unusual for you? Why? How?

INTERVIEWER INSTRUCTIONS: After he selects the first event and tells you who was there... READ THIS.

Okay, now I'm ready to hear about what went down step by step.

I want to get the exact order of things just as they happened that day.

What happened first? Second? Third? Etc.

Tell me what you were thinking as this stuff was going down. Tell me what you was saying, what you was doing.

Tell me what he said, what he did. Tell me what any other people around the situations were doing or saying.

I'll try to guide you with a few questions so that I can really understand what was happening in the beef. Okay?

**\*\*STEPS OF EVENT**

EVNT9. What happened? Describe the situation. How did it happen?

EVNT10. WHO made the first move toward violence.

EVNT11. WHAT was the first move.

EVNT12. Okay, after you knew that it was "on", what happened next? What did you do? What did he do?

EVNT13. What happened next after that?

**\*\*WHO DID WHAT:**

EVNTTP4. IF YOUR BOYS WERE THERE, What were YOUR BOYS doing or saying during the incident.

EVNTTP5. What were HIS BOYS doing or saying during the incident?

EVNTTP6. What were INNOCENT BYSTANDERS OR THIRD PARTIES doing or saying during the incident?

EVNTTP7. How did you feel about what these other people were doing/saying? (PROBE: Were you glad? Were you afraid?) How did your opponent react to them?

EVNT14. About how long did this dispute go on between you two? how long do you think did the actual fight took? How did you know how much time had past?

**\*\*WEAPONS**

Can you explain how weapons were involved, if they were?

EVNTW1. What type of WEAPON did you have?    IF NO, SKIP TO EVNTW6.

EVNTW2. Why did you have it on you that day?    Do you usually carry a weapon when you are in the 'Hood?

EVNTW3. IF YES,What did you do with the weapon in the violent situation? (show it, threaten with it, use it, etc.)

EVNTW4. IF FIRED, How many times did you fire your weapon?

EVNTW5. IF JUST THREATENED. How did it make you feel to threaten THE OTHER GUY with the gun?

EVNTW6. What were you hoping he would do next in that situation? [PROBE: run, mouth off more, apologize, back down, show fear, set it off, other]

EVNTW7. IF OPPONENT HAD WEAPON, What did YOUR OPPONENT do with his weapon during this dispute?

EVNTW8. IF OPPONENT FIRED, How many times did he fire his weapon?

EVNTW9. When you realized that he had a gun too what were you thinking at the time? Were you afraid for your life?

EVNTW10. Did you ever think that a WEAPON might be needed in this situation?

EVNTW11. IF NO GUN, Do you think you would have handled this beef differently if you had had a GUN that day?

EVNTW12. IF SQUASHED, Who decided to squash it? Did you decide not to use violence in this situation, FIRST? Or did YOUR OPPONENT decide not to use violence first? Or did a THIRD PARTY push you into deciding not to hurt anyone?

EVNTW13. IF SQUASHED, What was it that made you decide not to hurt your opponent in this situation?

## **ALCOHOL AND/OR DRUGS

I'm also interested in any involvement you might have had with drugs/alcohol on the day of the dispute.

EVNTAD1. Did you use any TYPE OF DRUGS OR ALCOHOL on the day of the GUN confrontation?

EVNTAD2. Did you feel you were high (drug name) and or drunk on the day of the incident? What about your opponent, do you think he was high or drunk at the time?

EVNTAD3. What was you smoking or drinking? [PROBE: Alcohol, marijuana, cocaine, crack, herion, PCP --angel dust, LSD, acid, any other drugs?] Anything else besides just _____(drug named)?

EVNTAD4. Do you remember about what time you started using that day? (drug name)

EVNTAD5. How much of (drug name) would you say you used from that time on up until the incident occurred?

EVNTAD6. Do you think the situation was related in any way to your using alcohol or drugs? Why or why not? How about your opponent?

EVNTAD7. Do you think the violent incident was in any way related to the drug business? Explain. How so? Were you selling drugs at the time it started?

EVNTAD8. IF THIRD PARTIES, Do you know if any of the OTHER people were under the influence of drugs or alcohol at the time of the violent incident? If YES, who /how many /what types of drugs/alcohol did they use?

## **INJURIES:

INJURY1. Did anyone get seriously hurt? Who? Was anyone injured in this incident? Who was injured?

INJURY2. IF YES, How serious was the wound?
[PROBE: very serious injury, shot in the (part of the body),
seriously cut, cut in the (part of the body),
seriously beat up, minor injury, bruises and scratches]

INJURY3. Did anyone need to go to the hospital to get medical attention because of the incident? Who went the hospital?

INJURY4. Do you know how long you (OR OTHER INJURED PEOPLE) were in the hospital?

## **OUTCOMES OF EVENT

EVNTOUT1. How did the situation end? What was the outcome? WHAT HAPPENED? (HOW?)

EVNTOUT2. Was the conflict settled THAT DAY? Why or why not?

EVNTOUT3. DID you gain or lose status from this incident? What did you gain? What did you lose?

EVNTOUT4. Was Your REPUTATION improved by this event? How?

EVNTOUT5. Was His REPUTATION improved by this event? How?

EVNTOUT6. After the fight did you change anything about where you "hangout" or who you associate with?

EVNTOUT7. After the fight, did you do anything extra to protect yourself? WHAT?

EVNTOUT8. *IF CHANGE,* Why was it necessary to do that?

EVNTOUT9. *IF NO CHANGE,* Why wasn't it necessary to do anything extra?

EVNTOUT10. Was there any need to retaliate or get back at your opponent after this event? Did anyone retaliate after the event was over? Who retaliated and what did they do?

EVNTOUT11. What sort of relationship did you and THE GUY have after the fight?

EVNTOUT12. IF TALK, Other than THE GUY, did anyone start treating you differently because of the fight?

EVNTOUT13. IF TALK, Was there any talk during the days or weeks after the fight? What were people in the street (or at school) saying about the fight?

EVNTOUT14. How did you feel about what was being said in the street or at school?

EVNTOUT15. How long did all of this gossip go on? When and how did it stop?

EVNTOUT16. Do you think you will have drama with this guy again in the future? Why or why not?

EVNTOUT17. Did you drink or use drugs after the incident?

EVNTOUT16. Did anyone get arrested or taken in by the police for this incident? Who? What happened?

## **POLICE

EVNTPOL1. Did the police come to the scene of the incident? [IF NO, SKIP TO EVNTPOL5.]

EVNTPOL2. What did the police say/do? [PROBE: Did they investigate? Did the police find any weapons? ]

EVNTPOL3. Did anyone get arrested or taken in by the police for this incident? Who? What happened?

EVNTPOL4.   IF POLICE, What happened after the police left?   Did the conflict heat up again?

EVNTPOL5.   IF POLICE, Do you think this approach is effective?   Why or why not?

EVNTPOL6.   Do you think the police could have done something to make the situation better if they had shown up?   What should they have done?

**\*\*WHY**

EVNTWHY1.   Thinking back, why do you think you did what you did?

EVNTWHY2.   What was it about this situation that made it necessary for you to take of this beef the way you did?

EVNTWHY3.   Was there a specific point when you realized that you were going to have to (get violent) resort to violence in this situation?

EVNTWHY4.   What were you trying to accomplish when you shot or threatened him with the gun?

EVNTWHY5.   Have you handled similar BEEFS in the same way before? Explain.

EVNTWHY6.   Looking back, do you think that you handled the situation in the right way?

EVNTELSE1.   Is there anything else that you forgot to tell me ABOUT this event? [USE EVENT REVIEW SHEETS  --END OF GUN EVENT GO TO OTHER WEAPON EVENT] REPEAT AS NEEDED

**\*\*OTHER SHOCKING LIFE EVENTS**
**\*\*ACCIDENTS / INJURIES**
LH32. Serious fall or accident
LH33. Beaten up by family member
LH34. Beaten up by a friend
LH35. Beaten up by someone in the 'Hood
LH36. Knifed by someone
LH37. Shot by someone
LH38. Was hospitalized for injury
LH39. Drug overdose / Bad trip

**\*\*EXPOSURE TO VIOLENCE**
LH40. Saw someone shot
LH41. Saw someone knifed
LH42. Saw someone beaten badly
LH43. Saw someone killed
LH44. Lost a family member
LH45. Lost a close friend

LH46. Lost someone from the 'Hood
LH47. Saw family member or friend's death

## **CRIMINAL ACTIVITY
Tell me about your criminal activity.
CRIME1. What types of crimes have you been involved in?
CRIME2. Have you got a record man? IF YES, What things have you been convicted of? (What's on your record?)
CRIME3. How many of the cases where juvenile cases? How many were adult?
CRIME4. Do you have any ACTIVE CASES on you now? FOR WHAT?
CRIME5. If he has been locked up, How many times you been locked up in your life? What facilities? How long? How was that experience for you?
I would like for you to tell me about any illegal activities you might have been involved in during your lifetime. Tell me about stuff that got you into trouble with the law for and stuff that did not get you into trouble for.

## CRIME TYPE
CJ1. Drug business -- at any level.
CJ2. Shoplifting or boosting
CJ3. Stealing Cars. (Car-Jacking)
CJ5. Hitting anyone -ASSAULT
CJ6. Robbing anyone or stick ups -ROBBERY
CJ8. Breaking into a home or store -BURGLARY
CJ9. Illegal WEAPONS possession.
CJ10. Illegal WEAPONS DEALING.
CJ11. Setting fires for money –ARSON
CJ12. ATTEMPTED MURDER
CJ13. Disorderly Conduct
CJ14. Other (specify) _____
INSTRUCTIONS: ASK FOLLOW-UP QUESTIONS AS APPROPRIATE.
[REPEAT AS NEEDED: --Were you ever involved in that? YES OR NO --
AGE WHEN INVOLVED? --HOW OFTEN INVOLVED? --HOW LONG
INVOLVED? --WAS VIOLENCE A PART OF IT? --WAS A GUN AS PART
OF IT? --USE ANOTHER WEAPON AS PART OF IT?
--ARRESTED FOR IT? --CONVICTED? --SENTENCE OR BID?

## **SCHOOL
S1. Good points
S2. Bad points
S3. Favorite subjects

S4. Are you in school now? IF YES, What grade?

*S5. IF NOT IN SCHOOL,* How far did you go in school? [Probe: graduated from 8th Grade, graduated from high school, enrolled in G.E.D. program, completed G.E.D., enrolled in college, enrolled in training school or program.

S6. Do you (did you) like school much?

PROBE: S7. What do (did) you like about it? What don't (didn't) you like about it?

S8. What is (was) the important issue for you in school?

S10. Looking back, is there anything that could have made the school experience better for you when you were younger? What should be done to improve schools in your neighborhood?

S11. Did you ever get any awards or special attention for your talents in school or the community? What achievement have you had? [PROBE: Sports, Art, Music, Creative writing, talent contests, public speaking, or religious activities]

**\*\*ROLE MODELS** (good and bad)

ROLE1. Who were your influences when you were growing up? (PROBE: family, older guys on the street, coach, teacher, religious figure, sports celebrity?)

PROBE: ROLE2. Why did you look up to that person?

PROBE: ROLE3. How did that person influence you?

ROLE4. When you were growing up did you know any real positive COMMUNITY LEADERS or activists from your neighborhood? Did you know any PROFESSIONAL PEOPLE who were successful and still lived in your neighborhood?

PROBE: ROLE5. How well did you know him/her/them? Did he/she ever talk with you about the future and doing positive things? How often?

ROLE6. Are you a role model to any kids in your 'Hood? How? In what ways?

**\*\*JOBS**

JOB1. Do you currently have a job? (If he has a job) What do you mainly do for MONEY? (PROBE for legal work) IF NO JOB, SKIP JOB3.

JOB2. Was it easy for you to find this job? How did you get it?

JOB3. Are you aware of any other job opportunities available to you?

JOB4. Are you currently looking for work? How long have you been looking? What have you done to try to find a job?

JOB5. What type of work are you looking for? What kind of job do you feel qualified to do?

FREE1. What kinds of things do you like to do in your free time? PROBE: Hang out on the corner, play ball, hang with his girl, go out, etc.

## **RELATIONSHIPS

REL1. When was your first major relationship? When was your first time having sex?

REL2. Do you have a wife or steady relationship now? How's that?

REL3. How long have you been together? Do you intend to stay together?

REL4. Is this the only relationship you have with a female, or do you still see other girls too? Are you exclusive with her?

REL5. Do you have any children? How old is your child? Does he/she live with you? Do you take care of him/her/them? How?

REL6. What are your plans as a father? What kind of life do you hope for your child or children?

## **FUTURE GOALS

FUT1. What do you hope for the future? What do you want for yourself? (PROBE: Career, family, security, being on your own, staying out of trouble, etc.?)

FUT2. Do you plan to continue your education within the next couple of years?

FUT3. Where do you think that you will be living one year from now?

FUT4. What kind of work do you think that will be doing to support yourself one year from now?

## **POSSIBLE SOLUTIONS

SLTN1. How can fights on the streets be reduced? (PROBE: ask for strategies including social programs, job programs, etc.)

SLTN2. What do you think should be done to protect young men like yourself, from violence?

SLTN10. Is there anything that you think SOMEONE could do during a violent situation to squash it when two individuals are already heated up? What do you think could be done in that type of situation? Do you think it would work? How?

SLTN3. Do you feel that community leaders in your neighborhood are doing their part to reduce the violence in your neighborhood? Why or why not? What should they be doing?

SLTN4. Do you feel that young people in your neighborhood are doing their part to reduce the violence in your neighborhood? Why or why not? What should they be doing?

SLTN5. Do you feel that religious leaders in your neighborhood are doing their part to reduce the violence in your neighborhood? Why or why not? What should they be doing?

**SLTN6.** Do you feel that the criminal justice system is doing it's part to reduce violence in your neighborhood? Why or why not? What should they be doing?

**SLTN7.** Do you feel that the police department is doing it's part to reduce violence in your neighborhood? Why or why not? Do you think this approach is effective? Why or why not? What do you think they should do?

**SLTN8.** Is there anything that you think the police could be doing to help stop the violence in your neighborhood? What would you suggest?

**SLTN9.** Is there anything that you think ANYONE could be doing to help stop the violence in your neighborhood? What would you suggest?

**\*\*CLOSING**

**END1.** Is there anything else that you would like to tell me about your experiences with violence and guns?

**END2.** Do you have any questions for me about the interview?

**END3.** What did you think of the interview? Was it interesting to you?

**END4.** Do you feel like you would like to talk to SOMEONE further about any of the stuff we talked about today? [PROBE: a peer counselor, a professional counselor, a drug treatment provider, recovering drug addict or alcoholic, or a researcher]

**END5.** Are you interested in finding out about programs in your neighborhood that exist to help young men like yourself make a better future for themselves? If yes, give him a list of community organizations and service providers.

THIS CONCLUDES THE FORMAL PART OF OUR INTERVIEW.

AT THIS POINT, I WOULD LIKE TO THANK YOU FOR YOUR HONESTY AND OPENNESS IN ANSWERING THESE QUESTIONS.

YOUR PARTICIPATION IS GREATLY APPRECIATED! THANK YOU

# A Dictionary of Slang Terms

**Slang Term or Phrase:** Meaning
**Amp / Amped:** hype / instigate
**Ass out:** flip the script / do the opposite of what is normal
**Assed out:** beaten severely / dead / going hay-wire
**Back in the days:** a while ago
**Beat me in the head:** don't lie to me / or don't play me for a fool.
**Bee, son, kid:** a term of kindness like a buddy
**Beef:** conflict, fight, shootout
**Bid:** jail sentence
**Big Willy:** big time / tough guy / getting money
**Blasted / barking / busting /bucking / spraying / wetting / letting off:** shot or shooting
**Blazzay-blazzay:** so on, so forth / etc. / whatever
**Blunts:** a cigarette of marijuana
**Boated / jetted:** run or running your fastest /fleeing
**Bodega:** corner store
**Boom:** a conjunction equivalent to: so, therefore, and or then.
**Boosting:** shoplifting
**Bounce:** leave the scene, motivate
**Break it down:** explain something to a person, talking
**Buck /bust at /let off:** shoot at
**Bugged out:** confused / going crazy
**Busted:** caught / ugly
**Cat:** a guy / referring to a person
**Catch rec.:** To beat some people or someone up for fun.
**Check yourself:** stop and analyze yourself before going any further
**Cheese / cream / loot / Benjamins /cash / cheddar / beans /dough /greenbacks :** money
**Chicken head:** girl / bitch / low class female or male
**Chill / chilling:** cool down / hold your head / maintain / basically to stop / relaxing with the guys
**C-Low:** dice game
**Clique / crew / posse / homeboys:** a group of guys that hang out together
**Clocking me / ice grill / icing / screwing you:** looking hard at a person / Hard stare/ poker face

*283*

**Cock-block:** cut throat
**Coke / yey-yo:** cocaine
**Coming off:** got through, a success
**Connect:** connection / networking /meet up
**Crib:** your house or place of residence
**Cut-throat:** kick dirt / destroy one's name or rep.
**Desert / Q-Borough:** Queens
**D- L:** down low / secretive
**Diss / Dissed / Disrespected:** disrespected / treated badly / dishonored
**Doffing dopes:** to get rid of a person
**Dolo:** solo or alone
**Dope:** smack / boy /heroin
**Duce Duce:** twenty-two gun
**Drama / beef / trauma:** conflict / fight / shooting
**Fams:** friends or family
**Fell off / falling off:** someone who lost everything or is about to lose everything.
**Flake :** fake person
**4 Pound / :** 45 Magnum gun
**Fronting / faking moves or jacks :** faking / pretending / simply just starting a fight / acting as if you are going to do or did something that one wouldn't even do.
**Get down:** do things
**Ghat / pistol /burner / steel / cronze / toolie / toast / heat / joint:** gun
**Ghost / Muerto / Elvis:** dead
**Gi'mme Feet:** give someone room or space
**Glock:** type of gun / popular brand of 9mm
**G.P.:** general purpose
**Grills:** keep looking at you hard.
**A Head / Zombie:** crackhead
**Herb / Herbus Cannibus / Punk :** weak / soft / push over / sucker /victim
**Homes or homie / homeboy:** friend
**Hood / N'hood / 'Round my way:** neighborhood or block
**Hoopty:** an older model car / beat up / something that might get you to A or B.
**House:** a building in jail or prison
**It's all good? :** It's alright or okay / rationalization
**Jects / PJs:** the projects

**Joint:** jail / years / guns / a cigarette of marijuana
**Jump off / Set off:** make happen / happen suddenly / or develop suddenly
**Keep it real:** no playing games / being honest / truthful
**Kicking or kick it:** talking or flirting / politicing
**Lace:** put together or finesse with ease
**Legit:** legitimate
**Lingo:** conversation
**Mad:** crazy / a lot of something / a great deal
**Madina / Bucktown / Crooklyn / Brooknam:** Brooklyn
**Make a def.:** definite
**Mecca / City:** Manhattan
**Money / scrams:** referring to a person
**The Monster:** AIDS
**No doubt /no diggity:** agreeing with a statement (emphasizers)
**Off the hook:** Bugging out, out of hand
**Off point:** completely unaware of any situation at hand.
**On point:** aware at all times / prepared
**Parlay:** relaxing / steady in the situation
**Paranoid / p'noid:** scared / shook / nervous / fearful
**Peeps / boys / "Ace Boone Coon":** very close friends / people in your crew or clique / immediate friends
**Pelong / Boogie down / BX:** Bronx
**Perpetrator:** phony / fake person
**Pet. / pettro:** short for petrified
**Phat :** nice/ expensive / good / excellent
**Pistol whip / gun butt:** getting hit with a gun
**Playing someone:** treat you like a sucker
**Po Po / 5-0 / Po-9 / c-cipher / Teddy /Bonton:** Police
**Posse:** friend
**Props:** getting attention / rewards / reinforcement / proper treatment / esteem / credit / points
**Rah rah:** talking trash or riffing
**Ranking:** jokes on each other / out joking
**Rap:** talk
**Rep:** reputation
**Re-up:** re-supplying drugs for a drug spot
**Scandal:** ditry information about a person
**Scrams boogie:** referring to a person /girl

**Sell me no dreams:** making up stories or fantasies / lying
**Shook:** scared / nervous / scaredy cat / pussy
**Shorty:** a female or a young kid
**Shotty:** type of gun
**Sling / pitching / clocking dough:** sell drugs / making money
**Smoked:** shot at, killed or smoked / hit hard
**Snitch / pigeon / herb:** one who tells on another that doesn't last long
at all / considered weak.
**Snuffed:** hitting a person unexceptedly "a cheap shot"
**Spilly:** the "spot"
**Squashed / deaded:** settled or stopped conflict
**Stomping grounds:** grounds that have already been pioneered / one's
place of dwelling or business spot.
**Stunting:** showing off / fronting
**Suspect:** victim / fishy person
**Sweeting someone:** hounding someone, constantly annoying
**"The game":** selling drugs
**Trees /weed / scammas / smoke:** Marijuana
**Trick:** a person who spends money for sex
**True that:** when agreeing with a statement
**Weeded / blunted / charged / blazed:** high on marijuana
**Weedgate:** weed spot
**Word up?/ Word?:** really?
**Wife or wifey:** steady girlfriend
**Wilding:** bugging, doing something stupid, going all out
**X:** unknown or dead person
**Zombie:** crack head

# REFERENCES

Anderson, E. (1978). *A Place on the Corner*. Chicago: University of Chicago Press.

Anderson, E. (1990). *Streetwise: Race, Class, and Change in an Urban Community*. Chicago: The University of Chicago Press.

Anderson, E. (1994). The Code of the Streets. *The Atlantic Monthly*(May), 81-94.

Anderson, E. (1999). *Violence and the Inner City Street Code*. Chicago: University of Chicago Press.

Becker, H. S. (1998). *Tricks of the Trade: How to Think about Your Research While You're Doing It*. Chicago: The University of Chicago Press.

Bernard, T. J. (1990). Angry Aggression among the "Truly Disadvantaged." *Criminology, 28:*, 73-96.

Biernacki, P., & Waldorf, D. (1981). Snowball Sampling: Problems and Techniques of Chain Referral Sampling. *Sociological Methods and Research, 10*(2), 141-163.

Billson, J. M. (1981). *Pathways to manhood: Young black males struggle for identity*. New Brunswick, NJ: Transaction.

Black, D. (1983). Crime as Social Control. *American Sociological Review, 48*, 34-45.

Black, D. (1993). *Crime as Social Control*. New York: Cambridge University Press.

Blumer, H. (1969). *Symbolic Interactionism: Perspective and Method*. Englewood Cliffs, NJ: Prentice-Hall, Inc.

Blumstein, A., (2002). Youth, Guns, and Violent Crime. *The Future of Children*. Volume 12(2): 39-54.

Blumstein, A., & Rosenfeld, R. (1998). Explaining Recent Trends in U.S. Homicide Rates. *The Journal of Criminal Law & Criminology, 88 Number 4*, 1175-1216.

Brown, B. (1990). Peer Groups and Peer Cultures. In S. S. F. a. G. R. Elliott (Ed.), *At the Threshold: The Developing Adolescent*. Cambridge, MA: Harvard University Press.

Brown, B. B., Mory, M. S., & Kinney, D. (1994). Casting Adolescent Crowds in a Relational Perspective: Caricature, Channel, and Context. In R. Montemayor, Adams, G.R., and Gullotta, T.P. (Ed.), *Personal Relationships During Adolescence* (pp. 123-167). Thousand Oaks, CA: Sage Publications.

Burt, R. (1987). Social Contagion and Innovation: Cohesion Versus Structural Equivalence. *American Journal of Sociology, 92*, 1287-1335.

Cairns, R. B., & Cairns, B. D. (1994). *Lifelines and Risks: Pathways of Youth in our Time.* New York: Cambridge University Press.

Campbell, A. (1984). *The Girls in the Gang.* New York: Basil Blackwell.

Campbell, A., & Gibbs, J. (Eds.). (1986). *Violent Transactions: The Limits of Personality.* New York: Basil Blackwell.

Canada, G. (1995). *Fist, Knife, Stick, Gun.* Boston, MA: Beacon Press.

Chambliss, W. (1977). The Saints and the Roughnecks. *Society, 11*(1), 24-31.

Clarke, R. V., & Cornish, D. B. (1985). Modeling Offenders' Decisions: A Framework for Research and Policy. In M. Tonry & N. Morris (Eds.), *Crime and Justice: An Annual Review of Research* (Vol. 6).

Cloward, R. A., & Ohlin, L. E. (1960). *Delinquency and Opportunity.* Glencoe, IL: Free Press.

Cohen, L. E., & Felson, M. (1979). Social Change and Crime Rate Trends: A Routine Activity Approach. *American Sociological Review, 44*(August), 588-608.

Cook, P. (1983). The Influence of Gun Availability on Violent Crime Patterns. In M. T. a. N. Morris (Ed.), *Crime and Justice: An Annual Review of Research* (Vol. Volume 4, pp. P. 49-90). Chicago: University of Chicago Press.

Cook, P., & Laub, J. (1998). The Unprecedented Epidemic in Youth Violence. In M. T. a. M. Moore (Ed.), *Crime and Justice: A Review of Research* (Vol. Volume 24 on Youth Violence, pp. p. 27-64). Chicago: University of Chicago Press.

Cook, P. J. (1980). Reducing Injury and Death Rates in Robbery. *Policy Analysis, 6*(1), 21-45.

Cornish, D. (1993, May 26-28,1993). *Crimes as Scripts.* Paper presented at the Second Annual Seminar on Environmental Criminology and Crime Analysis, University of Miami, Coral Gables, FL.

Cornish, D. (1994). The Procedural Analysis of Offending and Its Relevance for Situational Prevention. In R. V. Clarke (Ed.), *Crime Prevention Studies* (pp. 151-196). NY: Criminal Justice Press.

Decker, S., & Pennell, S. (1995). *Arrestees and Guns: Monitoring the Illegal Firearms Market:* Washington, DC: National Institute of Justice.

Decker, S. H. (1995). Reconstructing Homicide Events: The Role of Witnesses in Fatal Encounters. *Journal of Criminal Justice, 23*(5), 439-450.

Decker, S. H., Pennell, S., & Caldwell, A. (1997). Illegal Firearms: Access and Use by Arrestees. Washington, DC: *National Institute of Justice Research in Brief* (January).

Denzin, N. K., & Lincoln, Y. S. (Eds.). (1994). *Handbook of Qualitative Research*. Thousand Oaks, CA: Sage Publications, Inc.

Dilulio, J. J. (1995). The Coming of the Superpredators. *The Weekly Standard, November 27*, 23-28.

Dilulio, J. J. (1996). How to Stop the Coming Crime Wave. *Manhattan Insititute Civic Bulletin, 2*, 1-4.

Dunlap, E., Johnson, B., Sanabria, H., Holliday, E., Lipsey, V., Barnett, M., Hopkins, W., Sobel, I., Randolph, D., & Chin, K.-L. (1990). Studying Crack Users and their Criminal Careers: The Scientific and Artistic Aspects of Locating Hard-to-Reach Subjects and Interviewing Them About Sensitive Topics. *Contemporary Drug Problems*, 121-144.

Eder, D., & Enke, J. (1991). The Structure of Gossip: Opportunities and Constraints on Collective Expression among Adolescents. *American Sociological Review, 56*, 494-508.

Eder, D., Evans, C. C., & Parker, S. (1995). *School Talk: Gender and Adolescent Culture*. New Burnswick, NJ: Rutgers University Press.

Eder, D., & Kinney, D. A. (1995). The Effect of Middle School Extracurricular Activities on Adolescents' Popularity and Peer Status. *Youth and Society, 26*(3), 298-324.

Elikann, P. (1999). *Superpredators: The Demonization of Our Children by the Law*. New York: Plenum Press.

Fagan, J. (1992). Drug Selling and Licit Income in Distressed Neighborhoods: The Economic Lives of Drug Users and Dealers. In G. Peterson & A. Harrell (Eds.), *Drugs, Crime and Social Isolation*. Washington, DC: Urban Institute Press.

Fagan, J., & Chin, C. (1990). Violence as Regulation and Social Control in the Distribution of Crack. In M. d. l. Rosa, E. Lambert, & B. Gropper (Eds.), *Drugs and Violence*. Rockville, MD: National Institute on Drug Abuse Research Monograph n. 103. DHHS Pub. No. (ADM) 90-1721.

Fagan, J. A., & Freeman, R. B. (1999). Crime and Work. *Crime-and-Justice, 25*, 225-290.

Fagan, J., Wilkinson, D., & Davies, G. (2000, May 11-12). *Social Contagion of Violence*. Paper presented at the Youth Violence in Urban Communities, Boston: Harvard University.

Fagan, J., & Wilkinson, D. L. (1998a). Guns, Youth Violence, and Social Identity in Inner Cities. In M. T. a. M. Moore (Ed.), *Crime and Justice: A Review of Research Volume 24:* (pp. 105-187). Chicago: University of Chicago Press.

Fagan, J., & Wilkinson, D. L. (1998b). The Social Contexts and Functions of Adolescent Violence. In D. S. Elliott, B. A. Hamburg, & K. Williams (Eds.), *Violence in American Schools* (pp. p. 55-93): Cambridge University Press.

Feeney, F. (1986). Decision Making in Robberies. In R. V. Clarke & D. B. Cornish (Eds.), *The Reasoning Criminal*. New York: Springer-Verlag.

Felson, R. B. (1982). Impression Management and the Escalation of Aggression and Violence. *Social Psychology Quarterly, 45*(4), 245-254.

Felson, R. B. (1984). Patterns of Aggressive Social Interaction. In A. Mummendey (Ed.), *Social Psychology of Aggression: From Individual Behavior to Social Interaction* (pp. 107-126). New York: Springer-Verlag.

Felson, R. B. (1993). Predatory and Dispute-Related Violence: A Social Interactionist Approach. In R. V. Clarke & M. Felson (Eds.), *Routine Activity and Rational Choice, Advances in Criminological Theory* (Vol. 5, pp. p. 103-126). New Brunswick, NJ: Transaction Press.

Felson, R. B., & Steadman, H. J. (1983). Situational Factors in Disputes Leading to Criminal Violence. *Criminology, 21*(1), 59-74.

Fingerhut, L. A. (1993). Firearm Mortality among Children, Youth and Young Adults 1-34 Years of Age, Trends and Current Status: United States, 1985-1990. *Advance Data from Vital and Health Statistics, No. 231.*

Fingerhut, L. A., and Christoffel, K., (2002). Firearm-Related Death and Injury among Children and Adolescents. *The Future of Children.* Volume 12(2): 25-37.

Fleisher, M. S. (1998). *Dead End Kids: Gang Girls and the Boys They Know.* Madison: University of Wisconsin Press.

Fox, J. A. (1995). *Homicide Offending Patterns, 1976-1993.* Atlanta: American Academy for the Advancement of Science.

Fox, J. A. (1996). *Trends in Juvenile Violence: A Report to the United States Attorney General on Current and Future Rates of Juvenile Offending.* Washington DC: Bureau of Justice Statistics.

Furstenberg, F. (2000). The Sociology of Adolescence and Youth in the 1990s: A Critical Commentary. *Journal of Marriage and the Family, 62,* 896-910.

Gibson, C., Zhao, J., Lovrich, N., and Gaffney, M (2002). Social Integration, Individual Percpetions of Collective Efficacy, and Fear of Crime in Three Cities. *Justice Quarterly,* 19: 537-564.

Goffman, E. (1959). *The Presentation of Self in Everyday Life.* Garden City, NJ: Doubleday & Co.

Goffman, E. (1963a). *Behavior in Public Places: Notes on The Social Organization of Gatherings*. New York: The Free Press.

Goffman, E. (1963b). *Stigma: Notes on The Management of Spoiled Identity*. New York: Simon & Schuster Inc.

Goffman, E. (1967). *Interaction Ritual: Essays on Face-to-Face Behavior*. New York: Pantheon Books.

Goffman, E. (1983). The Interaction Order. *American Sociological Review, 48*, 1-17.

Goldstein, P. J., Brownstein, H. H., Ryan, P., & Belluci, P. A. (1989). Crack and Homicide in New York City, 1989: A Conceptually-based Event Analysis. *Contemporary Drug Problems, 16:*(651-687).

Gottfredson, D. (2001). *Schools and Delinquency*. New York: Cambridge.

Guerra, N., Nucci, L., & Huesmann, R. (1994). Moral Cognition and Childhood Aggression. In L. R. Huesmann (Ed.), *Aggressive Behaviors: Current Perspective* (pp. Pp. 13-32). New York: Plenum Press.

Guerra, N., & Slaby, R. G. (1990). Cognitive Mediators of Aggression in Adolescent Offenders: Illinois Interventions. *Developmental Psychology, 26*, 269-277.

Hagedorn, J. (1997). Frat Boys, Bossmen, Studs, and Gentlemen: A Typology of Gang Masculinities. In B. Forst (Ed.), *Masculinities and Violence*. Thousand Oaks: Sage Publications.

Hagedorn, J. M. (1988). *People and Folks: Gangs, Crime, and the Underclass in a Rustbelt City*. Chicago, IL: Lakeview Press.

Hamburg, B. A. (1974). Early adolescence: A Specific and Stressful Stage of the Life Cycle. In D. A. H. G.V. Coelho, and J.E. Adams (Ed.), *Coping and Adaptation* (pp. Pp. 101-124.). New York: Basic Books.

Hannerz, U. (1969). *Soulside: Inquiries into Ghetto Culture and Community*. New York: Columbia University Press.

Harris, L. (1993). *A Survey of Experiences, Perceptions, and Apprehensions about Guns among Young People in America*. Cambridge, MA: School of Public Health, Harvard University.

Heise, D., (1979). *Understanding Events: Affect and the Construction of Social Action* (New York: Cambridge University Press.

Hersch, P. (1998). *A Tribe Apart: A Journey into the Heart of American Adolescence*. New York: The Ballantine Publishing Group.

Hindelang, M., Gottfredson, M., & Garofalo, J. (1978). *Victims of Personal Crime*. Cambridge, MA: Ballinger Publishing Company.

Huff, R. (1998). *Comparing the Criminal Behavior of Youth Gangs and At-Risk Youths. Research in Brief*. Washington, DC: National Institute of Justice.

Inciardi, J. A., Horowitz, R., & Pottieger, A. E. (1993). *Street Kids, Street Drugs, Street Crime*. Belmont, CA: Wadsworth Publishing Co.

Kagan, J. (1989). *Unstable Ideas: Temperament, Cognition, and Self*. Cambridge, MA: Harvard University Press.

Katz, J. (1988). *Seductions of Crime: Moral and Sensual Attractions of Doing Evil*. New York: Basic.

Kennedy, D. (1993). Guns and Youth: Disrupting the Market. Cambridge, MA: John F. Kennedy School of Government, Harvard University.

Kinney, D. A. (1993). From Nerds to Normals: The Recovery of Identity among Adolescents from Middle School to High School. *Sociology of Education, Vol. 66*(January), 21-40.

Kotlowitz, A. (1991). *There Are No Children Here*. New York: Anchor Books.

Kvale, S. (1996). *Interviews: An Introduction to Qualitative Research Interviewing*. Thousand Oaks, CA: Sage.

Land, K. C., McCall, P. L., & Cohen, L. E. (1990). Structural Covariates of Homicide Rates: Are There Any Invariances Across Time and Social Space? *American Journal of Sociology, 95*(4), 922-63.

Luckenbill, D. F. (1977). Criminal Homicide as a Situated Transaction. *Social Problems*. 5: 176-186.

Luckenbill, D. F. (1980). Patterns of Force in Robbery. *Deviant Behavior: An Interdisciplinary Journal, 1*, 361-378.

Luckenbill, D. F., & Doyle, D. P. (1989). Structural position and Violence: Developing a Cultural Explanation. *Criminology, 27*(3), 419-436.

Majors, R., & Billson, J. M. (1992). *Cool Pose: The Dilemmas of Black Manhood in America*. New York: Simon & Schuster, Inc.

Massey, D. S., & Denton, N. A. (1993). *American Apartheid: Segregation and the Making of the Underclass*. Cambridge, MA: Harvard University Press.

McLaughlin, M. W., Irby, M. A., & Langman, J. (1994). *Urban Sanctuaries*. San Francisco, CA: Jossey-Bass.

Messerschmidt, J. W. (1993). *Masculinities and Crime: Critique and Reconceptualization of Theory*. Lanham, Maryland: Rowman & Littlefield Publishers, Inc.

Messerschmidt, J. W. (1997). *Crime as Structured action*. Sage Publications.

Miethe, T. D., & Meier, R. F. (1994). *Crime and Its Social Context: Toward an Integrated Theory of Offenders, Victims, and Situations*. Albany, NY: State University of New York Press.

Miles, M. B., & Huberman, A. M. (1994). *An Expanded Sourcebook: Qualitative data analysis*. Thousand Oaks, CA: Sage.

Miller, W. B. (1958). Lower Class Culture as a Generating Milieu of Gang Delinquency. *Journal of Social Issues, 14*, 5-19.

Moore, J. (1978). *Homeboys*. Philadelphia: Temple University Press.

Oliver, W. (1994). *The Violent Social World of Black Men*. New York: Lexington Books.

Polk, K. (1994). *When Men Kill: Scenarios of Masculine Violence*: Cambridge University Press.

Reiss, A., & Roth, J. A. (Eds.). (1993). *Understanding and Preventing Violence*. Washington, DC: National Academy Press.

Rosenberg, M. L., & Fenley, M. A. (Eds.). (1991). *Violence in America: A Public Health Approach*. New York: Oxford University Press.

Sampson, R. (1993). Linking Time and Place: Dynamic Contextualism and the Future of Criminological Inquiry. *Journal of Research in Crime and Delinquency, 30*(4), 428-444.

Sampson, R. J. (1997). The Embeddedness of Child and Adolescent Development: A community-level perspective on youth violence. In J. McCord (Ed.), *Violence and the Inner City* (pp. Pp. 31-77). New York: Cambridge University Press.

Sampson, R. J., & Wilson, W. J. (1995). Race, crime and urban inequality. In J. H. a. R. Peterson (Ed.), *Crime and Inequality*. Stanford, CA: Stanford University Press.

Sanders, J. (1994). *Gangbangs and Drive-bys*. New York: Aldine-deGruyter.

Schochet, P. Z., Burghardt, J., & Glazerman, S. (2000). *National Job Corps Study: The Short-Term Impacts of Job Corps on Participants' Employment and Related Outcomes. Executive Summary*. Princeton: U.S. Department of Labor.

Schwendinger, H., & Schwendinger, J. (1985). *Adolescent Subcultures and Delinquency*. New York: Free Press.

Sheley, J., & Wright, J. (1995). *In the Line of Fire: Youth, Guns, and Violence in Urban America*. New York: Aldine de Gruyter.

Sheley, J., Wright, J., & Smith, M. D. (1993). *Firearms, Violence and Inner-city Youth: A Report of Research Findings*. Washington D.C.: U.S. Department of Justice, National Institute of Justice.

Short, J. (1996). *Poverty, Ethnicity, and Violent Crime*. Boulder, CO: Westview.

Skogan, W. (1978). Weapon Use in Robbery. In J. I. a. A. Pottieger (Ed.), *Violent Crime: Historical and Contemporary Issues*. Beverly Hills, CA: Sage.

Slaby, R. G. (1997). Psychological Mediators of Violence in Urban Youth. In J. McCord (Ed.), *Violence and Childhood in the Inner City* (pp. p. 171-206). New York: Cambridge University Press.

Slaby, R. G., & Roedell, W. C. (1982). Development and Regulation of Aggression in Young Children. In J. Worrell (Ed.), *Psychological Development in the Elementary Years* (pp. Pp. 97-149). New York: Academic Press.

Snyder, H. N., & Sickmund, M. (1999). *Juvenile Offenders and Victims: 1999 National Report*. Washington DC: Office of Juvenile Justice and Delinquency Prevention, U.S. Department of Justice.

Sommers, I., & Baskin, D. (1993). The Situational Context of Violent Female Offending. *Journal of Research in Crime and Delinquency, 30*, 136-162.

Spergel, I. (1989). Youth Gangs: Continuity and Change. In N. M. M. Tonry (Ed.), *Crime and Justice: An Annual Review of Research, Volume 12*. Chicago: University of Chicago Press.

Steinberg, L., & Avenevoli, S. (2000). The Role of Context in the Development of Psychopathology: A Conceptual Framework and Some Speculative Propositions. *Child Development, 71*(1), 66-74.

Steinberg, L., & Caufmann, E. (1996). Maturity of Judgment in Adolescence: Psychosocial Factors in Adolescent Decision Making. *Law and Human Behaviors, 20*(249-272).

Strauss, A. L. (1987). *Qualitative Analysis for Social Scientists*. New York: Cambridge University Press.

Strauss, A. L. (1997). *Mirrors & Masks: The Search for Identity*. New Brunswick, N. J.: Transaction Publishers.

Strodtbeck, F. L., & Short, J. F., Jr. (1968). Aleatory Risks Versus Short-run Hedonism in Explanation of Gang Action. In J. James F. Short (Ed.), *Gang Delinquency and Delinquent Subcultures.* (pp. P. 273-291). New York: Harper and Row.

Sullivan, M. (1998). The Effects of Exposure to Violence on Early Adolescent Development: A Lifespace Approach. New York: Vera Institute of Justice.

Sullivan, M. L. (1989). *Getting Paid: Youth Crime and Culture in the Inner city*. Ithaca, NY: Cornell University Press.

Sullivan, M. L. (1997). *Social and Symbolic Interactionist Approaches to the Study of Adolescent Violence*. Paper presented at the American Society of Criminology, San Diego, CA.

Suttles, G. D. (1968). *The Social Order of the Slum*. Chicago: University of Chicago Press.

Taylor, R. B. (2002). Fear of Crime, Social Ties, and Collective Efficacy: Maybe Masquerading Measurement, Maybe déjà vu All Over Again. *Justice Quarterly*, Volume 19(4): 773-792.

Tedeschi, J. T., & Felson, R. (1994). *Violence, Aggression, and Coercive Actions*. Washington, D.C.: American Psychological Association.

Thrasher, F. M. (1927). *The Gang: A Study of 1,313 Gangs in Chicago.* Chicago: University of Chicago Press.

Tienda, M. (1991). Poor People and Poor Places: Deciphering Neighborhood Effects on Poverty Outcomes. In J. Huber (Ed.), *Macro-Micro Linkages in Sociology*. Newbury Park, CA: Sage.

Toch, H. (1969). *Violent Men: An Inquiry into the Psychology of Violence.* Chicago: Aldine Publishing Company.

Van Gundy, K. (2002). Gender, the Assertion of Autonomy, and the Stress Process in Young Adulthood. *Social Psychology Quarterly*. Vol. 65 (4): 346-363.

Walker, A. L., & Lidz, C. W. (1977). Methodological Notes on the Employment of Indigenous Observers. In R. S. Weppner (Ed.), *Street Ethnography*. Beverly Hills, CA: Sage.

Watters, J. K., & Bieracki, P. (1989). Targeted Sampling: Options for the Study of Hidden Populations. *Social Problems, 36*, 416-430.

Wells, W. and Horney, J. (2002). Weapon Effects and Individual Intent to Do Harm: Influences on the Escalation of Violence, *Criminology*. Vol. 40 (2), May 2002, pp. 265-296.

Whyte, W. F. (1943). *Street Corner Society*. Chicago: University of Chicago Press.

Wilkinson, D. L. (2001). Violent Events and Social Identity: Specifying the Relationship between Respect and Masculinity in Inner City Youth Violence. In D. A. Kinney (Ed.), *Sociological Studies of Children and Youth*. Stanford, CT: JAI Press.

Wilkinson, D. L., & Fagan, J. (2001a). A Theory of Violent Events. In R. Meier, Leslie Kennedy, and Sacco (Ed.), *The Process and Structure of Crime: Event Analysis: Advances in Criminological Theory Volume 9* (Vol. 9, pp. 169-195). New Brunswick, NJ: Transaction.

Wilkinson, D. L., & Fagan, J. (2001b). What We Know About Gun Use Among Adolescents. *Clinical Child and Family Psychology Review, 4*(2), 109-132.

Williams, T., & Kornblum, W. (1994). *The Uptown Kids: Struggle and Hope in the Projects*. New York: G. P. Putnam's Sons.

Wolcott, H. F. (1994). *Transforming Qualitative Data: Description, Analysis, and Interpretation*. Thousand Oaks, CA: Sage Publications, Inc.

Wolfgang, M. (1958). *Patterns of Criminal Homicide*. Philadelphia, PA: University of Pennsylvania Press.

Wolfgang, M., & Ferracuti, F. (1967). *The Subculture of Violence: Toward an Integrated Theory in Criminology* (1st ed.). Beverly Hills, CA: Sage.

Wolfgang, M., & Ferracuti, F. (*1982*). *The Subculture of Violence: Toward an Integrated Theory in Criminology* (2nd ed.). Beverly Hills, CA: Sage.

Wright, J. D., & Rossi, P. H. (1986). *Armed and Considered Dangerous: A Survey of Felons and Their Firearms*. New York: Aldine de Gruyter.

Wright, R., & Decker, S. (1997). *Armed Robbers in Action: Stick Ups and Street Culture*. Boston: Northeastern University Press.

Zimring, F. E., & Zuehl, J. (1986). Victim injury and death in urban robbery: A Chicago study. *Journal of Legal Issues, 15:* 1-40.

# NANE AND SUBJECT INDEX